Praise for *Vampyre*

MW00789138

"*Vampire fads come and go, emerging each decade in some new form. But for those for whom the vampyric mystique is a calling, the choices inspired become a life path.* Vampyre Sanguinomicon *offers a compelling and elegant presentation of the history, rituals, and customs of a specific spiritual movement. It has the quality of permanence, and it will likely make an enduring contribution to sanguinary lore.*"
—Dr. Katherine Ramsland, author of
The Science of Vampires and *Piercing the Darkness*

"*As a person who has studied and been involved in many different vampire philosophies, I find myself resonating with the Strigoi Vii more than any other because of their ability to evolve.* Vampyre Sanguinomicon *gives a fresh new voice to one of the oldest Vampyre pantheons out there and brings the tradition forth by cutting out the fluff and giving a more forensic view of Vampyrism. It is self-empowering and self-initiating without the need for a media guru. Kudos to Father Sebastiaan for giving us something truly original to sink our teeth into!*"
—Lady A, Marketing design manager, Anne Rice Vampire Lestat Fan Club

"*The* Vampyre Sanguinomicon *provides a unique and valid look at one of the oldest Vampyre traditions in the modern living vampire subculture. Full of rich descriptions and details of the past, it delves deep into the many aspects long whispered about in the shadows. Highly recommended.*"
—Corvis Nocturnum, author of *Allure of the Vampire: Our Sexual Attraction to the Undead*

"*A clearly and concisely written tome! It offers easily accessible information on the ethical and well-established ways of the Strigoi Vii. Heed well these words of wisdom and they will guide you to the gate of eternity. What you do, then, depends on you.*"
—Kaedrich Olsen, author of *Runes for Transformation*

VAMPYRE
SANGUINOMICON

VAMPYRE SANGUINOMICON

THE LEXICON
— OF THE —
LIVING VAMPIRE

FATHER SEBASTIAAN
Foreword by Konstantinos

WEISERBOOKS
San Francisco, CA / Newburyport, MA

First published in 2010 by Red Wheel/Weiser, LLC
With offices at:
500 Third Street, Suite 230
San Francisco, CA 94107
www.redwheelweiser.com

ISBN: 978-1-57863-480-4

Library of Congress Cataloging-in-Publication Data is available upon request.

Cover design by Frame 25 Productions
Text design by Donna Linden
Typeset in Ab Fang, Perpetua, and Venetian

Printed in the United States of America
TS
10 9 8 7 6 5 4 3 2 1
⊕ Text paper contains a minimum of 30% post-consumer waste material.

Warning and Disclaimer

The books of the *Sanguinomicon* are written for serious individuals who wish to unlock their own hidden potential. The rituals and Mysteries within these pages require the Seeker to be of sound mind and body. If you suffer from mental disorders, such as bipolar disorder or schizophrenia or serious physical ailments, such as heart disease, epilepsy, or other chronic illnesses, please, for your own safety, refrain from exploring the Strigoi Vii Mysteries. The authors, the Synod, and the publisher will not accept responsibility for the misuse of the material contained within. Nor do they condone or endorse underage sexual behavior or illegal or criminal activities of any sort.

This copy of the Vampyre Sanguinomicon *was formally*

consecrated on _____ *[date] and is the*

property of _____ *[Sobriquet].*

This book born of Love and Loyalty is dedicated to all who have heard the Calling—those yet to awaken, the Awakened, and the Ascended. I raise my chalice to honor you, my Family. So we begin . . .

CONTENTS

FOREWORD

I met Sebastiaan what feels like an immortal lifetime ago. It was 1996, and we were both at a taping of the *Ricki Lake* Show. The topic? You guessed it.

Instead of his now-trademark folded cowboy hat, Sebastiaan wore a more period-popular top hat, à la Gary Oldman in *Bram Stoker's Dracula*. At first glance, I thought he had to be another of the role-players—the audience and panel were filled with young "kids in capes." But Sebastiaan was different. His enthusiasm was almost infectious, and I didn't have to talk to him long to notice that, for him, this wasn't mere role-playing. Even at a young age, he "got" what the real power behind this whole scene was, even if he didn't know the word for it yet.

That word? *Psychodrama.*

I've made it pretty clear in *Vampires: The Occult Truth* that the evidence supporting the existence of movie-caliber immortal blood drinkers is sketchy at best. The case for psychic vampires is much stronger. Was blood a metaphor for beings that can take the energy of the living? More bizarrely, could these beings be either living or in a state that can only be called undead? The evidence sure seems to suggest this possibility.

What does this mean for those who pine for immortality of the Lestat or Edward type? (Okay, just the Lestat type—who really wants to shimmer and eat deer?) While some beautiful immortal may not carry you out the window and give you a dark kiss in an ancient tower or leaf-covered graveyard, it doesn't mean the power behind the vampire realm is forever closed off to you.

Again, that delicious word. *Psychodrama.*

All magic is psychodrama. Without extravagant rituals that speak to something deep in our subconscious, our minds simply can't reach the altered states necessary for accessing the unseen world. We live in a world that is dominated by daytime consciousness requirements. Few bosses ask how many spiritual planes you can travel through per minute or how many spells by Microsoft you've mastered. Mystical altered states are as repressed as can be, with drained BlackBerry batteries representing the only true down time for many.

I've seen psychodrama do eerie and wonderful things. It has healed me of a malformed vein that was threatening my brain and life, and MRIs don't lie. Psychodrama, when mastered, can result in more than just an altered state. With the right ritual structure, an altered state can result in powerful, real change in the physical world. Even quantum experiments in which individuals try to affect random number generators have proven that test groups with some kind of meditative preparation always do better. Amazing to see science "discovering" what occultists have always known and tabulating the results under controlled lab setups.

You hold in your hands a unique kind of book. Rather than claiming that vampires are born to some exotic bloodline or going on and on about why the author is special in some way that conveniently matches fictional vampires, this book gives you techniques for working with pure psychodrama. No ego or delusions required. The change you get out of it is directly proportionate to how deeply you let its structure affect you.

Since that day thirteen years ago, Sebastiaan and I have always stayed in reasonable contact. We've done a couple of Endless Night events in New Orleans together and plan to do more. We've had enough Jack Daniels and absinthe to facilitate the necessary quick catching up each time we get together. Over a couple of glasses recently, Sebastiaan reminded me of the first time he saw the term *Strigoi Vii*—literally "living vampire"—in my book. While the beings it described likely never existed, they do now, don't they? I'm delighted that Sebastiaan did what all occultists should do: he used psychodrama to bring something forth into reality.

As I type these last words, the last drops of water have erased the sugar cube in the absinthe glass in preparation nearby. With a swirl of the cloudy glass, and the promise of altered states it too can help provide, I raise my glass to the best example of a sane living vampire I know.

Konstantinos

PRELUDE

Ave,

Welcome to the public edition of the *Vampyre Sanguinomicon,* the core tome of the Mysteries of the Strigoi Vii, the Living Vampire. This book has been years in the making and represents a great amount of painstaking study, experimentation, and philosophical and spiritual reflection.

Both the mundane world and other vampire Legacies hold many misconceptions about the Strigoi Vii. Before proceeding, I would like to address and clear up these fallacies.

The Strigoi Vii exist within dualities. We are light and dark, male and female, primal and civilized, saints and sinners—all at the same time. We draw Our power from Our mutability and ability to "paradigm shift." We are unique amongst the vampire tribes. We are not psychic vampires or blood drinkers by nature, nor are we kids wearing capes or roleplayers taking a game too seriously. Vampyres *live.* We are amongst the Chosen, We are the Blessed, and We will not settle for just simply surviving. We are not cursed nor do We have "energy deficiencies" or "damaged, leaky chakras." Our subtle bodies work on a high spiritual vibration and require a higher amount of life force than those of other beings; this is why we employ the Art of Vampyrism. Many Strigoi Vii call this the Need, thirst, or hunger. Finally, although We are absolutely serious about Our nature, We also know when and how to lighten up and, of course, have a good laugh at Ourselves!

Now that has been said, let Us proceed. As you hold this book in your hands, you may very well be asking yourself why information that is considered secret can be revealed in a publicly published book. We Strigoi Vii, as a tradition and as a spiritual Family, have reached the point where We are willing to make Our basic teachings readily available. The Outer Mysteries that are contained within this book, known to Us as the Zadyrere, are open secrets. This comprises the Outer Mysteries of Prospectii, Jahira, Calmae, and MoRoii.

Imagine an audience watching an illusionist. The people in the audience will gasp and applaud while the magician performs his tricks. Yet when the show is over, only a very few in that audience, often curious children, will feel the desire to study the techniques or "secrets" behind the magic tricks and perhaps pursue stage magic as a career. Of those who do so, only the ones who possess talent and an understanding of the mechanics of stage magic will succeed. The Mysteries within this book are not tricks, but in a sense they are similar to illusions because the deeper secrets of Strigoi Vii lie beneath the surface of the glitter and metaphor. Setting these Mysteries in print frees them to evolve and will provide them with Immortality unto themselves.

By the 1930s, the Mysteries of the Hermetic Order of the Golden Dawn, one of the most influential orders of Western magick ever to exist, were almost forgotten. The order was many years defunct, and a handful of secretive successor orders maintained the Mysteries. However, to the enmity of many in the esoteric subculture, many of the Mysteries of the Golden Dawn were published by Israel Regardie in the late 1930s, so as to preserve the traditions of the Golden Dawn. To this day, these Mysteries form the basis for almost every Western esoteric tradition, from Aleister Crowley's Thelema to the religion known as Wicca that was founded by Gerald Gardner and others. The same intent is done with the publishing of the contents of the *Vampyre Sanguinomicon*.

One perspective, which may bring solace to the minds of older Strigoi Vii, is that the vast majority of people reading this book are exactly the same as the audience in a magic show. They may be thrilled and amazed, but they do not seek more, accepting what they have witnessed as either an unsolvable mystery or mere trickery. However, those with a childlike sense of wonder, as well as a spark of genuine curiosity, will seek to solve the magician's mysteries. In fact, the greatest magicians alive today, such as Chris Angel or David Copperfield, have spoken of particular magicians who inspired them to become magicians themselves.

The unawakened Strigoi Vii are like the entranced children in that audience. Some will become curious and play with magic tricks as any child would play with a favorite toy, then discard it and move on to something more interesting. On the other hand, there are a few with the drive, determination, and genuine interest to pursue their art and become the next great illusionists. They have a profound fascination with magic and are willing to tirelessly study, learn, and practice until they have achieved mastery and become skilled magicians. Such is it with the unawakened Strigoi Vii, who possess deep magick in the Current of their Blood and the commitment to become True Vampyres.

These Mysteries cannot be solved just by reading a book or seeking a Strigoi Vii teacher or mentor. Knowledge is useless unless you can personally apply it and gain results. Anyone can go out and buy a book on magic or spend thousands of dollars on the newest trick. Yet it takes true dedication and talent to become a true magician. The art of magic is this understanding. The potential Strigoi Vii must first have desire, endurance, and will for the Quest of Immortality, as well as the determination and drive to achieve personal evolution through these Mysteries.

Within the magician's code, magical secrets can be revealed to others determined to be magicians. So it is with the contents of this text. However, this book cannot teach talent or ability. All it can do is provide the reader with knowledge. Unless the reader has the ambition to solve and apply the Mysteries, they will remain pleasant and unattainable illusions. This book is a lexicon for those with sincere intentions and potential.

Many will ask by what intention have I endorsed and contributed to this book. Having already spent two decades in the Vampyre/vampire subculture, I have become inspired to make readily available this book and the teachings within. I have watched the mundane world's fear of Us metamorphose into a genuine fascination and love. I know it is time that a portion of these Mysteries in their original form be revealed to others, as they were to me. On my journey, I have met many who are truly like me and thus have added to Our vision. These "Vampyres" function on some frequency not shared by the rest of humanity. Increasingly more people like this are coming to the Sanguinarium and the Ordo Strigoi Vii (OSV), wanting to learn about Our perspectives on Vampyrism and, more specifically, Strigoi Vii. They come with a genuine wonder, love of life, and disagreement with what has been presented elsewhere. Thus exists the *Sanguinomicon,* which Seekers should read first and then ask questions once they are informed. Reading is an act of self-exploration. Seekers will draw their own conclusions from their interaction with the contents of this book. This book will resonate with the soul and spirit of the True Vampyre.

In addition, I have seen the Vampyre culture change from an underground, beautiful, and mysterious network of individuals to something that is very different. New traditions (Legacies) of vampyrism are becoming more commonplace. These new generations, sadly, often forget the original concepts, Mysteries, and traditions to which I had the pleasure of being introduced. The Vampyre lost its beauty and Glamour. My purpose in supporting and contributing to the *Sanguinomicon* project is to restore the old ways as well as to guide the Strigoi Vii into the future.

If a Strigoi Vii is genuine and sincere in their Calling to Our Current, they can see through the propaganda and make up their own mind. They are a True Vampyre! I must clearly state that I am not attacking any other traditions or Legacies. If a Seeker has the courage to be true to themselves and their inner nature, they will make the choices that will best aid their evolution, not their ego. They will draw conclusions about Us and Our traditions based on their own tangible results, not unexamined theories, rumors, or blind faith. Even should their exploration lead them away from Strigoi Vii, it will be for the right reasons, which is their own free will. This is why I encourage all those who come to me to read all they can about the subject of Vampyrism and vampyrism. I urge all Seekers to never limit themselves to only one mentor, but to see the fruits of knowledge from all—and to see all those above and below their current state of evolution to be teachers. Those who are True and genuine will know the truth of the phrase "If you love them, let them go, and if love is true, they will return." No knowledge should be forbidden.

However, beware . . .

Far too often in the "vamp scene" We hear Elders, Orders, houses, covens, and other groups or individuals say, "We are an ancient organization from the mists of time and our origins lie before the beginning of humanity. Our god/tradition/philosophy is the oldest in existence." As a fledgling, I fell for this as well. With hindsight, I can now view it for what it is: a foolish attempt to achieve ego gratification by trying to create an aura of illusionary superiority. The True Strigoi Vii I have encountered really don't care to engage in this sort of vampire one-upmanship. We know Our lineage and spiritual species has been with humanity for millennia in one form or another through many incarnations. Ours is one agreement and perspective on this. However, We have the collective strength to say, "We still don't know all the details." Many of Us have found little bits and pieces of the answer, and putting this together is like assembling a jigsaw puzzle with thousands of pieces. We have better things to do than engage in pointless debate about Our tradition like members of mundane fundamentalist religions. We would rather live Our lives to the fullest, look to the future, achieve personal mastery of the mortal coil, and seek results from the Mysteries.

Whenever an organization or group demands absolute and unquestioning faith from its members, they are exhibiting the first sign of being a cult. Free will is essential for true personal evolution, and discovery should come from within, not without. Most disappointing to me personally are those who succumb to the temptation of the vampire archetype for the purpose of filling spiritual or emotional voids in themselves. They form cults, claim false powers, and use the power of the Vampyre Glamour to brainwash others. Yes, those of the Family are drawn to each other and form deep-rooted and passionate bonds. Yes, the vampire archetype is absolutely sensual and erotic! However, one must be ethical and never use such power to violate the free will of others. What is a common factor linking the most successful movements and religions? It is free will. If any organization does not accord others complete freedom to follow or reject their teachings, they are doomed to failure. Strigoi Vii is not about deceit or manipulation. It is about freedom for the individual to test, validate, and explore the truth for themselves.

We Strigoi Vii are in agreement with mundane ethics on these points. Never let anyone try to seduce you with false knowledge or demand sexual favors in exchange for such knowledge. I have witnessed groups and Elders trading mentorship or Initiation for sex. Playing on the vampire fantasy in this way merely to seduce others is a point of weakness. Teachers should never manipulate their students! These kinds of power plays are repellent to the True Vampyre. The true Strigoi Vii knows We are all students and teachers for each other. No one has all the answers or is able to show them to you unless you have already discovered them for yourself. That is why We seek Immortality. We wish to have a conscious and timeless eternity in which to evolve and develop Ourselves.

The *Sanguinomicon* is canon only for the Strigoi Vii and no other tradition or path of Vampyrism. It does not speak to the entirety of the vampire/Vampyre community, but only to this specific path. However, in *Sanguinomicon* We briefly touch on other traditions and tribes in order to reveal the similarities and differences between Us and them.

It is quite true that Strigoi Vii has influenced and been influenced by many traditions, paths, and systems. Nothing in the world is completely original. Everything in history has been built on something from the past. Every great philosopher, artist, or scientist has been informed by the teachings and inspiration of all those who came before. Even Albert Einstein once said he was able to clearly see the nature of the universe only because he was standing on the shoulders of giants. This book comes from observations of years of experiences with my fang clients, occultists, fellow Strigoi Vii, and many other people I have met. Some of the Mysteries in this book were discovered by means of scrying, meditation, ritual, or deliberate and patient analysis. They are all tested and proven to function in reality for those of like minds. They have been woven together to reveal Our path, which is, in my opinion, the perfect blend for a specific type of individual.

It is important to make something clear. There are many complex terms in this book. Some of these are my interpretations of knowledge gleaned from divinations or Communion with the spirit guides of the Family. We have attempted to make these terms understandable to the reader, be it layperson, Elder, or scholar, and they are defined in the Vampyre Lexicon in appendix 1. Also, sometimes We use a word that may appear in other contexts or traditions. When this is the case, the meaning We ascribe to it is specific to Strigoi Vii only.

There are those who might think that the Strigoi Vii is a sect or cult. I can understand why some people might think so based on their first impression of Us. However, it would be absolutely impossible to have a cult of Strigoi Vii! We are each Cults of One. True Strigoi Vii are strong-willed individualists who would never be willing to submit to the mind control and brainwashing of a cult. In my view, running a cult is far too much work and a waste of energy. I've found that trying to work with Strigoi Vii is like herding cats: you can get a cat to agree with or pay attention to you, but it will never follow you like a sheep. A cat will simply refuse to do something it does not want to do; it will only do what you want if it was something it wished to do anyway.

Strigoi Vii cannot be sheep or followers, and therefore it is impossible to forge a cult of Strigoi Vii. However, they do find great pleasure in being with others of their own kind with whom they have a deep spiritual and philosophical bond. Strigoi Vii are truly individualists, yet highly social at the same time, and most definitely are not pack animals. Yet at times they can work together for a unified purpose, like a pride of lions hunting their prey, while remaining staunch individualists. This is free-willed agreement to achieve a goal. Like the lion on the hunt, many Strigoi Vii observe from a distance before committing to a group action.

Anton LaVey, author of *The Satanic Bible* and founder of the Church of Satan, learned this very lesson when he tried to form a central church for a movement of individualists. In my opinion, he should have focused on being an author and inspiring others, and thus his Church should have been a broad movement rather than a single organization. The creation of a movement should be based on the agreement of individuals. This is much more empowering, as it resonates with the true individualist on a deeper level.

To me, a church implies leaders and followers, and while that may suit those who desire beliefs, dogma, and faith, it just doesn't work for the highly individualist Strigoi Vii. In fact, I see the churches of most organized religions as cults! That is why at the end of the day the Strigoi Vii do not consider themselves postulants of a religion, but rather members of a philosophical and spiritual movement. Within the Strigoi Vii traditions, We maintain a university-like structure of learning and Initiation, which is more suited to inspire individualism, personal evolution, and freedom of thought than the dogma of organized religion. However, it must be noted that many countries, such as the United States, theoretically protect their residents' freedom of religion. We are more than happy to benefit from this protection, even if We do not agree with the terminology!

In summation: the main goal of the *Sanguinomicon* project is to inspire and challenge an individual's views and capture in writing the true spirit of the Strigoi Vii Mysteries and traditions of the Vampyre movement that evolved in the Gotham Halo (New York City). We are all still learning and evolving, yet the truth of Our core nature will remain the same. This evolution is pure Zhep'r, Immortality of the Self. Take what you need from this tome, learn, explore, and leave behind what doesn't work for you. This is your journey and your dream. Remember, Vampyres don't just survive. We *live*.

Those out there who agree with Us are truly Family, whilst the many who do not are simply on different paths. That is fine with me. I am following my own Quest of Family, not wasting my energy to amass a legion of followers. This Quest is my life's purpose.

If you are truly Vampyre, only through eternal effort and free will can you Awaken to your True Nature! Many will read these words; however, only a few will have the courage and endurance to embark on the journey of Zhep'r. The choice is yours.

Eternally,
Father Sebastiaan

ACKNOWLEDGMENTS

The "author" of the *Sanguinomicon* is officially Elorath, as this is a collective effort; there are many who have come together to make the *Sanguinomicon* project a reality. A great number of individuals contributed through actual writing, indispensable inspiration, or both. We are not seeking to disparage the invaluable role of any of Our contributors. Thus, one individual taking full credit would not be appropriate. By naming these collective contributors, Elorath demonstrates a unique approach seldom seen in a modern text. In Khem (Ancient Egypt), grimoires of magickal knowledge were always accredited to Thoth, the ibis-headed scribe and god of wisdom and magick, as well as to the author. The same is the case with this tome.

Father Sebastiaan, the founding father of the Ordo Strigoi Vii (OSV) and the Sanguinarium, is the inspirer of this project. Special thanks go to executive editors Lilith Madleh and Ziis for their gracious efforts in editing *Sanguinomicon*. They worked tirelessly to piece together this unique text.

Further acknowledgments also go out to other contributing members, which include my fang clients, members and supporters of the Sanguinarium movement, including Magister Mael, Nine, Lucius, Victor Magnus, Sheridan, Magister Mael, Aziza Rii, Bianca, Grimm, Jack Dean Stauss, Sascar Mina, Valeria Sinistrari, Irhandi, Lady~A, Lord Chaz, Chad Savage, Lord A., Maven, Goddess Rosemary, Kalliope, and countless others, for without them this text would not have become a reality. Special thanks to Our friends and conspirators, including Michelle Belanger, Vincent, Katherine Ramsland, Seth, Crudelia, Nemo, Daemonox, Rez, Madame X, Jason Crutchfield, and Shishain. We sincerely thank all the many individuals, far too many to name, who have helped this project reach fruition, including a very special dedication to Kinma, who made the first edition of the *Vampyre Sanguinomicon* possible.

The Strigoi Vii Charge

I AM Strigoi Vii.
In Love and Loyalty.
I am the Ruler of My Dream and seek never to die.
When in My Dayside, I am rational and materialistic.
Yet, by My own Will, I can enter the world mystic
And move to My Nightside, beyond the Veil.
I realize all things are possible and by My Will I prevail.
Within the equilibrium I find My Twilight.
I move closer to Zhep'r with every Flight.
I understand the difference between knowledge and belief.
Death is My only true enemy——it shall never conquer Me.
I am Immortal, and Life I embrace.
I lead, explore, and feed to My taste.
I create, I love, and I celebrate,
For I know Life's pleasures all surely await!
I shall always uphold The Black Veil, My Covenant,
The basis of Our Mysteries and beginning of My imprint.
Though I sit atop the food chain, I respect all other living things,
For they have their place due to the Energy they bring.
Thus I honor those who give Me the most precious gift.
Strigoi Vii is My spiritual Family, My sacred Heritage.
None shall keep Me from Zhep'r, for I am My own God!
I rejoice in My nature, Myself I applaud!
With Love & Loyalty.
I AM Strigoi Vii . . .
HAIL ELORATH!

Mortal-minded——"There are many beliefs and perspectives"
Immortal-minded——"I know no beliefs or faith that
lead to gnosis. Only results equal knowledge"

Book I

LIBER FLORATH

THE VAMPYRE PROSPECTUS

Chapter 1
SO WE BEGIN

Some are born to sweet delight,
Some are born to endless night.
—William Blake, "Auguries of Innocence"

Since the dawn of civilization, the vampire has danced through the dreams and nightmares of every culture. These whispers have been expressed over the past four aeons through Our Glamour, evident in folklore, literature, art, and the media, as well as many other spheres. Each new generation recognizes and embraces some new masque of the Immortal vampire archetype.

Why is this so? Is there not truth in every myth? There truly is, but it is most often hidden beneath metaphor and thus not immediately recognized. Therefore, your first task is to put aside what you already believe or think you know about "vampires" and listen carefully. What lies within these pages may initially seem for many readers to be sheer nonsense. However, for some rare few it will ring of familiarity. These blessed individuals have the unique potential to experience the world in a manner quite unknown to the rest of humanity. It is for those with this Dark Flame that this book has been written.

"The Vampyre Prospectus" is the cornerstone and the first of a series of core syllabus texts of the Strigoi Vii written from the perspective of the Ordo Strigoi Vii (OSV) and the Synod. Each tome of the *Sanguinomicon* is organized into a regimented system that disseminates the core

Mysteries, traditions, philosophies, and teachings of the Strigoi Vii. Thus, each book is intended to be a spark that ignites the Awakening of the Dark Flame, or the hidden potential, that may lie within you. That Awakening is the first step on the journey into the magickal, spiritual, and philosophical system We call Strigoi Vii. Whether you are a Seeker exploring the possibility of Strigoi Vii Initiation or a curious scholar of the esoteric, this book is the foremost authority and resource on the Mysteries of the Strigoi Vii.

This manifesto will set you on the first steps of understanding Zhep'r, or the evolution from a mortal's perspective to that of the Immortal. When beginning on this Great Work, you must first look within yourself as you would into a mirror, reading beyond the myths perpetuated in the mortal mind throughout history, and truly understand your own soul. Many splendid gems of truth are buried in the dull earth of history and legend. Consider the film *The Matrix*. Morpheus offers his student Neo a choice. He could explore the world beyond his ken by swallowing a red pill or instead take a blue pill and return to the mundane world. The original advertising campaign for *The Matrix* asked: "What is the Matrix? You will have to see it to understand!" Strigoi Vii is no different. At this very moment you are faced with the choice between living a complacent, "normal" life or rising above the world to transcend ordinary experience and gain a profound and extraordinary perspective.

In order to achieve success, you must test and experiment with the Strigoi Vii Mysteries. You shall begin to see through and beyond the mirror, a Quest which can only be embarked on in solitude. Only a few can possibly see past the enthralling Glamour that has seduced the mortal-minded for centuries. As one of Our mortal patrons has said, "This reality is beyond fiction." You must forget all you think you know about the vampire in order to comprehend the world known to the Family of the Strigoi Vii.

When reading and exploring the books of the *Sanguinomicon*, you may not agree with or feel drawn to some of the Mysteries that lie within. This is only natural, and skeptical questioning is the first step to unlocking this knowledge and comprehending how you may best apply it for yourself. We are catalysts of transformation for Our Family as well as others Awakened to the subtle world.

Those pursuing the Mysteries must be willing to study, analyze, and test the material presented in these texts. If you read the *Sanguinomicon* and do not experiment with or attempt to solve the Mysteries yourself, it will be as if you took the trouble to perfectly learn all the rules of chess yet never played a single game. You will be just another bibliophile who adds the *Sanguinomicon* to their collection. Results are inarguable. They are the only way you will ever know the truth of the Mysteries and determine if you are of the Family. This is the first step toward experiencing Awakening and Initiation. Achieving these results will take time, patience, and effort. Yet without validation, you will never know the potential power of the knowledge that lies within your hands at this very moment.

> *The one glimpse he had had of the title was enough to*
> *send him into transports, and some of the diagrams set in*
> *the vague Latin text excited the tensest and most disquiet-*
> *ing recollections in his brain. He felt it was highly necessary*
> *to get the ponderous thing home and begin deciphering it,*
> *and bore it out of the shop with such precipitate haste . . .*
> —H. P. Lovecraft, "The Descendant" (describing the *Necronomicon*)

The *Sanguinomicon* refers to the collection of texts containing the written Outer Circle teachings of the spiritual and philosophical meta-paradigms of Strigoi Vii, as defined by the Ordo Strigoi Vii (OSV) and the Synod. Strigoi Vii are engaged with and dedicated to spiritual and material mastery of this mortal coil and beyond. They are willing to tread the path necessary to guarantee the Immortality of the Self and serve the Quest of Family.

The *Sanguinomicon* is essentially the modern equivalent of earlier works on the same subject, including the *Pert em Hru,* or *The Book of Coming Forth by Day,* better known today as the Egyptian Book of the

Dead. It may also be likened to other sacred texts such as the Tibetan Book of the Dead and the Buddhist Sutras.

The Outer Strigoi Vii Mysteries focus on achieving the equilibrium of the *Dayside* (Corporeal, materialistic, rational, and skeptical), *Nightside* (Ethereal, spiritual, and magickal), and *Twilight* (Astral, a condition of balance). "The Vampyre Prospectus" is the foundation for and introduction to the *Sanguinomicon.* Each subsequent book explores deeper and deeper Mysteries through exercises and lessons. The second book, "Coming Forth by Day," explores the Corporeal Dayside Mysteries of Strigoi Vii. The third book, "Coming Forth by Night," explores the Ethereal Nightside. Finally, the fourth book, a discrete text for members of the Sanguinarium, explores the processes of "Coming Forth by Twilight," which completes the Outer Mysteries of the Vampyre. Upon completing these Mysteries, the Strigoi Vii establishes a solid foundation from which to secure personal Immortality of the Self. This is a transformative journey from the mentality of the mortal-minded to that of the Immortal. We Strigoi Vii call this journey of transformation Zhep'r.

The name *Sanguinomicon* is indeed inspired by the *Necronomicon,* a fictional and nonexistent magickal grimoire created by American horror writer and fantasist H. P. Lovecraft (1891–1937) and often mentioned in his stories. The etymology of the word *sanguinomicon* is based in Greek and Latin. The word *sanguine* in Latin means "of blood"; the word *nom* means "law" in Greek. Thus, one approximate English translation of *Sanguinomicon* would be "Book of the Laws of Blood." For the Strigoi Vii, it is the core sacred text.

> *The Revelations of the Devout and Learn'd*
> *Who rose before us, and as Prophets burn'd,*
> *Are all but Stories, which, awoke from Sleep,*
> *They told their comrades, and to Sleep return'd.*
> —Edward Fitzgerald, *Rubiyat of Omar Khayyam*

Strigoi Vii is the plural for *Strigoi Viu,* the Romanian word meaning, approximately, "living vampire" and/or "vampire witch." This is the word from which We take Our name. In Romanian mythology the word *strig* (*strega* in Italian) translates to mean "witch." One source of this word is the ancient Roman mythological shrieking vampire bird known as the *strix*. We feel this name is best suited to describe Our Family and Its traditions, magickal systems, Mysteries, and philosophies. Strigoi Vii is Our distinct form of Vampyre witchcraft. It shares many elements with modern neopaganism and other esoteric systems, yet still remains completely unique.

Many great thinkers such as Aristotle, William Blake, Carl Jung, Friedrich Nietzsche, Albert Einstein, Ayn Rand with her philosophy of Objectivism, and Ragnar Redbeard (author of *Might Is Right*) have expressed elements of Our Corporeal Dayside perspectives in various ways. However, it must be noted that the Dayside Vampyre philosophy is only partially revealed by these viewpoints or thinkers. Moreover, many of these personages unfortunately incorporate objectionable sentiments (such as racism and sexism) into their more excellent philosophies. You can also see elements of Our Ethereal Nightside perspectives reflected throughout history in the esoteric realms, including the Chaos Magick of Peter J. Carroll, Sumerian and Egyptian magic, Hinduism, Buddhism, the Thelema of Magus Aleister Crowley, Gnostic teachings, Judeo-Christian mysticism, and Hermetic Magick from ancient times.

We define the process of *syncretism* as reading between the lines and seeing the elements of the Mysteries in disparate myths, stories, and thoughts, and then putting these fragments back together into greater and more practical truths. As Strigoi Vii, that is what We do, seeking truth and reason through Our own insight as well as that of other wise ones.

For the last millennium, and even during the days of Sumer and Khem (better known as today as Ancient Egypt), the forefathers of the Family have been in the shadows, working in secrecy with Our Ancestors. However, all of this is changing now. With the guidance of Our Ancestors, a new generation of the Family is finally deliberately revealing Our collective heritage. We are gathering together and slowly coming out of the shadows in order to take part in the future and embrace Our past as One.

Vampyre or vampire? As members of a tradition rooted in parcels through history, We Strigoi Vii make a clear differentiation between the words *Vampyre* and *vampire*. We use the terms *Vampyre, Strigoi Vii,* and *Living Vampire* interchangeably, usually with capitals to refer to Ourselves. Many of the original Vampyre covens of Angael Halo (Los Angeles) and Gotham Halo (New York City) were the "Old Guard" who employed the spelling of *Vampyre* with a *y*. This subtle spelling difference may be confusing at first; however, Our traditional spelling denotes a significant and profound difference between fantasy and reality. Thus the Strigoi Vii, when speaking in short text, spell Vampyre with a capital *V* and a *y*. We use the *y* spelling to designate the term representing Our existence and Our Mysteries. For example, when referring to the practice of energy tapping from the Strigoi Vii perspective, one would say *Vampyrism*. When We spell vampire with an *i* and lowercase *v,* it traditionally refers to the mythological, literary, or popular concept of the vampire.

Vampyre is also the older and more classic spelling popularly used in the nineteenth century, originating from the Latin word *vampyrus*. The word *vampire* came into the more modern usage with the translation from Eastern European names such as *upior, upyr, vampire,* and *vapir.* Some members of the Family feel the words *Vampyre* and *vampire* are both somewhat cliché and simply prefer to refer to themselves as Strigoi Vii. We Strigoi Vii are proud of and honor Our heritage and traditions, yet look to the future with vigor and excitement.

As proposed by a Sanguinarium contemporary Jack Dean Stauss of Fang Club Hollywood fame, a little research would show you that *Vampyre* with a *y* was the Eastern European spelling of the word, based on *Wampyr* and *Valkrye*. John William Polidori is often given credit for the first English depiction of a modern-day Vampyre in his classic short story "The Vampyre," written in 1819.

An interesting sidenote about this story is that Lord Byron was erroneously given credit for this original tale, even though he and Polidori both stated in several press conferences that it was written by Polidori. This tale was written on the same weekend and on the same vacation Polidori shared with Mary and Percy Shelley, during which she inked a little story called *Frankenstein, or the Modern Prometheus*. Lord Byron, Polidori, Claire Clairmont, and the Shelleys were on a vacation in Switzerland when they decided to try and scare each other with ghost stories over dinner . . . The end results became the classics "The Vampyre" and *Frankenstein*.

Later on, during the end of Victorian era and right after Jack the Ripper terrorized the Whitechapel district of London, Bram Stoker was getting ready for the release of his famous novel, *Dracula*. His publisher thought it would be best that he change all the mentions of the word *vampyre* in his novel to *vampire*. *Vampyre* seemed too ethnic, and the main suspects in the Whitechapel murders were two Eastern European men named Seweryn Kłosowski and Aaron Kosminski. (The Whitechapel murders were committed in 1888, but the official investigation wasn't until 1894. This incited an 1895 race riot on the east end of London due to Scotland Yard's inability to convict a suspect.) Stoker's novel was completed in 1894, refined and rewritten in 1895, excerpts were released to the public in various newspapers from 1895 through 1898, and the official book was published in 1897. Removing any ethnic overtones was not only socially acceptable in the English Victorian era, it was prevalent amongst members of high society at the time. After that, the word was popularly spelled with an *i*.

Chapter 2
THE BLACK VEIL

*[T]here are two types of laws; just and unjust. I would
be the first to advocate obeying just laws. One has not
only a legal but a moral responsibility to obey just laws
. . . a just law is a code that squares with the moral
law . . . rooted in eternal law and natural law.*
—Dr. Martin Luther King, Jr., "Letter
from Birmingham City Jail"

The Five Principles

1ST PRINCIPLE: LAW. Strigoi Vii are not criminals.

2ND PRINCIPLE: RESPONSIBILITY. Strigoi Vii are adults.

3RD PRINCIPLE: BLOOD. Strigoi Vii see Blood as a metaphor for
something far more subtle.

4TH PRINCIPLE: QUEST. Strigoi Vii have a unified cause—the Current and the Quest.

5TH PRINCIPLE: SECRETS. Strigoi Vii is an open secret, hidden in plain
sight.

The Black Veil lies at the foundation of the Mysteries and contains
Our most sacred Principles. It has been created in order to ensure

Us the freedom of a solid, real-world, Dayside foundation. The edition presented here pertains exclusively to the Strigoi Vii and the Sanguinarium.

The Black Veil has been the source of Our ethics and power and is Our staff and Our shield. It exists for the preservation and prosperity of Our Mysteries, Family, and the Sanguinarium and is endorsed by the Synod and the OSV. Those who are not Strigoi Vii or with the Sanguinarium are not expected to uphold these Principles, as they are not bound to them. Of course, We of the Strigoi Vii encourage even those who are not of the Family to recognize and respect the common sense inherent in Our Black Veil. These simple guidelines provide Us with the freedom to maneuver unhindered through the mundane world.

The initial version of the Black Veil was originally written in late 1996 by the first Synod and Father as the code of conduct for the Gotham Halo's first Noir Haven, the Long Black Veil, and the members of Clan SABRETOOTH. The first editions of the Black Veil were based on a mix of the fetish scene's codes of conduct from the Eulenspiegel Society (TES) and the elegance of Renaissance faire etiquette, as well as containing elements of chivalry and romantic overtones in order to raise the Vampyre Glamour. Over time, several revisions and drafts of the Black Veil were created, the most notable being the "13 Rules of the Vamp Community," by Michelle Belanger, and the revision of an edition by Lady Melanie. These versions of the Black Veil were highly influenced by the role-playing game *Vampire: The Masquerade,* from which the vampire community drew on in these early years for terminology and community structure. Many different groups and individuals within the vampire subculture have created their own variations on the Black Veil, including the "7 Ethics of the Community" (which the Strigoi Vii refer to as the "Kherete Veil") a revision of Michelle Belanger's earlier version. This revision was endorsed by the Synod in order to create an edition of the Black Veil that would accommodate all those outside the Sanguinarium in the vampire community. However, the current Strigoi Vii Black Veil presented here represents the fundamental core ethics of the original Black Veil. It is the final version of the Black Veil embraced and endorsed by the Strigoi Vii and the Sanguinarium.

Why are there so many different versions of this text, and what makes this edition the most useful? From the perspective of the Strigoi Vii, the other editions of the Black Veil have high merit; however, they have not fully captured or expressed in words how to avoid potential liabilities faced in the tangible Dayside realities of the everyday world. Also, many of the earlier versions of the Black Veil are now quite out of date. Contemporary Dayside reality must be addressed in order to ensure the security and prosperity of the Family. It is unwise and self-defeating for a Strigoi Vii or Black Swan to betray themself by violating the common sense of these Principles. These simple guidelines should not be seen as restricting, but instead as empowering, as they offer Us the means to exist and thrive responsibly and judiciously within mundane society.

If a Strigoi Vii violates the Black Veil, they will suffer not only obvious consequences within the Sanguinarium and amongst the Family, but, most importantly, a condition of negative Zhep'r known as *khaskt,* which means "loss of opportunity." In effect, those who violate the Veil are robbing themselves of their own Zhep'r and actually reversing their opportunity for Immortality of the Self. Khaskt can be seen as the Strigoi Vii equivalent of negative karma. Yet it is much more potent for those attuned to the Current of Elorath through Initiation, or by employing the Mysteries on any level.

Strigoi Vii promotes social responsibility and recognizes that the consequences of Our actions may have various, often negative, repercussions as We become more visible to the mundane world. Those who proudly bear the Legacy Ankh close to their hearts, be they Strigoi Vii or Black Swan, make the statement that they are in agreement with the Principles of the Strigoi Vii Black Veil. These Principles are innate common sense for the responsible members of Our Family. The Black Veil gives Us the freedom and foundation to live and thrive within mundane society without offending or placing fear into Our source.

1st Principle: Law

Strigoi Vii are not criminals.
Adherence to the laws of Our local governments, even if We disagree with them, is essential to provide Us with the freedom to explore Our nature. Criminal or illegal behavior is greatly condemned within Strigoi Vii culture. By this, We do not refer to minor legal infractions such as parking violations. We are referring to serious crimes such as drug dealing, murder, rape, assault, and theft. Strigoi Vii are free spirited and individualistic. However, all Strigoi Vii are expected to act with common sense and practice social responsibility. It is the duty of every Strigoi Vii to conduct themselves in a manner that will not bring negative consequences upon the Family.

2nd Principle: Responsibility

Strigoi Vii are adults.
We must honor the need for minors to establish a skeptical, objective, and rational Dayside foundation before exploring and embracing the Nightside. Those who have not reached the age of majority (eighteen in the United States) must not be encouraged or permitted to explore Our Mysteries, participate in Vampyre ritual, or enter Our Sanctums under any conditions. Thus no child shall ever be formally Initiated into the Mysteries of Strigoi Vii, either privately or publicly.

Those children curious about Our Mysteries should explore the basics of yoga, quantum physics, theology, paganism, magick, Reiki, martial arts, and the works of philosophers such as Charles Darwin, Frederick Nietzsche, and Ayn Rand. This way, they build a solid foundation that shall better prepare them to pursue Zhep'r upon coming of age.

3rd Principle: Blood

Strigoi Vii see Blood as a metaphor for something far more subtle.
From the perspective of the Strigoi Vii, the Art of Vampyrism occurs

purely on a subtle energetic level, and thus Strigoi Vii do not drink of Corporeal, physical blood for tapping energies. The word *Blood* with a capital *B* is merely a metaphorical term for the subtle vital life force better known as *Prana* in Sanskrit, *Chi* in Chinese medicine, or *Ki* in Japanese martial arts. Within the Sanguinarium, *Sanguine* symbolizes the spiritual Current and Blood (heritage) of the Family; however, in the online vampire community outside the Sanguinarium, this has come to refer to blood drinkers. Be careful to clarify this potentially confusing distinction. On the Nightside perspective, We practice other, more subtle forms of absorbing and obtaining energy, which We find much more efficient and pertinent to Our Mysteries. On a Dayside level, the decision not to drink blood leads to a clear avoidance of legal liabilities and health risks such as blood-borne diseases, including hepatitis, syphilis, HIV / AIDS, and many more.

4th Principle: Quest

Strigoi Vii have a unified cause—the Current and the Quest.
The Current is the "Blood" that is the signature of Our Family. The collective duty of all Strigoi Vii is the Quest of Family. We must search out those with potential to Awaken, yet who are not aware of their potential. However, We never force a potential to follow Our way, as Vampyres are not mindless followers. Potentials must be allowed to come to the Family in their own way and in their own time. The Strigoi Vii should always use one of the proven tools for supporting the Quest of Family, as to not degrade Our Mysteries. Give the Seeker a hint, let them feel the Calling, and come when and if they are ready. Never support or join an organization or individual that actively opposes the Family or Our Quest. Never enter into debates with the mortal-minded or try to convert them to Our ways, as such behavior is in conflict with the Glamour and a waste of time and energy. Betraying the Quest of Family is not only betraying the Family, it is betraying yourself.

5th Principle: Secrets

Strigoi Vii is an open secret, hidden in plain sight.

Secrets protect and bind Us. Our Mysteries are Our own, and those who wish to explore them should seek them out alone, through personal initiative and action. As a sleight of hand magician employs the Principle of "hidden in plain sight," so does the Living Vampire.

Here follow three examples of the Black Veil Principle of Secrets. Firstly, take example from the Magisters. Honor your Sorors' and Fraters' right of privacy, such as in respect to their mundane identity. Never disclose their personal information to anyone, especially to the mortal-minded, but even to other Family members, without their explicit permission. The only circumstance under which the Synod would disclose the given name and identity of any Strigoi Vii is if such information was required under the legal jurisdiction of the proper authorities.

Secondly, public discussion of Strigoi Vii and the Mysteries outside of the Sanctums, such as with the media, on social networking websites, in public, or with those not of the Blood, is an obvious violation of this Principle. At all times speak only for yourself and never represent the greater Family outside of the guidelines of the Quest of Family. Leave that to those select members of the Magistry who are properly trained in public relations. Supporting this Principle furthers the Glamour and protects Our Mysteries.

Finally, one of the most important aspects of this Principle of the Black Veil is avoiding discussion of the Mysteries with someone who has not had the opportunity to read the *Sanguinomicon* and reflect on the contents. Respect free will and let Seekers gain a first impression of the Mysteries and formulate an opinion on their own. When an individual has the opportunity to read a text, they shall draw their own conclusions, whilst if you tell them about it, they will more likely only be able to see it from your perspective.

Summation

The Strigoi Vii Black Veil is Our code and applies only to the Strigoi Vii or those involved with the Sanguinarium. Employ these proven Principles, and you will have a solid foundation for Zhep'r. Do not debate with others who disagree or cannot see the common sense outlined here. As they are not in agreement, simply smile and say, *"We must agree to disagree, for free will is the whole of the law."*

Chapter 3
VAMPYRE PHILOSOPHY

There are more things in heaven and earth, Horatio,
Than are dreamt of in your philosophy.
—William Shakespeare, *Hamlet*

Vampyre philosophy is difficult to explain in a few or even many words. First and foremost, Strigoi Vii are passionate about life and seek its continuance. Strigoi Vii philosophy has at its core Immortality and preservation of the Self, whilst being in touch with Our core primal and animalistic nature and simultaneously finding empowerment in modern society.

We employ a philosophical stance called that of the "Immortal-minded," centered on Our Quest for Immortality of the Self. This ethos is in direct contrast to the common "mortal-minded" perspective on life. This is why you see references to "mortals" in Strigoi Vii literature. Additionally, in Our daily life We seek an equilibrium between Our *Dayside* and Our *Nightside* philosophies. We call this equilibrium the *Twilight*. Without the Twilight, it is impossible to fully achieve Zhep'r.

The Dayside is the beginning of the journey of Zhep'r and deals with the material coil of reality as perceived and experienced through the five senses. Here the Strigoi Vii seeks individual mastery of the Self and achievement of a strong-willed, autonomous, objective, and rational foundation. Yet mastering the Dayside also involves a strong awareness of an instinctive, primal inner nature of every human and Vampyre. This is the cornerstone of mastery of the Self and the Dayside. The Strigoi Vii takes a responsible approach to the Corporeal world and associated indulgences. They are aware and in control of the duality of their primal animalistic urges and their civilized, refined nature. The Strigoi Vii is mindful of their similarities to, as well as their distinct differences from, the mortal-minded. The Strigoi Vii also seeks dominion over the *mortal coils,* such as happiness, a long and healthy Corporeal life, accumulation of life experience and knowledge, and material mastery in prosperous living circumstances (including financial freedom and a high standard of living). The True Vampyres look to the future with ambition and excitement, yet do not deign to mortgage their present for future hopes.

By nature, Strigoi Vii are very independent and individualistic. However, they may also be highly social beings when they so choose or when the mood strikes them. For the Strigoi Vii, the personal, *inwardly empowered ego,* which focuses on preservation and evolution of the Self, always comes before all else. In essence, their knowledge of who they are comes from within. The Strigoi Vii draws a clear distinction between this inwardly empowered ego and the insecure, *externally gratified ego.* Individuals with an externally gratified ego have no intrinsic sense of Self. Instead, their Self is shaped and changed by their personal interactions, Corporeal circumstances, and how they are perceived by others. In a vain attempt to fill the void within them, they set about controlling and manipulating others for a burst of temporary, hollow ego satisfaction. Such an approach to life has nothing to do with personal evolution. Strigoi Vii philosophy encourages the personal self-mastery of knowing and controlling oneself first, not controlling others. Free will is amongst the highest of all virtues to the Strigoi Vii, and thus We respect the free will of all sentient beings.

In order to truly live life, you must fully experience it with all your senses. However, before this can be achieved, you must first break free of subjugation to mortal slave bonds such as destructive drugs, unhealthy

liber Elorath

relationships, mind-numbing television shows, escapism through video game or Internet addictions, and constant indulgence in unhealthy fast foods, to mention just a few. Such things are merely distractions which, when practiced to excess, only dull the senses, harm the body, and thus prevent you from truly living. The True Strigoi Vii know how to amuse themself in a nondestructive manner and control their possessions, finances, and pastimes instead of being controlled by them.

In true postmodern fashion, the Strigoi Vii see constructed boundaries and social roles for what they are and seek to live life as they choose without being bound by artificial conventions. Strigoi Vii are very sensual, romantic, and passionate and may often have a taste for the ways of the libertine. An important element of Strigoi Vii is carnal pleasure and worship of the flesh and seeing one's body as a temple of flesh. Many Strigoi Vii deliberately subvert or deny the gender and sexual roles and class strictures found in mundane society. Strigoi Vii love the finest pleasures of life, such as conversation and debate, art, music, gourmet food, dance, and literature. They will never force others to adopt their views or actions, always respecting others' free will above all else. However, they will also try to inspire and encourage others to live a more unfettered and fulfilling life.

Strigoi Vii are not victims of blind faith, and thus strive to break the conditioning of mortal-minded beliefs and dogma, seeking knowledge only through results. In this sense, the Strigoi Vii is very similar to the scientist who constantly investigates and tests the world around him before drawing conclusions or fashioning laws of nature.

Money and monetary gains are not seen as evil by the Strigoi Vii unless they control and warp the Self through avarice and greed. The Strigoi Vii view money and capital as a form of Corporeal energy that is neither beneficial nor harmful in itself. Thus they call such currencies "monetary energy." The Strigoi Vii are very careful to never allow themselves to be controlled by their possessions.

Common amongst the Strigoi Vii is the modern application of historical and long-lost forms of customs and chivalry. These can range from holding elegant masquerade balls or Victorian tea parties to the study of dead languages. Taking inspiration from the code of chivalry of medieval knights, many masculine Strigoi Vii embrace gentlemanly codes of conduct, strive for individual nobility, and treat all others with courtesy. It is also common to find feminine Strigoi Vii embracing the role of truly elegant ladies and sincere witches. They draw directly upon the feminine aspect of Kalistree as a source of their empowerment and mastery. However, it is worth noting that Strigoi Vii recognize and respect alternative lifestyles and "abnormal" conceptions of individual gender roles. Even though the yin and yang of masculine and feminine may be seen as distinct yet balanced opposites, many Strigoi Vii have varied understandings and applications of masculinity and femininity.

The above examples and behaviors reflect only a portion of the Dayside perspectives found within the Family. As always, Strigoi Vii encourages individuals to define their own attitudes and paths in life.

The Nightside is the equal opposite of the Dayside in Strigoi Vii philosophy. In the Nightside, the Strigoi Vii moves beyond the Mysteries of rational reality such as science and the laws of physics. The Strigoi Vii must have an absolute grounding in the Dayside to effectively explore the Mysteries of the Nightside. In the Nightside, the Strigoi Vii can investigate the many subtle worlds that intersect with our Corporeal world. The Nightside encompasses the *Ethereal,* the domain of Prana (vital life energy) and many forms of energy sensitivity and manipulation. The mortal-minded view Our Nightside as occultism and mysticism. The beginnings of Strigoi Vii theology lie in the Nightside. Our theology is not a trendy new-age blind acceptance of crude belief and faith, but rather a scientific approach to exploration of the subtle worlds. In the Nightside, the Strigoi Vii deeply explores quantum physics, meditation, energy work such as Reiki, Tantra, and yoga, and sacred geometry. Individual experience and achieved results form the foundation of Strigoi Vii theology, not antique articles of accepted dogma.

The Twilight represents a higher level of the Vampyre Mysteries and is detailed in the tome "Coming Forth by Twilight." The Twilight is the contrasting balance between the Dayside and Nightside, allowing the Strigoi Vii who becomes adept in Twilight to fully enjoy the pleasures and benefits of both. With such mastery, the Strigoi Vii can rise to fully embrace the experiences of the Astral, dreamwalking, and higher planes of existence.

Gnosis is the personal experience of divinity, spirituality, and the Self. A most important part of Gnosis for the Strigoi Vii is the Quest for Immortality. The Strigoi Vii strives for personal survival and preservation of the Self beyond the First Death of the Corporeal body. To this end, the Strigoi Vii always seek to increase their own Zhep'r and master an evolved state that may be described as timeless, nonlinear, and transcending ordinary reality. Yet the Strigoi Vii must first ignite the Quest of Immortality of the Self through a deeply rooted foundation in the Corporeal Dayside perspective. Through mastery of the Dayside and the Nightside, as well as the equilibrium between them, known as Twilight, the Strigoi Vii may truly discover personal Immortality of the Self.

> *An adoration of Osiris, Un-nefer, god great within Abydos,*
> *king of eternity, lord of everlasting, traversing millions of*
> *years in the duration of his life, son eldest of the womb of*
> *Nut, engendered by Seb the chief, lord of* ureret *crown, lofty*
> *of the white crown, prince of gods and of men, he hath re-*
> *ceived the crook [and] flail and the dignity of his fathers. . . .*
> *Eternity it is and Everlastingness, Eternity is*
> *the day, Everlastingness is the night.*
> —*The Papyrus of Ani,* or *The Egyptian Book of*
> *the Dead,* E. A. Wallis Budge (trans.)

Zhep'r is the Strigoi Vii word for evolution, transformation of the Self, and the Quest of Immortality. This term is formed from two words: the Egyptian *Kheperi* (transform) and the Greek *Zephyr* (the god of the West Wind.) The word *Kheper* is also related to the terms *Kheperi* and the Egyptian transformation of *Kheperu* and can be translated as "to come into being," "to become," and "transformation." Another source of the word is *Khepera,* the name for the morning incarnation of the Sun god in Egyptian mythology. The associated Egyptian symbol or hieroglyph is a scarab beetle. The scarab beetle lays its eggs in carrion, which gave the Ancient Egyptians the impression that these insects were born from death. Thus, the scarab came to represent rebirth. Although Our term *Zhep'r* has a different phonetic value than the original Egyptian word (the Egyptian word is pronounced *khef-fer,* and Our term is pronounced *zef-hur*), it carries a similar definition and meaning. There is another spelling of this word, *Xeper,* which is employed by the Temple of Set, a left-hand path esoteric order founded in 1975.

Strigoi Vii are agents of change, beings of evolution and transformation. Zhep'r is this process of change. Nothing in the universe is absolutely fixed and eternal. Strigoi Vii revel in evolution. To the Strigoi Vii, Chaos is freedom!

From the Dayside perspective, Zhep'r is self-mastery and improvement. Dayside Zhep'r focuses on furthering the material coils such as financial freedom, improving one's personal Glamour, and living a prosperous, healthy, and long and vital life. From the Nightside perspective, Zhep'r is the Awakening and mastery of the Strigoi Vii's psychic abilities, connection to the subtle worlds and the achievement of spiritual Immortality of the Self. The core of the Strigoi Vii Quest is conquering the Second Death, which is the dissolution of the consciousness that occurs some time after the Corporeal body has ceased to function. Strigoi Vii call this the *Oblivescence,* or the process of forgetting, as the soul is washed in a spiritual amnesia or is fully energetically dispersed, depending on your perspective. Zhep'r is further expressed in the process of self-deification. This involves solving the Mysteries on a personal level, Awakening the Dragon (higher Self), and Coming forth by Twilight.

For the Strigoi Vii, Zhep'r is not a goal but a constant journey. There is no end to the Quest of Zhep'r except Second Death. Thus the Second Death is the only true enemy of the Vampyre.

Belief is a Tool.
—Peter J. Carroll, author of *Liber Null & Psychonaut*

Is Strigoi Vii a religion? Yes and no. Vampyrism is an action performed by the Strigoi Vii. Our philosophy and traditions, as well as Our Art of Vampyrism, are a group of tested concepts and applications, not a belief system. Thus Strigoi Vii is not a religion in the common sense of the word. Its reality is far more complex.

The Mysteries are a spiritual and philosophical *metaparadigm* or *metabelief system,* which is based on the ability to *paradigm shift* (utilize various belief systems and methods, based on applicability, to achieve a specific purpose). For the Strigoi Vii, belief is a tool that can be applied at will. Thus, the Strigoi Vii may adopt and discard different epistemological systems and philosophies as it suits their needs, rather than acting unconsciously on inescapably ingrained belief.

One of the characteristics of those naturally attuned to Our nature is that they cannot truly be of another "religion." So it is incorrect for an Awakened Strigoi Vii to say, "I am a pagan" or "I am a Satanist." The Awakened Strigoi Vii has come to the collective agreement that religion is a system of arbitrary belief used by humans to attempt to understand the reality around them as well as to control others' behavior. Our use of religion is different. Strigoi Vii employ belief systems, known as paradigms or ideologies, to adopt a temporary view that will aid them in Zhep'r or employment of the Glamour. They then discard the system when it is no longer useful. This viewpoint is very similar to the mechanics of Chaos Magick.

To make an analogy, Strigoi Vii is like the core operating system of a computer, whilst each paradigm is like a separate program or application. The program you employ depends on your need. To navigate the Internet, you choose a web browser. A word processing program is useful only if you wish to create a text document. For example, a

Strigoi Vii may love the practices and traditions of Asatru, or Norse paganism. Thus they may employ the rituals and magick of that particular paradigm to further their sense of Self and increase their Zhep'r. However, this does not make that Strigoi Vii truly an Asatru; they are simply employing or "wearing" Asatru beliefs and traditions as one would wear an article of clothing. Many of the feminine Strigoi Vii appreciate the goddess-centered elements found within many traditions of neopaganism. Thus, they can make use of the beliefs of myriad pagan religions and enjoy the pleasures of feminine goddess-oriented empowerment. Many members of Our Family may have a preferred paradigm as a mortal might prefer a specific type of cuisine or genre of literature.

Today, We are seeing a new movement sometimes known as "Traditionalist Strigoi Vii" or "True Vampyres" developing within the Family. These pioneers find existing without beliefs or paradigms and recognizing their true Self is most beneficial to them. To these traditionalists, any belief, even a temporarily adopted one, can be seen as a crutch. However, Strigoi Vii are nothing if not mutable and flexible. They may wear many masks, not only in their spiritual existence, but in their everyday lives as well. Strigoi Vii are Sunday school teachers, politicians, university professors, doctors, artists, religious leaders, and police officers. There are even Strigoi Vii within the ministry of the Catholic Church!

Such seeming paradoxes are possible because, whilst personal paradigms have strong meanings for these individuals, they clearly realize they are Strigoi Vii first and foremost. How else do you think so many members of the Family have walked through the history of mankind so easily and gracefully?

A monster then, a dream,
A discord. Dragons of the prime,
That tare each other in their slime,
Were mellow music match'd with him . . .

What hope of answer, or redress?
Behind the veil, behind the veil.
—Alfred, Lord Tennyson, "In Memoriam"

The Dragon has long been associated with mystery, magick, power, nobility, and divinity. The Dragon is a powerful symbol that is as deeply ingrained in the world's mythology and legends as the vampire. Within each Strigoi Vii, the Dragon exists as a higher consciousness of the Self. This Divine Spark breathes forth the Dark Flame for each member of the Family and is the Throne from which all perception is experienced.

Within Strigoi Vii theology, the Dragon represents Our pacts with ancient divinities, the spiral helix of the divine potential existing in Our subtle bodies, Our higher Self, and Our animalistic primal nature. Thus Elorath, Our spiritual Blood, is seen as a "Dance of Dragons" by many within the Family.

The concept of the higher Self has been recently popularized by contemporary new-age and occult movements. However, it was recognized long before. Aleister Crowley spoke of the higher Self as the "Holy Guardian Angel" within each person, or the manifestation of true will. Other cultures have called the higher Self or similar concepts by various names. The Hermetic Order of the Golden Dawn called it the *Genius,* and it was named the *Daemon* in Greek mythology. It is not completely dissimilar to what many religions call the soul. An early appearance of the term occurs in the fifteenth-century grimoire entitled *The Book of the Sacred Magic of Abramelin the Mage.*

The Corporeal manifestation of the Dragon is the reptilian brain, which is the portion of the brain first identified by Dr. Paul D. MacLean. It is also known as the brain stem, or the lower part of the brain. The reptilian brain controls essential involuntary functions such as the cardiovascular and respiratory system. We share the structure of the brain stem with reptiles, and it is also believed to be responsible for primitive rage and flight-or-fight responses. In the mammalian brain, the brain stem represents the most ancient and unchanged part of the brain structure. Other, more highly evolved, portions of the brain exist in their present form due to the process of mammalian evolution. The reptilian brain may be seen as the seat of primitive and animalistic functions.

For the Strigoi Vii, achieving Communion with the Dragon is to see the world through the Dragon's emerald eyes: to see beyond our set conceptions and engage in pure *perception,* unhindered by ingrained mortal-minded ideas of what is and what is not. Such Communion may be achieved through meditation, development of the Self, and the furthering of Zhep'r. For the Strigoi Vii, experiencing and maintaining this Communion is a great point in personal evolution and the core of self-knowledge. Awakening the Dragon of the Self is one of the core Principles of the Strigoi Vii Mysteries.

Chapter 4
THE ART OF VAMPYRISM

Energy is the only life, and is from the Body; and Rea-
son is the bound or outward circumference of Energy.
Energy is Eternal Delight.
—William Blake, "The Marriage of Heaven and Hell"

Every living being transfers energy. This transfer occurs in every interaction, be it as simple as two people trading glances across a room, a
conversation between a mother and child, or even one animal devour-
ing another. As Albert Einstein explained in his theory of relativity,
matter and energy are incontrovertible ($E = mc^2$). Everything in the
Corporeal world contains energy and can be transformed into energy,
from the lightning in the sky during a thunderstorm to the chair you
are sitting in as you read this book. Moreover, as Newton stated, energy can never be created or destroyed, only transformed. When you
eat, the food does not "disappear." Instead, part of it is transformed
into energy that powers your physical body, and part of it remains as
waste products. The transformation and transmission of energy is an
endless cycle. The Arts of Vampyrism are among many energy manipulations We call "techniques."

Every person who has been in a large group of people knows the
experience of collective energy. The "energy of the crowd" can be
sensed in various circumstances, such as a concert, political rally, sport-
ing event, or university lecture. When a group of people gather for

one focused purpose, a huge amount of collective emotional and Corporeal energy is produced. Many people will report feeling "psyched up" or "enervated" after taking part in such a gathering. Humans are amazing beings! When a large number of humans come together and share a thrilling or emotionally charged experience, they release huge amounts of energy. We, as Strigoi Vii, can sense and tap this energy. We call collective energy generated by large crowds *Ambient Energy,* and learning how to tap and absorb this energy is the most elementary form of the Art of Vampyrism.

Anyone working in a performance-oriented profession, such as a musician, DJ, tour guide, professor, or politician, experiences a flow of energy between themselves and their audience. Many who choose such professions or even become celebrities do so because they have a deep hunger for this experience. They feel charged and exhilarated in front of an audience. The emotions of the audience, whether approval or disdain, provide the Astral "flavor" of the energy during such a performance. That is why so many of these individuals are drawn to Strigoi Vii.

You may ask if this applies on a subtle level for divine entities. Absolutely! The gods and goddesses of mortal religions absorb Ambient energy on a grand scale from their worshippers. For example, the godform Allah receives energy from the daily prayers of millions of Muslims. More than 1.1 billion people send immense amounts of energy toward the godform Jesus every Sunday morning. Could it be that when humans worship their deities with such loving free will they are really giving life to and feeding the most successful vampires in history?

The Art of Vampyrism, at its core, is an exchange of energies. As practiced by the Strigoi Vii and defined by the *Sanguinomicon,* the Art of Vampyrism is a series of methods for ethically and honorably tapping the surplus subtle life energies radiated by the human body. The Art of Vampyrism is an integral part of the nature and existence of the Strigoi Vii. All Strigoi Vii who move toward the Nightside practice this sacred Art, usually instinctively at first, then consciously as an Initiate, and finally without effort once they have Ascended to a high level of mastery. Please note that the purpose and intent of Our Art of Vampyrism is completely distinct from that practiced by traditional psychic vampires. One of the biggest misconceptions is that all vampires and Vampyres drink blood. This is simply not true, as Strigoi Vii of Romanian myths and in reality are not blood drinkers. Our Vampyrism takes place exclusively on a subtle level. From the Dayside perspective, there are the obvious health risks like contracting HIV, hepatitis, or infection and the fact that in many cultures drinking blood is not only taboo—it is considered an act of cannibalism and assault as well. From the Nightside perspective, blood drinking is not an efficient technique to provide the large amounts of energy required to fuel transformation. For the Living Vampire, all references to blood are strictly metaphorical and symbolic.

The purpose of Our Vampyrism is, first and foremost, to fuel direct Offerings of life force in Communion with Our Ancestors and to connect and achieve awareness of Our Dragon. Communion is the main catalyst to ignite Zhep'r and the most sacred and private act within all the Strigoi Vii Mysteries. Communion is the gateway to Immortality of the Self. On a more advanced level, the life force procured is used for the application of Nomaj Sorcery, a multidimensional vibrational system that is at the core of the Inner Mysteries. However, at the most basic level, Vampyrism takes place in order to fuel Zhep'r and to raise the metabolism of the subtle body, which aids in the process of achieving Zhep'r.

The human body is the most evolved Corporeal entity, and thus creates a specific, high-intensity frequency of Prana (the Sanskrit word for vital life force), which is the most suited to the energetic system of the Strigoi Vii subtle body. Prana is thus the source and fuel of life, that is why We consider Ourselves Living Vampires. Other frequencies of Prana, such as that from animals, plants, or objects, have their uses. However, they are simply not compatible with and cannot be of use in fueling Zhep'r. Nor are they suitable for the Offering in Communion.

Many un-Awakened Living Vampires practice Vampyrism unconsciously, as their subtle bodies vibrate on a higher frequency than the average human and create an instinctual thirst for life force. Through the disciplines of the Art of Vampyrism—will, intent, and training—the un-Awakened Vampyre can learn to master Vampyrism as an art. This "need" for subtle energy is akin to the "thirst" or "hunger" in vampire literature. As Zhep'r increases, so does the Need for more energy.

The Art of Vampyrism can be seen by the uninformed as a maliciously predatory act. However, We are not without a deep-rooted system of ethics. Although the Art of Vampyrism is an action that intentionally and consciously draws energy from the subtle bodies of humans, it is not a parasitic act, as is the case with traditional psychic vampirism. Through Our Art of Vampyrism, as in the transfer of energies within the web of life, the flow of energy is actually healthy, advantageous, and very pleasurable for the human. This is a highly symbiotic relationship and has truly evolved beyond what most would consider true predation. Within the Strigoi Vii Mysteries, the tapping of energies from subtle energies never involves the drinking of physical blood, ending the life of any living being, or causing physical harm of any kind. If done with respect and care, the Art of Vampyrism is not physically, emotionally, or spiritually harmful to the human subtle body in any way. The Art of Vampyrism is beneficial and affirming for the Strigoi Vii and the mundane alike.

As a rough analogy, one might consider the pilot fish that attaches itself to a shark. The pilot fish consumes parasites and bits of undigested food that would otherwise potentially cause harm to the shark. Despite the fact that sharks are often seen as consummate predators, it is extremely rare for a shark to consume a pilot fish, even when it swims into the shark's mouth to remove pieces of food from its teeth (thus preserving them from decay.) Both the pilot fish and the shark benefit from and mutually thrive due to their symbiotic relationship. So is it with the mortal-minded and the Vampyre.

Throughout history, many subtle energetic techniques such as Reiki, Tantric workings, and yoga have utilized similar processes as the Art of Vampyrism. Vampyrism, in Our view, is an exchange of energies.

Performers such as actors or musicians exchange energy with their audience every time they perform. The only difference is that the Strigoi Vii has a specific intent and purpose in collecting this excess energy. One can also witness this relationship and exchange of energies reflected in the symbiotic relationship between deities and their worshipful followers, or celebrities and their starstruck admiring fans. Such acts are, in Our worldview, unconscious applications of Our basic Arts of Vampyrism.

In effect, Vampyrism can, from Our view, be considered a healing act. It may be seen as beneficial to the mortal world, for We remove and unblock stagnant energies and inspire the flow of radiant energies through the subtle world and humanity's collective consciousness. This is why so many are unconsciously seduced by Vampyres. However, Strigoi Vii do not slaughter or torture for pleasure or any other purpose! Any such act is always reprehensible within the ethical system of the Strigoi Vii. We respectfully take what We need due to a pure love of life. Our clear intent is that Our sources live happy, fulfilled, and content lives.

> *All we have to go upon are traditions and superstitions.*
> *These do not at the first appear much . . . Yet must we*
> *be satisfied, in the first place because we have to be, no*
> *other means is at our control, and secondly, because, af-*
> *ter all these things, tradition and superstition, are every-*
> *thing. Does not the belief in vampires rest . . . on them?*
> —Bram Stoker, *Dracula*

> *For it is the life of all flesh; the blood of it is the life thereof . . .*
> *Ye shall eat the blood of no manner of flesh: for the life of all*
> *flesh is the blood thereof: whosoever eateth it shall be cut off.*
> —Leviticus 17:14

Chapter 5

FAMILY

Blood is thicker than water.
—Proverb

Frater, We are of the same Current of Blood, the same frequency
of spirit. We are those with the drive, courage, love of life, will,
and desire to embrace the opportunity for Immortality of the
Self. Never forget this is the agreement which bonds Us as Fam-
ily. As you experience Zhep'r, you will come to understand this.
—Magister Dimitri, August 1997

Strigoi Vii, as a collective of individuals and a Family, are bound by an
unbreakable spiritual and metaphysical bond. To reflect this bond, We
metaphorically refer to those of the Strigoi Vii Family as "of the Blood,"
or simply by the Latin word for blood, *Sanguine*. The Family of Strigoi
Vii does not exactly correspond to a biological mortal family. We experience a far stronger bond with other Strigoi Vii that is difficult to
explain to those who are not of the Blood.

When encountering another of Our Legacy, We often immediately recognize them through the *Radiance,* or a subtle intuition of
who and what they are. The strength of the Radiance depends on
several factors. A Strigoi Vii who has reached a high level of Initiation, is strongly in tune with the Current of Elorath, or has recently

been sated with Prana or made Communion may emit a Radiance that burns like a flame. Un-Awakened individuals will often exhibit a dim glimmer of the Radiance, whilst for some it will shine like a lighthouse in the darkness. Some Strigoi Vii have described the experience of sensing the Radiance as being strongly and seemingly inexplicably drawn to another or feeling a deep-rooted and unexplainable sympathy with or liking for someone. Many Strigoi Vii have also reported that others of the Family emanate a sort of subtle "glow," hence the term *Radiance.*

The Currents that surge within Our souls are deep rooted and, from a certain perspective, quite ancient. Our sense of pride in Our Family and Our connection with others of Our Family is a reflection of this agreement. We do not know the origins of the Current, nor do We dwell on this. We look toward the here and now as well as the future, yet recognize Our commonality as Family.

Awakening as a process comes to members of the Family in three different forms: Latent Vampyres, Born Vampyres, and Made Vampyres. Such experiences affect each Vampyre differently, as not everyone is at a point of self-awareness when they realize the Current is present within them.

Latent Vampyres are formally known as *Klavasi.* This is the most common type of awakening within the Current—when a True Vampyre realizes their Radiance. It occurs at some point after puberty. One theory on the origins of Latent Vampyres is that during or shortly after the conception of their Corporeal bodies, an Ancestor implanted the seed of the Current within them while they were in their mother's womb. Another possibility is that one or both of their parents carry a spiritual gene of the Current in their subtle bodies and passed it on to their child, thus giving them the potential to Awaken as a Latent Vampyre. The awakening is usually triggered by experiences like trauma, being fed on deeply by another Vampyre, being in the vicinity of a large Communion rite, being exposed to one of the many avenues of the Quest, having a sexual encounter with another Vampyre, or a series of bizarre events that seem akin to fate. Most Seekers are Latent Vampyres and many describe the awakening as akin to the realization one is gay or that they have a calling. Latent Vampyres may always feel drawn to the others of the Family. *Sanguinomicon* primarily caters to Latent Vampyres. and the Initiation structure aids them in their awakening and furthers their Zhep'r.

Born Vampyres are formally known as *Quissain* and are very rare. Such individuals were virtually born Awakened and instinctively are aware of what they are. As children, the Quissain are usually very eccentric and will most often have multitudes of symptoms such as dyslexia, antisocial disorders, hyperactivity, and more. Born Vampyres will almost always display psychic abilities and excel in energy work such as yoga and Reiki. What is most interesting is that Quissain make up the most Ronin and rarely Initiate. Amongst the Family they manifest mostly as pure Ramkht in frequency and behavior, with a strong sense of confidence and natural talents at the Art of Vampyrism.

Made Vampyres are formally known as *Ardetha* and undergo a series of rites and conscious Initiations—or they have been touched on such a deep level that they Awaken. The ritual for made Vampyres is only known to select Magisters and is rarely used. Sometimes this is known as the Kiss of Elorath. There are many controversies regarding Ardetha amongst members of the Strigoi Vii Family, some believing that we can only be born to what We are (purebloods), whilst others feel that in this time and age it is important to allow mortals (or "half-breeds") the opportunity to become. Whatever the story, the individual must demonstrate potential and a sincere interest in joining the Family. Such an Awakening is usually very traumatic and cannot occur without the agreement and involvement of a Strigoi Morte who is willing to become the Patron of the individual who is to receive the Kiss.

Paths constitute the variety of ways people interact with the Strigoi Vii Mysteries. There are three paths within the Strigoi Vii Mysteries: *Black Swans, Ronin,* and *Initiates.*

Black Swans are those who do not consider themselves True Vampyres or Strigoi Vii, yet are drawn to the Mysteries and Our Glamour. Black Swans can be involved in the Sanguinarium and often benefit from elements of the Mysteries. Most often Black Swans are friends, lovers, companions, or mundane family members of a Strigoi Vii Ronin or Initiate. Many Black Swans have read the *Sanguinomicon* and are in at least partial agreement with Our Outer Mysteries. It is very common for Black Swans to offer themselves as consensual energy donors in order to benefit from the Awakening and healing powers of the Art of Vampyrism or to experience energy transfer on a sensual level. Black Swans who feel the Calling and Awaken to the Mysteries may choose to embrace the Mysteries on their own terms as Ronin or through formally Initiating at a later point.

Ronin are individuals who do not follow the standard Initiatory formulae of Strigoi Vii, yet are in agreement with Our Mysteries. The word *Ronin* originates from the Japanese samurai of the Tokugawa era and means "to be without a lord." The term thus befits the solitary Strigoi Vii. Ronin are the equivalent of solitaries in other esoteric systems, and they often do not involve themselves directly in the Sanguinarium movement. Being solitary and independent, yet still "of the Current," Ronin consider themselves Strigoi Vii but have not formally Initiated. Ronin most often focus solely on the Outer Mysteries and may have their own personal system of achieving Zhep'r. It is not uncommon for a Ronin to eventually become a formal Initiate of the Mysteries.

Initiates are the most common type of Strigoi Vii and closely work within the standard formulae of Ordeals as detailed within the *Sanguinomicon*. They find the sequential system of Initiation greatly complements their own Zhep'r and use the Mysteries as a powerful personal tool. However, based on their own personal predilections, Initiates still pursue individual approaches to building Zhep'r and empowering their will. Being an Initiate of Strigoi Vii by no means limits individuality or the pursuit of Zhep'r. The Initiate's commitment to the Mysteries allows them to easily interact with and relate to others of the Family through the common perspectives of personal validation and organization. Initiates are the members of the Family most often Initiated into the Ordo Strigoi Vii or who sit on the Synod, due to their clearly stated qualifications and intent. One can compare Initiates to those who have gone through a university system and earned a formal degree, whilst Ronin are most often self-taught. To extend the analogy, Black Swans would be prospective students who have expressed an interest in attending a particular university or starting a course of study but have not yet committed themselves.

We know each other
by secret symbols,

. . . .

there is subtle appraisement;
even if we [speak] a brief greeting

or do not speak at all,
we know our Name

we nameless initiates,
born of one mother,

companions
of the flame.
—H.D., "The Walls Do Not Fall"

A Sobriquet is a "Vampyre Name," and Strigoi Vii tradition encourages that, upon the Prospectii validation, the Initiate adopt this fresh, new name for exclusive use amongst other Strigoi Vii. This is quite similar to the *magickal motto* used within the Hermetic Order of the Golden Dawn. Sobriquets should reflect a piece of the Initiate's personality and are used within ritual and magickal workings. Such names can reflect the individual's Current, vision of themselves, or identification with an ancient or obscure god or goddess. Examples include Mael ("prince" or "king" in Gaelic), Irhandi ("sorcerer" in Sumerian), and Lilith (Hebrew/Sumerian goddess).

When a Magister is Initiated, they take a second Sobriquet as their Magister name, which is their "true name" and never revealed to anyone outside the Family. The Sobriquet is to be used for correspondence with other Strigoi Vii, within the Sanctums of the Sanguinarium, and as a working tool in ritual and meditation. Sobriquets are similar to magickal names in mortal-minded esoteric traditions or a "handle" on the Internet. The Strigoi Vii Sobriquet also provides additional security and privacy, as addressing a Strigoi Vii by their legal or given name is rude and disrespectful, unless they specifically request it in an open forum or you have a personal friendship with them and are interacting in the mundane world. In addition, the Sobriquet allows the Strigoi Vii to enter a new state of mind where they are free to express themselves amongst other members of the Family.

A Sobriquet is different from an assumed "scene name," which is used for social purposes, or a "given name," which is a legal name used in the Dayside and the mundane world. The Sobriquet should be unrelated to any previous aliases, magickal names, or other names the Strigoi Vii has used. Thus when the Strigoi Vii make the Prospectii Rite of Dedication, they should from that point on use a completely new and fresh name specifically for the Strigoi Vii. It should reflect a point of personal empowerment and a new beginning for the Strigoi Vii. This name is chosen in Sanguinarium virtual sanctums as a user name and maintains privacy and focus on Zhep'r.

. . .And I have felt
A presence that disturbs me with the joy
Of elevated thoughts; a sense sublime
Of something far more deeply interfused,

. . . .

A motion and a spirit, that impels
All thinking things, all objects of all thought,
And rolls through all things . . .
—William Wordsworth, "Lines Composed
a Few Miles above Tintern Abbey"

The Current of Elorath, or simply the "Current" of the Strigoi Vii
Mysteries, flows through each member of the Family and is symbol-
ized by the number XXIII (23). The reason for this numerical linkage is
revealed in the Higher Mysteries. The Current is the Blood that
attunes and unites the Family to the Egregore of Elorath. Egregores, in
occult parlance, are beings comprised of the collective will, purpose,
and group mind and soul of a gathering of individuals focusing their
specific intent into the creation of the Egregore. The Egregore of Elorath represents the lineage and collective "Current" of the Strigoi Vii.

Being of the Current, or metaphorically "of the Blood," implies
the possession of a subtle gene that cannot be found in the DNA of the
Corporeal body. It is something far more subtle and complex and can
only be understood by solving the Mysteries. The Current is a spiritual
frequency, and Elorath is the collective soul that manifests through this
potential. Being an Egregore, Elorath is the result and Current of the
collective will, soul, karma, and dharma of the Family. It is singularly
manifested with various aspects.

Others who are Awakened or knowledgeable about the occult
can identify Elorath as an Egregore. Yet only those of the Blood can

liber Elorath

fully understand and experience the intimacy of Awakening to the Current of Elorath. Those who are Awakened to the Current or accept the *Calling* are aware of their True Nature. Elorath is the commonality of the Strigoi Vii. Many will ignore the Current, often thinking themselves to be misled or merely harboring fantasies, and are thus unable to accept what lies within them. In religions such as Santeria, the postulant seeks to find their "head," or their attunement to an Orisha (one of the divinities of that religion). In Christianity, one may relate to a specific patron saint. This is the same as hearing the Calling and discovering one's attunement to the Current of Elorath. However, all Strigoi Vii are free and encouraged to attune to other Currents and paradigms; this is within the nature of the Blood of Elorath.

Once a Strigoi Vii has recognized the Current within themselves, they proceed to higher levels of attunement, such as recognizing their Patron Strigoi Morte guides, which can be any godform or Ascended Master, whether known to humankind or not. Awakened and un-Awakened Strigoi Vii alike can recognize the Radiance or Calling of the Current within others of their kin. The Radiance draws those of the Family to each other. This mysterious attraction cannot be explained, yet it creates a deep bond of love and loyalty that runs deeper than mortal perceptions and alliances.

The full origins of Elorath are unknown. Suffice to say that Elorath has a discrete subtle conscious behind It. Many who cannot understand Elorath create fabricated stories to explain Its origin or nature and may even deny Its existence. However, Elorath cannot be weakened by such petty disbelief, and through the many who employ Our traditions or Mysteries, It becomes stronger and more Awakened.

There are various sub-Currents and aspects of Elorath known as *Choirs*. The singularity is Elorath Itself. The next level of Choirs is the *Duality* of *Mithu* (masculine) and *Kalistree* (feminine). The foundation of these Currents is known as the *Trinity*, containing three different aspects: *Kitra* (weaver/councilor), *Mradu* (guardian/warrior), and *Ramkht* (priest/inspirator). The archetypes behind the Trinity Choirs in their modern conception were inspired by the Kheprians; however, Strigoi Vii employ them in Our own vision.

Whilst there are many who carry the Strigoi Vii "gene," only a few will show the potential to follow their True Nature, and, of those, even fewer will "take the red pill" and pursue the steps to fulfill their Awakening.

The Trinity, or the *Kharrus,* lies at the foundation of the Current of Elorath and consists of the Currents of Kitra, the weavers and councilors; Ramkht, the priests and inspirators; and Mradu, the warriors and guardians. Each Strigoi Vii contains within themself elements of all three of these Currents. However, a few select Strigoi Vii are drawn to and identify with a specific one, which they discover through their journey of Zhep'r. These rare individuals are known as the *Chorus of Elorath,* or Kharrus. Each Current's core signature determines how an individual Strigoi Vii interacts with and processes energy. The Chorus of Elorath maintains equilibrium within the Family and the Current of Elorath. Only Magisters can be formally be ordained into these Currents, yet all Strigoi Vii can easily engage with the characteristics of these Currents in order to experiment with processing energy and to test their talents. These Currents are also known as "Roads."

Please note that those who hear the Calling to the Kharrus represent only a very small portion of the Awakened Family. Since the vast majority of the Family is solitary and works on an individual basis, they have no need for Initiation into one of these Roads, as the essential function of the Chorus is within group ritual. In contrast, however, there are also those who are formally ordained into two or more Currents. However, some Strigoi Vii who attempt to fully master more than one Current sometimes experience a lack of focus in their ritual experience and journey of Zhep'r.

Councilors and Weavers of Elorath, formally addressed as *Kitra,* are by nature catalysts of energy flow and cycling.

Energetically, their techniques focus on weaving, cycling, healing, flowing, and sensuality. They are often drawn to and talented in dance, music, poetry, lovemaking, performance, and healing. They are by nature highly sensual and are often physically attractive or possess a strong physical presence. Kitra have an essential need to be loved. Weaver energies are often very feminine in nature, yet it is not uncommon to meet male Kitra. The regalia of the Kitra is the crown and chalice, and they will usually wear their ritual cord over the hips. Kitra formal garb, such as ritual and temple robes, will often be very flirtatious and erotic, similar to that of a belly dancer or Romani ("gypsy").

Warriors and Guardians of Elorath, known formally as *Mradu,* are charged with protecting the Family within and without. Mradu are loyal, grounded, protective, often manifest a fondness for strategy of many kinds, and are drawn to the energetic techniques of defense, grounding, shielding, filtering, and defending the Family. They are also excellent at mediating disputes and have a strong need to provide love, thus complimenting the Kitra. Their energies are very masculine in nature and their Corporeal bodies are often large in size so as to facilitate the process of grounding energy. Many Mithu are male; however, it is not uncommon to encounter female Mradu. The regalia of the Mradu is a specially consecrated long black hilted, double-bladed tirual blade known as an *ar'thana.* Mradu guardians often wear their cord from shoulder to waist, like a nineteenth-century military sash. Mradu ritual and temple robes may incorporate military-like design or vestiges of medieval armor.

Priests and Inspiration of Elorath, who are known formally as Ramkht, fuel the intent of the Current. Their energies partake of the duality of masculine and feminine, so both men and women are equally drawn to this Road. Of all the Currents, the inspirators focus on the energy techniques of dreaming, inspiration, manifestation, guiding, and leading the Family. The Ramkht are often seen as the most intellectual and scholarly of all the Trinity Choir, yet this is an over-generalization. Individuals associating with the Ramkht Current are frequently natural teachers and leaders and drawn to literary and philosophical matters. The regalia of the Ramkht includes a consecrated and attuned wand or rod. In ritual Ramkht often wear a ritual cord around their shoulders like a priestly vestment. Ramkht ritual and temple garb is often long and flowing, almost androgynous in appearance.

It was meet that we should make merry, and be glad: for this thy brother was dead, and is alive again; and was lost, and is found.
—"The Parable of the Prodigal Son," Luke 15:32

The Quest of Family, or the *Family Quest,* is the duty of each and every Strigoi Vii Initiate. The dual purpose of the Quest is to advance the individual and the collective of the Family through mutual inspiration and support. The Quest of Family involves finding others of the Blood and introducing them to their heritage subtly, without force or the "conversion" techniques practiced within mortal religions.

The central element within the Family Quest is respect for the free will of all sentient beings. The Family Quest should be executed only through subtle hints and inspiration. Thus, no Strigoi Vii should ever shame the Family by proselytizing like a member of a desperate religious cult. This is against the nature of the Quest. Power comes only from free will and independent thought.

The Legacy Ankh is the sigil that represents the Living Vampire, the Strigoi Vii Mysteries, the Covenants of the Black Veil, and the Current of Elorath. This precious artifact is proudly worn, discreetly in public and openly in ritual, by both Strigoi Vii and Black Swans to symbolize their support and dedication to the Sanguinarium, the Strigoi Vii Mysteries, and the Family.

The ankh, or, in Latin, the *crux ansata* (cross with a handle), was originally the Egyptian hieroglyph meaning "life." Many Ancient Egyptian artworks, especially funerary art, depict gods and pharaohs bearing this symbol. The ankh was also associated with Osiris, the god of death and rebirth, and mummies were often adorned with ankhs in order to symbolically convey the gift of life after death. Over time, the ankh came to symbolize Immortality and can even be seen as a key to unlocking the gates of death. The Rosicrucians and members of Hermetic orders often use this symbol in their rituals. The Coptic Christians, as well, employed it as a symbol of life beyond death. Ankhs incorporating mirrors into their design have sometimes been used to symbolize perception of the subtle reality.

The bladed ankh first surfaced in popular culture in the 1983 film *The Hunger,* directed by Tony Scott and based on the novel by Whitley Strieber, who also, significantly, wrote the novel *Communion.* With its historical symbolism, cultural significance, and esoteric nature, the ankh was the obvious symbol for the Strigoi Vii. In 1996, Master Metal Manipulator D'Drennan was commissioned by Father Sebastiaan to make an exclusive version of a bladed ankh to represent the Mysteries and Our Family. Thus was born the Legacy Ankh, the most commonly recognized international symbol of the Vampyre movement and the Family. Since there are so many imitators of Our sigil, the Legacy Ankh is legally copyrighted and trademarked by the Ordo Strigoi Vii in order to protect it and to avoid any misuse of the symbol. We wish to make it clear that this particular scimitar-bladed ankh is the exclusive symbol of Strigoi Vii as defined by the *Sanguinomicon* and is to be recognized and respected as such.

The Mundane refers to the mortal world outside the gates of the Sanguinarium and the Strigoi Vii Mysteries. This is the "normal" world whose inhabitants are not aware of who and what We are or of the metaphysical realities to which We are Awakened. Other Awakened tribes, such as various vampire/Vampyre Legacies and Initiates of other esoteric systems, are not counted within the mundane. They are simply "Others," and may be seen as spiritual cousins of the Strigoi Vii. Terms such as *dane, mortal-minded,* or *hyle* (the Gnostic term for an un-Awakened individual) are used to refer to members of the mundane world.

The Dayside aspect of the Strigoi Vii Mysteries is the main tool We use to master Our Corporeal Self and achieve a strong interaction with the mundane world. We employ Dayside philosophies in Our everyday mundane lives in order to improve and further develop Our Self. This grounding in the Dayside is known as the Dayside Principles and is studied in the Jahira Mystery.

Strigoi Vii refer to their "mundane" or "mortal" families as their birth family. Many Strigoi Vii's birth families cannot understand or accept their nature, so the Strigoi Vii can only interact with their birth family on a strictly Dayside level. However, some fortunate Strigoi Vii have understanding birth families who accord them the luxury of openly expressing their nature. The process of disclosing one's Strigoi Vii nature to birth family or friends is sometimes rather humorously called "Coming out of the Coffin." This term originated from the Long Black Veil events in NYC in the 1990s, which were held on Thursdays in a gay club called MOTHER. In order to evolve in Zhep'r, the Strigoi Vii must learn to accept and balance their Dayside birth families as well as their Strigoi Vii Family.

See worlds on worlds compose one universe,
Observe how system into system runs,
What other planets circle other suns,
What varied beings people every star . . .
—Alexander Pope, *Essay on Man*

Other Tribes, or *Others,* comprise those who are not directly of Our Current. They include Awakened or un-Awakened individuals, traditions, or groups that are drawn to the vampire archetype, yet are not Strigoi Vii. It is not uncommon for Strigoi Vii to be confused with these "Others." While there are similarities between the Strigoi Vii and other tribes, We are still very distinctly different from them.

The Others and associated tribes and organizations have manifested mostly on the Internet since about 1996 or 1997. Many of these online groups spell *vampire* with an *i* and lowercase *v.* These groups are often known collectively as the "online vamp community" (or OVC), as most community interactions take place online, or simply as the "vamp community" (VC). The OVC rarely represents the old-school, in-person, real Vampyre community that has existed in fellowship for decades, mostly in large cities such as London, New York, and Los Angeles. The OVC and the Sanguinarium are becoming more and more distant as of this printing. Cities are energy nodes that We call *Halos* due to the large amounts of Ambient Prana that collects about them. The following discussion and definition of some tribes of Others takes place from the Strigoi Vii perspective and is as objective as possible.

Tribes, also known as *Legacies,* are the Strigoi Vii terms for traditions in other occult and pagan systems and specifically refer to the different paths and traditions of vampyrism. Each Legacy comprises a specific paradigm of rituals, philosophies, and traditions. Increasingly more Legacies are emerging in recent years. They include the *Tiamantis* (Temple of the Vampire, or TOV), *Setian* (Ordo of the Vampyre from the Temple of Set), the *Sahjaza* (a focused sub-Legacy of Strigoi Vii), the *Kheprians,* the *Sekhtrians,* and many others. Please be aware that psychic vampires do not, to Strigoi Vii, constitute a Legacy, but rather are a different tribe of Others.

Traditional psychic vampires are termed *asarai* by the Strigoi Vii. Traditional psychic vampirism is clearly defined in

Dion Fortune's book *Psychic Self-Defense* and Anton LaVey's 1969 magnum opus *The Satanic Bible*. Asarai are also discussed in Konstantinos's contemporary book *Vampires: The Occult Truth*. Traditional psychic vampires are parasites who truly drain others of their emotional and Pranic energy, and there is nothing positive about them. Asarai are individuals who intentionally or unintentionally create psychological drama and harmfully siphon energy from others. They can Awaken and become ethical psychic vampires, but most asarai are un-Awakened, unable or unwilling to confront and manage their nature. Many of the ethical psychic vampires consider asarai to be un-Awakened to their nature and thus not able to manage their condition.

Asarai fulfill the traditional archetype of the psychic vampire. Their vampirism may take many forms, including emotional or even sexual predation. Most asarai are found in everyday life in many guises. They rarely identify with the Glamour or are even aware of the Sanguinarium. Some examples of asarai include a lover or friend who is emotionally damaged and continually creates psychodrama in the lives of others. Such individuals will leech on to people around them, playing on their sympathies, and drain them of their resources. A classic asarai may manifest as a patient in a nursing home who is horribly bitter and negative about her life. Nurses and caregivers will often feel literally drained as they care for these individuals and find these asarai occupying all of their resources and attention. A particular student who intimidates the other members of the class and monopolizes the teacher's attention may very well be an asarai. Cancer patients or people suffering from terminal illnesses often manifest very powerful symptoms of traditional psychic vampirism, though generally without knowledge or malicious intent. People who claim to be "sex addicts" are often actually asarai as well.

However, there are some asarai who identify with the vampire image or lifestyle, so be cautious and aware of these individuals! They will sometimes flock to the contemporary gothic subculture or assume the new-age persona of an individual with a "damaged aura" or "leaky chakras," often leading others to confuse them with responsible and ethical psychic vampires who wish to manage their condition. Many asarai who have attempted to enter the sphere of Our Family are truly craven, negative, and energy-deficient beings. It should be noted that the Strigoi Vii do not agree with redefining terms such as *psychic vampire* to accommodate contemporary social trends created by people who do not remember or wish to respect the old ways as properly defined by notable logicians such as Dion Fortune and Aleister Crowley. This is why We recognize the differences between traditional psychic vampires (asarai) and their ethical counterparts.

The best defense against asarai is to completely avoid them! However, this may not be possible when you have an asarai as a colleague, supervisor, or member of your immediate mundane family or social circle. When interaction with an asarai is unavoidable, you must not cater to their games. Becoming involved in their machinations only feeds their parasitism and causes them to want more. Endless circling arguments, unhealthy attempts at gaining attention, "guilt trips," or unnaturally intense emotional reactions are all tactics of traditional psychic vampires. Energy filtering and shielding may also offer some defense, but it is best to simply avoid them altogether. Both Dion Fortune and Anton LaVey outline excellent and time-tested defensive techniques against these traditional psychic vampires in their respective books.

Ethical psychic vampires are the most common and numerous tribe of Others. These oft-Awakened energy sensitives have an energy deficiency or damage to their subtle energy bodies. They must feed from the life force of other humans in order to maintain their physical, emotional, and mental well-being. The abbreviations *psi* or *psy* for ethical psychic vampires are very common in the OVC, and these individuals have formed their own support networks and organizations. They share a great deal of terminology with the Strigoi Vii and employ similar energy-work techniques. The vast majority of individuals who are aware of their condition as psychic vampires (the process of which they also refer to as Awakening) have formed their own ethical codes, including versions of the Black Veil, and strive to find solutions for and a balance within their condition. To them, vampyrism is a condition brought about by a damaged or inefficient subtle body that cannot generate enough vital life force on its own. In contrast, the Strigoi Vii are not ethical psychic vampires. While We have some superficial similarities to this tribe, Our intent and motivation for tapping life force is completely different. Strigoi Vii seek to harvest the excess life force of humans in order to evolve in Zhep'r and to increase the frequency and metabolism of Our subtle bodies.

Kheprians and the *Kherete* represent a special case as a Legacy amongst ethical psychic vampires. Kheprianism is a tradition of vampyrism that has brought many of its members great success, and individual Kheprians have frequently maintained good relations with individual Strigoi Vii and many other Legacies. Kheprians believe that their founder modified their chakras during their previous lives, allowing them a better footing in the subtle reality. Thus, they believe they have a stronger control over the ability to avoid the Second Death and reincarnate with their subtle bodies intact from incarnation to incarnation. They believe this modification in their subtle bodies has caused symptoms of psychic vampyrism. The Kheprians should also be recognized as an influential Legacy, as their groupings of warrior, priest, and councilor helped further define and develop the Strigoi Vii Currents of Mradu, Ramkht, and Kitra. The *Kherete Path* is a new term reflecting groups and individuals who follow the Kheprian traditions, yet are not members of House Kheperu or the Kheprian Order.

Tiamantis is the name We Strigoi Vii have assigned to another Legacy of energy vampires known as the Temple of the Vampire, or TOV. The TOV consider themselves "Satanic Vampires," as they have been heavily involved with the Church of Satan since the death of Anton LaVey. Publically, the Church of Satan is a completely separate entity from the TOV, yet they do have many members in common. Members of the TOV spell *vampire* with a capital *V.* These individuals share many of the philosophical perspectives of the Strigoi Vii, and thus may be similar to Us in certain ways. Magister Dimitri claimed to be a TOV Adept, and His previous experience informed some of the terminology of Strigoi Vii, such as Communion, Twilight, the Dragon, Dayside, and Nightside. However, the Tiamantis' main difference from Us is their elitist belief that vampires are superior to and the predators of all others.

Gaja are "wannabe vampires" who have always been present in the Vampyre community and around the Sanguinarium, often as victims of the Glamour. Strigoi Vii are often amused by these irresponsible posers who lurk on the periphery of Our Sanctums or in the general vamp community. Many gaja wear gauche Dracula capes, cheap store-bought plastic fangs, and spend their nights moping about the local darkwave nightclub claiming to be hundreds of years old. It is not rare to find a traditional psychic vampire who is also gaja. Very often gaja will either attach themselves to Strigoi Vii, begging to be "turned" into a vampire, or, conversely, childishly and comically insult Strigoi Vii, claiming We are not "real vampires." Gaja often manifest as "dark gurus," claiming nonexistent powers, and deluded role-players who take their hobby too seriously. Far too commonly, they adopt Our terminology and claim to be Awakened, when in fact they have only learned a few elements of Strigoi Vii and have no actual understanding of Our Mysteries. Do not confuse gaja with "fashion vampires," who simply enjoy the dramatic, aesthetic, and romantic trappings of the vampire archetype. Such individuals are merely enjoying themselves and are not truly gaja. The true Strigoi Vii can identify gaja with little effort.

Sanguinarians, or *sanguine vampires,* are individuals who feel they need to consume physical human blood to maintain their spiritual, physical, and mental health. Sanguinarians are one of the most controversial groups of Others within the online vampire subculture. From the perspective of the OSV and the Synod, the consumption of blood contains extreme risks (such as blood-borne diseases) and is an inefficient form of obtaining Prana. In reality, the majority of people who claim to be blood drinkers usually have only ingested Corporeal human blood once or twice in their lives, if at all. At the time of this writing, the Synod and the OSV have only encountered a few rare individuals who truly practice sanguinarianism as more than a sexual fetish or as a consequence of Renfield's syndrome (a psychological disorder in which the individual believes they must consume blood). Claiming status as a sanguinarian vampire is sometimes done solely for social shock value or as a misguided attempt to relate to the vamp community. However, a fair number of Sanguinarians are blood fetishists who enjoy the vampire archetype for the purpose of enhancing their sexual fantasies. Please refer to the principle on blood drinking in The Black Veil (chapter 2) and the discussion of blood drinking for the Strigoi Vii position on this practice.

Occultist Vampires are those who practice vampyrism as an esoteric path. These include the members of the Temple of Set's Order of the Vampyre, Michael Ford's Order of Phospherous, and some practitioners of the various left-hand path traditions. Such individuals are not necessarily Strigoi Vii, but many do come to the Family, as such groups will act as a trigger of their Awakening to the Current.

Fashion Vampires are individuals who often cross over with Black Swans and/or fans, but are most commonly individuals who love the imagery and concept of the vampire archetype. They often dress up on Saturday nights and hit their local gothic club or Noir Haven. Fashion vamps are not all gaja, which is a big misconception; most are realists and know they are not True Vampyres—they simply enjoy the aesthetics. Fashion vamps sometimes end up Awakening to one of the tribes.

Fans, or *literary vampires,* are not just one tribe but many different groups of fans who are attracted to specific writers or cinematic works. They are mostly not spiritual in any way. Two examples of well-organized and outstanding groups of literary vampires include the fans of *The Vampire Chronicles* by Anne Rice and the *Twilight* novels (known as Twilighters) by Stephanie Meyer. Some members of these tribes may even be nararim and introduced to the Family through research into the vampire culture. They do provide an excellent source of willing donors and prepare mortals for Awakenings as Black Swans. Fans can also be considered any organized or unorganized tribe who enjoys series such as *Dark Shadows, True Blood,* and others.

Other tribes include the many Others out there who are Awakened to the Current but identify as being part of other traditions and do not claim their kinship to Our Blood. They may be similar to Us, Awakened to the same subtle worlds and perceptions that We are privileged to know. There cannot be an absolute list or measure of the characteristics of Our Blood, so there are many of the Family who are on paths that bear different names but are truly the same. When you encounter them, you will know them by their Radiance and spiritual signature of the Dark Flame. Always seek to know the individual beyond the group to which they may belong. Our real Sorors and Fraters will speak through wisdom, humbleness, results, and achievement. Those truly of the Blood will not try to control others before they can control themselves.

However, bear this caution in mind! Those who speak of themselves in grandiose or self-glorifying terms are not of the Blood or worthy of your attention, as they are obviously insecure and claiming powers they do not have. Wisdom dictates that you avoid unwittingly falling into the orbit of such pretenders. Just keep your subtle eyes open and your Fellows will be revealed.

Chapter 6
THE SANGUINARIUM

Let me not to the marriage of true minds
Admit impediments . . .
—William Shakespeare, Sonnet 116

The Sanguinarium could be described as the culture and movement of the Strigoi Vii, whilst the Family refers to the Blood and Current. The etymology of the word *Sanguinarium* roughly translates from Latin to mean "guild of the blood." It is the international covenant network, and tribe of Family individuals, businesses, and gatherings, which are focused on the Mysteries of Strigoi Vii. At the core of this movement is the *Ordo Strigoi Vii* (OSV), which is the Inner Circle of the Family and the spiritual leadership and administrative authority, the *Synod*. The Sanguinarium began in the early 1990s and is now an international movement, which in some respects is very separate from and in contrast to the majority of the online vampire community.

The Sanguinarium represents the social aspect of the Family. Ronin, as solitary individuals, practice Strigoi Vii and potentially Initiate into the Mysteries on a private basis and rarely interact with the more social forum of the Sanguinarium. Many will enter the Sanguinarium for various periods of activity and then leave, only to return at a later time to network with and discover others of the Family.

Those coming to the Sanguinarium are treated as individuals above and beyond any organizations to which they belong or affiliations they hold. The Sanguinarium no longer focuses on Initiatory groups such as clans, covens, or households, as they distract from the unity of the Family and the focus on the individual. The core of the Sanguinarium is the Strigoi Vii Black Veil. Initiates of Strigoi Vii who violate the Principles of the Black Veil are deemed destructive to themselves and the Family, and will most likely call down the *khaskt* upon themselves. This is a self-imposed curse that can be best equated to the mortal concept of negative karma. Other consequences may include excommunication for serious crimes, such as using one's status in the Family to manipulate minors or take part in major criminal activities such as drug dealing, rape, abusing animals or humans, or murder.

The Ordo Strigoi Vii (OSV) is the Inner Circle of the Sanguinarium movement and began as a small collective of individuals from a mix of spiritual traditions who obtained fangs from SABRETOOTH in Gotham Halo. The ritual of making fangs allowed personal interactions with and connections to each individual. At this time, fangs were one of the primary symbols employed by like-minded individuals involved in Vampyrism when networking with each other. What made those who would eventually be the seeds of the OSV stand out amongst these fang clients is that they were unified in having a more spiritual approach to Vampyrism. One of these clients, who offered the initial influence and guidance, was the late and now Ascended Magister Dimitri. His Vampyre-pagan coven, known as Haven, all obtained fangs and became the nucleus of the origins of the Strigoi Vii movement, which inspired Father Sebastiaan to found the coven of Sahjaza with Goddess Rosemary. In fact, the very term *Strigoi Vii* was brought to the attention of the Family by Magister Dimitri, who claimed Slavic lineage from the Balkans in Eastern Europe.

Eventually, a convergence of individuals from diverse traditions and perspectives came together to painstakingly test and experiment with various philosophies and esoteric systems. Over time, individuals in this group each verified the reality of Communion and the Strigoi Morte, as well as many other aspects of the Corporeal and subtle realities.

This movement formed the foundations of what is now the system of Strigoi Vii as outlined within this book.

Today, membership to the OSV is strictly by invitation only and of such secrecy that some claim the OSV and the Synod many not even exist. Every invitee must have a personal invitation from the Synod or a Magister. Invitations are presented discretely and secretly, and it is considered a great honor amongst the Strigoi Vii to be invited into this exclusive order of the Family. Such invitations are reserved only for the most dedicated and exceptional role models, who are generally Traditionalist Strigoi Vii. The vast majority of members are anonymous and very private about their affiliation, as the OSV is a secret society.

The Synod is spiritual leadership of the Current and the OSV, and its members are the architects of the Sanguinarium. The Synod's primary focus is the preservation and prosperity of the Family. They tirelessly further the Quest of Family and act as examples for upholding the principles of the Black Veil.

The members of the Synod are responsible for moderating and organizing virtual Sanctums, dealing with public relations and media representation, approving and updating publications and the Strigoi Vii websites. Many members of the Synod offer their services as ministers, advisors, or teachers of the Mysteries. They may preside over ceremonies such as Initiations, weddings, and consecrations for the Strigoi Vii community.

But if ye sholde youre trouthe kepe and save.
Trouthe is the hyeste thing that man may kepe . . .
—Geoffrey Chaucer, *The Canterbury*
Tales, "The Franklin's Tale"

Traditions and etiquette are at the heart of Strigoi Vii culture. The Strigoi Vii have their own traditions of etiquette. The old-school traditions of formality and chivalry are highly respected by the sincere members of the Family. There are no absolute or steadfast laws of etiquette, but these traditions are tools of communication and charming demonstrations that show one is of the Current. However, as so many Strigoi Vii are solitary, only a few actually employ this etiquette frequently. Yet it is still helpful to know in case of an eventual meeting between members of the Family.

As a sign of respect, those present who hold the most junior level of Initiation should show their respect and dedication by making the first action in any application of etiquette.

First and foremost, when in Sanctums, never address a Strigoi Vii or any of their guests by their given name unless they present it first. Only use their Sobriquet or whichever name they prefer.

Written correspondence is greatly valued amongst the Strigoi Vii, and a handwritten letter carries much more weight than electronic correspondence. Spending time and energy on the presentation as well as the content is a sign of patience and regard. Of course, this is not always possible. When written correspondence takes place between two Strigoi Vii, whether it be online or through letters, it is traditional to begin with the Latin *Ave,* which means "greetings," and close with "Eternally," "Forever," "I Remain," or whichever formal salutation the Strigoi Vii prefers. When addressing other Strigoi Vii, *Soror* or *Frater* (Latin for "brother" and "sister," respectively) is the appropriate title for those Initiated into the Outer Mysteries. Those Initiated into the Inner Mysteries should be addressed as *Magister* or *Magistra.* When addressing Magister Templi it can be formalized as *Reverend* or *Godmother* or *Godfather,* depending on your taste and how the Magister requests to be addressed.

The Sanguine Greeting, conceived of by one of the Sanguinarium Founding Fathers, Lord D'Drennan, may take slightly different forms in varying locations. However, all forms of this greeting should begin with each Strigoi Vii steadily looking into the Throne behind the other's eyes, and thus facing each other's Dragon within. Then, once the gaze has been broken, the greeter, usually the individual who has attained Initiation junior to the other, takes the hand of the senior Strigoi Vii and kisses the back. This is then repeated by the other party.

When entering a Halo, it is customary to announce oneself to the active members of the Family if one has the intention of entering Sanctums or Noir Havens. If the Strigoi Vii is present on mundane business related to their Dayside or merely taking a personal holiday, this is not necessary. However, many Strigoi Vii consider it good manners to announce oneself in all cases.

In the case of a personal invitation to a private event or domicile, many Strigoi Vii deem it proper etiquette to bring a bottle of absinthe or fine red wine. Absinthe is highly regarded by the Strigoi Vii and was an important part of the vampire/Vampyre culture long before it became popular in Europe and amongst poets and artists. Absinthe was often brewed by individuals sometimes referred to as "alchemasters" or "alchemistresses." The Strigoi Vii absinthe ritual is a wonderful and secretive ceremony used to celebrate important events such as birthdays. Today, due to modifications in U.S. laws, true absinthe is available for purchase in America. The Bloodbath, a drink created by Soror Ambrosia at the Long Black Veil (LBV) Noir Haven in Gotham, is also a wonderful toasting drink and a tradition amongst the Strigoi Vii. The LBV recipe for the Bloodbath is one-third Chambord or other raspberry liquor, one-third red wine, and one-third cranberry juice. Both drinks are wonderful for Moots and as after-ritual cocktails. Many Strigoi Vii also enjoy the aptly-named Romanian Vampire wine, available in many large cities. However, if the personal tastes of the Strigoi Vii do not include alcohol, flowers or gourmet food or candy also make excellent "hostess" gifts.

As in vampire folklore, a Strigoi Vii should never enter another's home without first being invited. However, the reason for this is merely simple courtesy and not an unholy curse! It is considered a serious breach of etiquette for a Strigoi Vii to attend a gathering to which they have not received an invitation, especially if the gathering takes place within a Sanctum. Similarly, an invited Strigoi Vii should never bring guests, whether mortal or of the Family, to any gathering without first consulting the Host. However, Strigoi Vii should also be hospitable to other members of the Family and include them in group activities if possible. It is not at all uncommon for a Strigoi Vii to generously offer their resources and services to a Soror or Frater if they are needed.

Quorums are face-to-face, private gatherings of Strigoi Vii for the purposes of ritual, feasting, Initiation, discussion of the Mysteries, socialization, and the pursuit of special interests. Members of the Family are charged with taking the initiative to organize such gatherings on a regional and international level. Quorums may occur with varying frequencies, such as one-time only, weekly, monthly, bimonthly, or annually. The most secure place to network and announce Quorums is on the Synod-endorsed Sanguinarium message boards.

Quorums are different from organizations such as covens or lodges because they are discrete cabals, which are fluid instead of fixed, organized groups into which individuals Initiate. Quorums are intended to promote individualism, action, and flexibility rather than solid structures. The elasticity of the Quorum system allows for a high level of freedom and comfort among the participants, as opposed to the many obligations that may be associated with covens or lodges. The Sanguinarium remains fixed as an international movement; Quorums occur as necessary.

The organizer of a Quorum is simply known as the *Host,* and it is the Host's duty to coordinate the location and date, distribute invitations, and choose the purpose of the Quorum, such as a discussion circle (sometimes known as a *Kull*), social meet-up, or full ritual. Proper tradition and etiquette requires all attendees to assume responsibility for their own expenses such as food, ritual supplies, or transportation. For example, if a space such as a hotel room or dance studio must be rented for a ritual, the cost should be shared amongst the attendees.

Quorums are best held in private, away from the mortal-minded, in order to further a sense of secrecy and privacy. In Quorum, members of the Family must be able to speak freely and openly without violating the Black Veil's Covenant of Secrets. *Open Quorums* welcome all those who are Initiated into the Family as long as they RSVP with the Host, whilst *Closed Quorums* are open only to specifically invited individuals. The Host of any Quorum must be at least Initiated as a Calmae in order to organize or "call forth" the Quorum, whilst a group ritual may only be led by an Adept or Magister.

Group rituals should only take place in Quorums, and those in attendance must have at least read the *Sanguinomicon* and secured the approval of the Host. It is in the best interests of everyone that the un-Initiated and those unfamiliar with Our Mysteries not attend Quorums. They will not be able to take part in the discussion or activities, and thus will feel out of place. Not only may this make them uncomfortable, it will act as a distraction from the intended focus of the Quorum.

Moots differ from Quorums in that they function as social events. Examples of Moots include preplanned meet and greets, discussions over dinner or coffee, or after parties following a formal Quorum. Gatherings such as these are perfect places to make in-person contact with others of the Family. Moots may also function as a way to screen others in a public place for potential inclusion in a Quorum. This is the only occasion when Black Swans may be in attendance, but, even so, their presence is discouraged and should always be announced to the Host in advance. Moots can be held in more exposed public places such as restaurants, taverns, cocktail lounges, coffee shops, or parks. Proper Moots should not be held in loud bars or during nightclub events, as a sense of intimacy is essential to the meeting. Whenever possible, avoid holding Moots in gothic-themed locations, as these cliché settings are not the best place to focus on the subjects at hand.

Remember that Moots are different from Quorums. It is possible to hold a Moot before or after a Quorum in order to make the gathering more flexible. However, Quorums where Communion ritual and deeper discussion of the Mysteries take place must be limited only to

Initiated members of the Family. Neither Quorums nor Moots are for those who are simply curious, looking for a social network, or wishing to "sightsee." It is essential to preserve the sanctity, integrity, and seriousness of any gathering.

Sanctums are sacred places to the Vampyre, be they physical locations temporarily created in a ritual, or virtual, such as websites like *Kaladra.org* or *Sanguinarium.net*. They are often used for Quorums and Moots when they can be secured from the mundane world. Some legendary Sanctums include specific sacred places and historical sites such as the Pyramid of Giza in Egypt, the Temple of Ur in southern Iraq, the Mayan pyramids on the Yucatan peninsula in Mexico, and the Minoan temple on the Greek island of Santorini. Some sanctums cannot be fully secured, so secrecy and discretion is necessary when assembling in these places. Outer Sanctums may include restaurants, parks, nightclubs, coffee shops, and art galleries. Moots and discreet rituals can be held in Outer Sanctums, as long as the mundane world is not alerted. Secret, or Inner, Sanctums are spaces away from the eyes of the mundane, such as private temples, back rooms of Noir Havens, private message boards, places created in ritual, or personal domiciles that have been consecrated. An Inner Sanctum must be a location where intimate conversations and group ritual between members of the Family may freely take place without distractions. When a Quorum involving ritual is in session, the space is considered an Inner Sanctum where only Initiated Vampyres and, depending on the circumstances, invited Black Swans may be present. In any Inner Sanctum, guardians are best posted in order to protect the sacred space. The moment an interruption or disruption by mundanes or the excommunicated occurs, the Sanctum is violated and exposed.

Noir Havens are semipublic, Outer Sanctum social events for celebration and pleasure and are most often held in lounges, nightclubs, or bars. These gatherings were originally organized specifically by Strigoi Vii and welcome members of other Awakened traditions, Legacies, tribes, and alternative/underground subcultures.

Noir Havens originally started in venues such as gay, gothic, or fetish nightclubs, but they are more commonly secret parties in the back room of a "mainstream" club. *Salon Noirs* (once called Courts) are a variation on Noir Havens and are essentially cocktail parties and a lounge of dark pleasures. The concept originated in the Belle Époque period in Paris, beginning in the 1880s through the onset of World War I. Often, Noir Havens will include the word *black* (in various translations) in their name. Some examples include the original Noir Haven, Long Black Veil of New York City; Black Trillium of Toronto; Black Xion of Amsterdam; and Lutetia Noir of Paris.

Noir Havens may be as small as a Monday club night at a local gothic club or dark lounge, or as large as an elaborate masquerade ball. It all depends on the desired audience and the determination of the organizers and promoters. However, Noir Havens are best held in exclusive venues as to avoid contact with mundane settings. Most often, such events will have an invite-only or restricted door policy and enforce a specific dress code such as costume, gothic, or fetish attire. Such regulations screen out those who are not serious or sympathetic attendees. More intimate gatherings such as Moots and Quorums should take place separately from Noir Havens. Havens are places for dancing, art shows, performance rituals, music, drinking, and celebration, not the sacred, intimate, and private Family gatherings.

The Vampire Ball events began at the BANK nightclub in NYC in January 1996 and have since spread across the world. They have inspired a style that mixes masquerade ball, pagan/esoteric gathering, and fetish ball. These events often have firebreathers; bands; DJs; ballroom, tango/salsa, Victorian, burlesque, and belly dancing; vendors selling unique wares and performance art with a strict masqued dress code. Vampire Balls are ceremonies, and no self-respecting vampire/

Vampyre would go without proper attire, nor would the producers tolerate those out of dress code. The most famous of the Vampire Ball events include the New York Vampire Ball and the Endless Night Vampire Ball in New Orleans over Halloween weekend.

Halos are sacred to the Strigoi Vii. Those Initiated into the Outer Mysteries are often attracted to cities due to the large fluxes of Pranic energy in these places. Areas with large populations contain immense reservoirs of energy that are constantly radiated outward, and thus are a perfect source of excess life force for the Vampyre. Strigoi Vii call such areas *Halos.* Specific cities have always been considered Halos and contain large populations of Strigoi Vii. The most notable Halos are Gotham (New York City), Angael (Los Angeles), Wyvern (Seattle), Morta (New Orleans), Avalon (London), and Lutetia (Paris). Other Halos exist and continue to grow in energy as more and more Awakenings take place. The activity of Strigoi Vii in these areas usually results in a spontaneous naming beyond the mundane name of the city and which often comes from a historical title or characteristic of the city.

In the late twentieth and the early twenty-first centuries, Halos hosted large communities of Vampyres who organized Courts, Quorums, Moots, banquets, and other such events. Seekers still often travel long distances to Halos in order to meet other Strigoi Vii in person. The communities of Strigoi Vii and other Awakened ones within Halos evolve, grow, or diminish according to the collective social interests of the Family.

Unlike Strigoi Vii who are Initiated into the Outer Mysteries, Magisters are often more solitary and less dependent on Halos. This is due to their mastery of Nomaj Sorcery and Astral workings. Thus, they are less attached to social structures and more often focused on personal interior Quests.

Gotham Halo, often called the "Rome of Vampyres," is the largest and most famous of the Halos. It is not restricted by geographic or civic boundaries, and so includes the five boroughs of New York City, northeastern New Jersey, Westchester County, and Long Island, or what is often called the New York metropolitan area. What makes the Gotham Halo so intense and powerful is that, after Tokyo and Mexico City, New York is one of the largest metropolitan areas in the world. Gotham also has been the seat of an incredible amount of history for the Vampyre/vampire subculture. Almost every tradition or tribe in the vamp community has members within the Gotham Halo.

Chapter 7
FESTIVALS

Festivals are the annual sacred holidays of the Strigoi Vii. The calendar of the Family is officially endorsed by the Synod and is used to mark the founding of the Sanguinarium. Traditionally this calendar is lunar (sundown to sundown), beginning with the Strigoi Vii New Year's Eve, the Twilight Festival or Im Zhep'r (Halloween). Thus, the Strigoi Vii year starts on November 1 and ends on October 31.

The Strigoi Vii calendar was formally adopted on the founding day of the Sanguinarium, November 6, 1992. Each year has a specific name given by the Synod. *S.Y.* is the abbreviation for Sanguinarium Year of this new Vampyric Age. There are many important Vampyre "holidays" officially recognized by the Synod for the Strigoi Vii, known as *festivals*. Each of these festivals was recognized by the Synod in order to mark the times when the members of the Family most often celebrate aspects of Our Mysteries and how they are reflected amongst mortals.

The Dark Moon is a sacred time for the Strigoi Vii. During this period, no moon appears in the sky, as sunlight does not reflect from it in a manner that is visible on Earth. The Dark Moon phase lasts approximately three days and occurs between the last visible sign of the waning moon and first appearance of the new crescent moon. This period of absolute dark is highly suitable for Nightside applications.

During the Dark Moon phase, Ethereal and Astral energies can be more easily harnessed and manipulated. This is excellent time for Communion with the Strigoi Morte and with the Dragon.

For many, the Dark Moon represents a period between life and death, a time of solitude, darkness, and self-contemplation. In Khem, or Ancient Egypt, periods such as this were known as the Hours of Tuat, when the sun god would enter the underworld and make his passage alone and in darkness before emerging with life once again.

The Dark Moon also represents the darkest aspects of the goddesses Lilith, Hecate, and Kali, creatrixes of the vampire mythology. From the perspective of the Outer Mysteries, this is a time of personal contemplation, soul searching, and solitude from the mundane.

Many Strigoi Vii prefer to spend the time of the Dark Moon in absolute solitude and restful quiet, and they pause to reflect before resuming their regular plans and activities.

Beyond the Dark Moon, the major festivals are the *Nightside Festival,* the *Dayside Festival,* the *Twilight Festival,* and the *Dragon Festival.*

The Nightside Festival or the "Long Night Festival" is the longest night of the year, which is recognized as the holiday of European pagans, or Yule. During this festival, We delve deeply into Our Nightside, celebrating freedom and distance from the metaphorical symbol of the light of the sun. The Nightside Festival is a celebration of Our Nightside Family and a time for exploration of Our magickal and primal natures before many of Us celebrate mundane holidays such as Christmas with Our birth families. The Nightside Festival takes place on December 20 or 21 in the Northern Hemisphere and June 20 or 21 in the Southern Hemisphere. On this night, We celebrate Kalistree, the feminine and goddess aspect of Elorath.

The Dayside Festival or the "Long Day Festival" is the shortest night of the year, the summer solstice, and the time when Sol (the sun) is dominant. This is a time for deep reflection on our Dayside natures and celebration of Our mortal families, materialistic achievements, and the Corporeal world. On this day, We should also reflect on Our personal Dayside weaknesses. Through contemplation, We understand how We may see these as challenges to be turned into tools to further increase Our Zhep'r. We revel in what the materialistic and Dayside life has to offer Us and plan our Dayside goals for the coming year, such as a career change or major purchase such as that of a car or home. The Long Day Festival takes place on June 20 or 21 in the Northern Hemisphere and December 20 or 21 in the Southern Hemisphere. On this night, We celebrate Mithu, the masculine god aspect of Elorath.

The Twilight Festival falls on October 30 (Halloween eve), October 31 (the Celtic Samhain), and the following day of November 1 (All Saints' Day). This three-day festival is often considered a Greater Festival by many and remains one of the most popularly celebrated festivals. These are the nights of balance and metamorphosis, as well as the Strigoi Vii New Year, inspired by the Celtic/pagan New Year. It is the gateway leading to the longer nights of the year and encompasses many diverse holidays such as All Hallows Eve, Samhain and Halloween, the Day of the Dead, and All Saints' Day. The Twilight Festival is most commonly celebrated on October 31. As of this writing, the Endless Night Vampire Ball in New Orleans is where the Strigoi Vii and many other vampire tribes gather for the "Grande Conclave." This is the largest vampire/Vampyre gathering in the world.

During this festival, We often enjoy expressing Our Glamour in full force and walking openly amongst the mundane. Even though this is officially not a Grande Festival, it is one of the most popular of all celebrations, since so many Strigoi Vii enjoy the theatrics of Halloween, or Samhain. On this night, the Shroud Between Worlds is most easily crossed. This is the time for the Strigoi Vii to celebrate the most important holiday of the Family. Many do so by attending carnival-style masques with a funereal theme and by saying farewell to the previous year. Traditionally, this is the night on which Magister Ascensions take place, and Twilight Festival celebrations are partially held in the Ascended Magisters' honor. Quorums of Strigoi Vii from around the world often meet at this time. In late September and throughout the preceding months, all of the Family begin to prepare costumes and masks for this night. During the Twilight Festival, We celebrate Elorath as a whole.

The Dragon Festival takes place during the night of April 30 or May 1. This celebration began as a pre-Christian European holiday and was later co-opted by the Christians. Traditionally this night, *Walpurgisnacht,* is the night when demons, faeries, banshees, and other such legendary creatures are said to hold their dark celebrations. To the Strigoi Vii, the Dragon Festival represents Our higher Selves and Our Dragons. This festival is also a major celebration of the Family when the Dragon Mass is held on a worldwide level. This night, We celebrate the Ramkht Current, the inspiration of fire and an aspect of Elorath.

There are also several minor Strigoi Vii festivals, including the *Crimson Festival,* the *Bast Festival,* and an individual's *Ascension Festival.*

The Crimson Festival takes place on February 14, St. Valentine's Day, and has become very popular within the Sanguinarium. From the Immortal's perspective, this the time when We celebrate Our deepest passions and romances, as well as past and present loves. Here We recognize the partnerships and marriages that helped Us in our personal evolutions. The Crimson Festival is also a festival of the Hunt, celebrating its seductive, civilized, and glamorous aspects. The symbolism of crimson is related to the concept embodied in the words *For the Blood is the Life,* which is a metaphor for sustaining Ourselves by feasting on Pranic energy. This night, We celebrate Kitra, the weaver and lover aspect of Elorath.

The Bast Festival takes place near the mundane pagan holiday Lammas and celebrates the deadly predators of the animal kingdom, especially felines, as a tool to attune Ourselves to Our primal natures. It is usually celebrated on August 1. This festival is about life and death, feeding and hunting. It is the primal twin to the Crimson Festival. The Bast Festival is often held far away from civilization, such as deep within a forest or in the desert around large bonfires. During these celebrations, one group takes on the roles of predators (hawks, cats, bears, eagles, lions, etc.) whilst another takes on the roles of prey (rabbits, mice, deer, etc.) and a simulated hunt is enacted. Due to its nature, this Mass is a Family or group celebration only. This night, We celebrate Mradu, the warrior aspect of Elorath.

Awakening Festivals are personal events that occur in accordance with the individual experience of the Strigoi Vii Initiate and celebrate their first Awakening. The most important of all personal festivals for any Strigoi Vii is their Awakening Festival, somewhat akin to a Vampyre's birthday. Whether the Initiate is a novice in the esoteric world or whether their Initiation into Strigoi Vii represents the consummation of prolonged exploration and study, the date on which each individual Strigoi Vii is consciously "born" to the Family is a most important anniversary. On this date, each Strigoi Vii personally celebrates and affirms their Awakening.

Chapter 8
THE GLAMOUR

Vampires, they say, blow an unearthly beauty,
Their bodies are all suffused with a soft witch-fire,
Their flesh like an opal . . . their hair like the float of night.
Why do we muse upon them, what secret's in them?
It is because, at last, we love the darkness,
Love all things in it, tired of too much light?
—Conrad Aiken, *The Jig of Forslin*

The Glamour represents the mystic powers of mesmerism, seduction, and control that legends and literature assign to the vampire. A "Glamour" may be described as a magic spell, or, most commonly, an alluring or fascinating attraction. The moth that immolates itself within a candle flame is irresistibly drawn to the burning glamour of the fire. In such a manner do the mundane flock to Us when We apply Our Vampyre Glamour. There are two levels of Our Glamour: the Outer Glamour and the Inner Glamour.

The Outer Glamour is often used by the newer Initiates or those embroiled in the aesthetics of gothic vampire imagery, such as fangs and dramatic attire. Mortals love such trappings, as they are eternally seduced by the fantasy of the vampire. A Strigoi Vii may use the Outer Glamour by attending a gathering dressed in a gothic or otherwise striking costume that is likely to fascinate people, thus drawing them and their associated energies to the Strigoi Vii.

Then, when the Strigoi Vii grows in Zhep'r, they begin to manifest the Inner Glamour, which is mastered only through experience, talent, and skill. The Inner Glamour comes from within and is not dependent on the Vampyre archetype for empowerment. This level of Glamour involves techniques such as neuro-linguistic programming (NLP), voice control, the art of seduction, deliberate body language, aromatherapy, and the application of psychological and subliminal cues. Many of the techniques of the Inner Glamour are used by public speakers, successful corporate executives, and sleight-of-hand magicians. Since the days of prehistoric humans, those who have fully mastered these techniques have been often elevated by mortals to the place of gurus, heroes, or gods. Even now, those who have this special "charisma" often find a place as politicians or celebrities. Beginning to be less dependent on the Outer Glamour, yet still being able to recognize and reflect on it and occasionally employ it when necessary, is a strong trait of a potential Magister.

Today, the Living Vampire can master this art of seduction and control of their personal presence in order to further their Zhep'r. All humans are instinctually disposed toward fascination and seduction. This can be seen in their courtship and mating rituals. Each Strigoi Vii must embrace their personal Glamour to fully be loved, desired, and revered. It is through proper application of the different levels of the Glamour that We maintain Our position as the rulers of Our own personal worlds.

We can employ and take advantage of the Glamour that appears in folklore, mythology, art, and literature. There are few archetypes more compelling and enduring than that of the vampire. Every culture has stories and legends of some sort of vampire. Through the Glamour, this archetype has been branded into the human collective unconsciousness. Mortals instinctively fear, love, and worship the vampire archetype. Our Family and Mysteries directly benefit from this fascination, which We tap with little effort.

Today, We begin a new open Glamour. Despite the legends, for centuries the majority of mortals did not believe We actually, physically, existed. Many of the mortal-minded today worship not only the Ascended Masters as their deities, but also the icon of the vampire. Our image pervades every aspect of mundane society, from bestselling novels to hit television shows and movies. Every Halloween party has at least a few "vampires" in attendance. We represent everything for which most people long: romance, power, mystery, freedom, and, most importantly, Immortality.

Also, the recent "metaphysical" and new-age fads have created an ethos in which the mundane are ready to accept Our existence with enthusiasm and passion. Every major bookstore contains a section on magick and the occult. Many write books describing their encounters with vampires. People claiming to be vampires today openly go on talk shows, write books, and are the subjects of documentaries. It is as if the world has been awaiting Us.

Be proud of your heritage, for the vampire archetype is truly Immortal, like Our personal Quest of Immortality. Employ the Glamour with skill and wisdom, and your own individual nobility will be realized.

Fangs aided me in my Awakening. Wearing fangs was something I always wanted to experience, and for me it was an incredibly profound event. When I first looked into the mirror with them, something just clicked, and a primal and empowering urge came over me! Of course, the fangs themselves were merely a placebo, but I embraced it! For me, like many other Strigoi Vii to whom I spoke, getting my fangs was a true rite of passage. Fangs cannot make a Vampyre, but they can sure add to one!
—Adrien Black Moon, Strigoi Vii Initiate and fang client of Father Sebastiaan, London, England

Fangs, a classic symbol of the Vampyre Glamour, can be a powerful tool and a rite of passage. They are also a long-standing Strigoi Vii tradition.

Many may find fangs cliché, yet this is not necessarily the case. Within the vampire mythos, fangs are a constant and important symbol. As with many aspects of the Glamour, this conditioning is intentional.

Fangsmiths (those who make custom fangs) have consistently noticed that when an individual gets their fangs and looks in the mirror for the first time, there is a subtle shift or transformation as they begin to view themselves differently. Thus, for many, going through the ritual of having a pair of fangs made by a Fangsmith is an Initiation into the subculture or Family. There is nothing metaphysical about this. It is a psychological metamorphosis that may ignite Zhep'r and be the first step to Awakening.

You should procure quality fangs made by a Fangsmith, not the ones made by Hollywood SFX artists or dentists. Special-effects fangs are usually made overlarge to create the proper camera image, and most dentists are not trained or skilled in fangsmithing. Your fangs should be caps, small and subtle, made without a bridge (so you can speak easily), and prepared from the highest-quality dental acrylics.

The best part is that, unlike the cheap, boxed fangs available in most Halloween shops, good fangs will be customized to your face and tooth color. This means they will be fitted for you, so you may feel that the fangs are a part of yourself. Many Vampyres wear their fangs often and feel incomplete without them, as fangs are a symbol of Our nature. This symbol can do many things. Fangs act as a tool of the Outer Glamour. They can be a tool of seduction, as everyone is attracted to vampires. Also, they are a symbol of the Blood and Our primal nature.

That is why so many Initiates consider that getting a pair of custom fangs from a proper Fangsmith or "Family Dentist" is an essential part of the Glamour and of Coming forth by Day.

Chapter 9

VAMPYRE INITIATION

Then took the tree of Mystery root in the World of Los
Its topmost boughs shooting a fibre beneath Enitharmons couch
The double rooted Labyrinth soon wavd around their heads
—William Blake, *The Four Zoas*

Ordeals are formalized rites of passage into the Mysteries, teachings, and traditions of Strigoi Vii for Initiates. Each of these psychological and spiritual equations is solved by the individual on a solitary basis or with the guidance of other Initiates and Magisters. The Ordeals are a regimented, sequential system of learning and Ascension that directs a Strigoi Vii through the Mirror Gates of Zhep'r. They may be likened to grades and degrees in a scholastic institution or within occult groups such as the Hermetic Order of the Golden Dawn or Freemasonry. The Seeker achieves Initiation by bringing the Strigoi Vii Mysteries into their sphere of understanding. Verification of this understanding occurs through the achievement of specific results.

Mastery of the Strigoi Vii Mysteries is an individual and personal process, not a Family endeavor. It is the achievement of a spiritual Ascension, not of a social label or title that implies one individual's superiority over another. Each Mystery is a form of agreement and attunement within the Current and should only be done at the individual's own pace.

The Ordeals are most often undertaken on a solitary basis, as only the Strigoi Morte, Our Ancestors, may truly judge an Initiate's worth. Some Strigoi Vii choose to formalize their Initiation through a ceremonial ritual witnessed by a Magister.

The Outer Mysteries are the elementary foundations of Strigoi Vii Initiation. They are preferably done as points of self-Initiation. Each should be done sequentially. It is traditional to take about six months before moving on to the next Ascension, and to do otherwise is generally considered hasty. It marks also someone as being without the patience or maturity for Immortality.

Vampyre Seekers, or *O ° Nasarim* are individuals who have shown a potential for Strigoi Vii and a subconscious curiosity for Awakening. They may or may not be aware of their potential. They often will search for others like themselves and explore various groups and traditions. The Seekers may be drawn to books on the subject of Vampyres, vampyrism, and vampires before acquiring an official copy of the *Sanguinomicon* and studying its contents as a first step toward personal validation. There are no expectations or formal Initiations of Seekers.

Vampyre Dedicants, or *I ° Prospectii,* are those who have shown a vested interest in the Mysteries and potential for Zhep'r. Seekers are individuals who have Awakened to a curiosity about their True Nature. They are in agreement with the Black Veil and have shown a sincere dedication and understanding of the Mysteries. Traditionally, these dedicates of Strigoi Vii are known as *Bellah,* or the beautiful ones. Prospectii first begin by building a personal foundation of experience and knowledge that may lead them to pursue formal Initiation. They may also choose to formally dedicate and validate their Initiation on a solitary basis or perform it before a Magister through the Prospectii Rite of Dedication found at the end of this chapter. Some Strigoi Vii Initiates wish to mark their Ascension by meeting with a fangsmith and having a pair of custom fangs made as a personal symbol of transformation and often will obtain and consecrate a personal Legacy Ankh pendant. What is most important to note is that becoming a Strigoi Vii dedicant is not considered a formal Initiation; it is considered an experimental stage of Zhep'r, where the dedicant is expected to maintain a skeptical and rational exploration of the Mysteries and personal validation is key.

Vampyre Initiates, formally known as *II° Jahira,* receive this title by Coming forth by Day. This level of Initiation is for those who have sincerely dedicated themselves to mastery of the Dayside foundations of Strigoi Vii philosophy in the Corporeal world of the five senses. The Jahira focuses on the five Dayside Principles: the cult of one, material mastery, corporeal immortality, personal glamour, and empowering the quest. They are expected to test the rational and pragmatic Dayside foundation before moving on to the Higher Mysteries, and have seriously chosen to shift from a state of the mortal mind to that of an Immortal-minded perspective. Those who have solved this Mystery often choose to display a crystal or white stone in their ankh. The ritual of Ascension for marking this initiation is known as the *Rite of Day* or the *Jahira Ascension.*

Vampyre Sorors/Fraters, or *III° Calmae,* are those who have Come forth by Night, moved beyond the Corporeal foundations of the five senses, and touched on the deeper Mysteries of the Ethereal realm of the subtle world. Officially, Calmae are referred to as Sorors (sisters) or Fraters (brothers) within the Family. The Calmae has been introduced to the Ethereal level of reality and is familiar with life force, or Prana. Those who are Coming forth by Night further work toward mastering the Immortal-minded perspective, energy work, understanding the Anatomy of Death, and the Art of Vampyrism and work with the Sanguine Mass Communion ritual. Traditionally, Calmae were addressed "Sir," "Madame," or "Lady" to reflect their level of Initiation, however; *Soror* or *Frater* is now more common. Those who have successfully danced within this Mystery often choose to display a crimson or red stone in their ankh upon their Initiation.

The ritual of ascension for marking this initiation is known as the *Rite of Night* or the *Calmae Ascension*.

Vampyre Adepts, or *IV° MoRoii*, are those who have successfully Come forth by Twilight, validated the existence of the Current within them, and testified to a true Recoiling in Communion with the Strigoi Morte. They have achieved true Flight (out-of-body experiences, or OBE) and mastered outer forms of the Art of Vampyrism, whilst demonstrating perceptual control and Awakening of their Dragon. To formally Initiate to MoRoii, one must balance the Dayside and Night side perspectives into a strong equilibrium of Twilight, living in all three perspectives. Those who have Come forth by Twilight may act, if they choose, as "deacons" and lead group Communion rituals, as at this point they should have enough mastery to handle larger amounts of Prana directed in the offerings. Those who have successfully solved this Mystery often choose to display a purple stone in their ankh. The ritual of ascension for marking this initiation is known as the *Rite of Twilight,* or the *MoRoii Ascension*.

Vampyre Acolyte, or *V° Azraelle,* are those who have passed through an ascension point or "portal degree" between the Inner and Outer Mysteries. This Ordeal is a prelude to becoming a Magister and begins with taking an Oath of Loyalty to the Family. It is completed by the mysterious *Rite of Transformation*, forever awakening the individual to the Current and recognizing complete Awakening.

Magisters are individuals who have formally mastered the Outer Mysteries and are taught the Inner Mysteries. These teachings are only administered to the most sincere and dedicated Initiates who have Come forth by Twilight and almost exclusively within the providence of the OSV. Magisters are the Inner Circle of the Sanguinarium movement and are taught the secrets of vibrational sorcery, or Nomaj, and maintain their own private orders, structures, teachings, and Initiations. Since details of the levels of Initiation within the Magister Ordeals are kept from the mundane and Outer Mysteries, as they cannot be described and are oral traditions; it is simply put that those who are not Initiated will not understand.

In Latin, *Magister* means "master" or "teacher." It was a title of respect given to highly educated individuals in the classical era, the Middle Ages, and the Renaissance. The female equivalent of this title is *Magistra*. They have made great progress in Zhep'r, as they have achieved full Awakening of their Dragon and dedicated themselves fully to their own personal Quest for Immortality. Magisters have experienced a full equilibrium of Twilight. Magisters have testified to possess the necessary skills to defeat the Second Death. All Magisters are shining examples of the Mysteries, traditions, and philosophies of Strigoi Vii.

Every Magister, by accepting the secrets, is bound to uphold the Black Veil and Mysteries of Strigoi Vii and support the Quest of Family. Magisters are dedicated to the evolution, preservation, and prosperity of the Strigoi Vii Mysteries and Family. Traditionally, Magister Initiations are held in private with only other Inner Circle members present and on a secret time of the year during a private conclave. However, they can be done elsewhere, if necessary. The Magister Ascension ritual is a private ceremony in which the Strigoi Vii seeking Ascension performs a personal Initiation rite before at least a Grande Magister and preferably the Keeper of Elorath.

Some Magisters choose to accept the duties of *Magister Templi,* a formal minister of Elorath. A Magister Templi ("master of the temple") can be equated to a rabbi in the Jewish faith, a padrino or padrina in Santeria, or a Gnostic bishop. They often lead rituals, witness Initiations, consecrate temples and Sanctums, preside over Blood and Roses ceremonies, and lead group Communion. Magister Templi are often addressed as *Godmother* or *Godfather* or, in some circumstances, *Reverend*.

Magisters have earned the right to wear an obsidian stone in Their Legacy Ankh if they so choose, but few actually do so. A genuine Magister has no need to advertise their level of Initiation. The true Magister has achieved an inwardly empowered ego and focuses exclusively on their own Zhep'r. Magisters, of course, may be at different levels of evolution based on their personal interests and dedication to their journey of Zhep'r.

The Ipsissimus have mastered the Outer and Inner Mysteries of Strigoi Vii are considered to have reached the highest level of Initiation within Family. They are often retired Magisters who focus on their own personal agendas and Zhep'r. Such Initiates are considered to be at a point where their level of Ascension cannot be measured within Initiations or degrees.

Ascending to Magisterhood is not the end of the evolution of Zhep'r for the Strigoi Vii. In reality, it is only the beginning of one's exploration of the Inner Mysteries and deeper secrets of the Strigoi Vii.

Prospectii Rite of Dedication

This simple ritual of self-Initiation is the most basic of all formal Initiations within the Strigoi Vii Mysteries. Ritual is a powerful tool of personal reflection and empowerment, as well as a rite of passage showing dedication to the Mysteries of the Living Vampire.

The only tools needed are a completely private, darkened room, a mirror, a black candle, and a Legacy Ankh pendant. The room should be as dark as possible and must be locked or otherwise secured so that you will not be interrupted during the ceremony. This ritual, if possible, should be performed at midnight during the New Moon. Hang the mirror on the wall or place it on a table or shelf so that it is at eye level and light the black candle to represent your journey into the darkness others fear. Then, with sincerity, look directly and deeply into your own eyes in the mirror and speak the Strigoi Vii Charge after making a declaration of your chosen Sobriquet. To further enhance the ritual experience, it may be empowering to wear your fangs (for the purposes of psychodrama) and a Legacy Ankh pendant whilst Nightklad (clothed only by the darkness to allow energies to flow) or while wearing a mask and black robe. Some Initiates may also choose to utilize music and incense to help set the mood. You should employ whatever tools will aid in making your Initiation a singular and profound experience.

This simple act of dedication is the first step on your journey of Zhep'r. It should be performed alone unless you have the luxury of knowing ordained Strigoi Vii Magisters. However, it is permissible to perform the Prospectii Validation Rite in the presence of an Initiated lover or partner who is already of a higher level of Initiation. In both cases, however, the entire Initiation must be performed by the individual. Be aware that any witnesses act as observers only and not "examiners" or "benefactors." It is your free will that must be exercised first and foremost. Thus you should preside over your own Initiation. You, and only you, are qualified to say if you are ready to advance to the next step in your journey of Zhep'r.

Prospectus Summation

Strigoi Vii is not a path for the masses, for mortals lack the gemlike flame of the Current of Elorath, the essence of Our Family. Many will come to challenge the Mysteries and fail, out of frustration, lack of potential, or lack of sincerity. Those who are dedicated to deciphering the Mysteries should advance carefully and without undue haste. Be sure that you are absolutely ready for each step of Zhep'r. Strigoi Vii titles are reflections of what the individual practices and that with which they agree. They are not invented titles in the hierarchy of a fantasy social club or role-playing game! Earning a title, be it Jahira or Magister, denotes a serious and personal experience of Ascension and journey through Zhep'r.

Many will initially come to Our Mysteries eagerly, be an active presence in the Sanguinarium for a short time, perhaps even express a desire to Initiate, and then abruptly or gradually drift away from Our Current. These half-hearted ones, known to us as *Phyle,* choose to remain bound to their limited, mortal-minded perspective. Phyle will never truly revel in the pleasures of Ascension through Zhep'r and thus cannot experience the Immortal's perspective of personal godhood. The journey of Zhep'r is arduous and, at times, frustrating. However, it is a journey the likes of which you have never even imagined before, with incomparable rewards to be gained through perseverance and application.

In conclusion, honestly evaluate your personal reaction to the *Sanguinomicon*. If what you have just read seems intimately familiar, if you can truly say, "I feel as if I somehow knew this already," and you possess a strong curiosity to know more, you are then indeed a true Seeker. The next step is up to you. Simply test and experiment with the Mysteries within. If you find your personal exploration results in enlightenment, then you are experiencing Zhep'r. To those few who are of Our Blood, you Shining Ones, welcome to the honor of Our Family.

Book II

UBER JAHIRA

COMING FORTH BY DAY

I have no faith, I believe in nothing:
I only come to knowledge and
find the truth in Gnosis . . .
—Magister Dimitri

Prelude to the Dayside
INTRODUCTION TO THE IMMORTAL MINDSET

The beginning of the chapters of coming forth by day, and of praisings and glorifications, of coming forth from and going into the under-world glorious in Amentet beautiful; to be said [on] the day of the burial going in after coming forth.
—The Papyrus of Ani, or The Egyptian Book of
the Dead, E. A. Wallis Budge (trans.)

Welcome to the syllabus of the aspiring Jahira, "Coming Forth by Day," entitled "Liber Jahira." "Liber Jahira" differs significantly from "Liber Elorath: The Vampyre Prospectus," which is a two-dimensional introduction that serves as a basic set of concepts regarding Strigoi Vii. "Coming Forth by Day" is a three-dimensional text, as it contains not only instruction but applicable and tangible examples, as well as exercises the prospective Jahiras can test for themselves. Thus, with this book, the Jahira will explore and validate the Strigoi Vii Dayside Mysteries.

To explain Vampyrism from the perspective of the Strigoi Vii, We begin with the basic Hollywood concept of the vampire as introduced in "The Vampyre Prospectus." While the Strigoi Vii Vampyre is rational and real and the Hollywood vampire fantastical, Our reality has much in common with its namesake archetype. Society is in love with the fictional vampire for a reason. The vampire possesses what humans recognize they do not: power, control, seduction, sorcery, and, perhaps most notably, *Immortality*.

Of all these traits, Immortality (in the sense that We understand it) is the most unattainable for the average human. Perhaps this is why they idolize the vampire archetype and attempt to become like it. However, as far-fetched as it may seem, the journey of the True Vampyre is as much about Immortality as its Hollywood counterpart, albeit from a very different perspective.

We all believe we understand death. Death, we are told from an early age, is the only certainty in life. So, aware of the restrictions of our bodies and the inevitability of their decay, we set our thinking to a timescale of one hundred years or less. This manner of thinking is called the mortal mindset. However, what if there were no such restriction? How would our lives change? How would we view our existence if we stopped racing against the inevitable clock? Would we rush less and perhaps accomplish more? Would we perceive our experiences and actions differently? What would our priorities be if there were no "deadline?"

To adopt the Immortal mindset is to break free of the limitations we place on our own minds and selves. To be Immortal-minded is to be timeless, to live in the moment. While thinking of the past and planning for the future have their place, often we fail to live at all because we constantly obsess over how to cram too much into the continually dwindling days of our lives. We find ourselves defaulting to the habit and routine that makes up many mortal-minded people's perception of a "normal life"—a cycle of sleeping, working, eating, and repeating. We measure out our lives with the spoonfuls of school, family, career, retirement, all rushing us to the inevitability of death. We rarely stop to consider our actions. Are they fulfilling? Fruitful? We seem to know what is expected of us by a mortal-minded world, but what do we really *want*?

To be mortal-minded is to live according to acceptable standards of the so-called norm, or as the great French philosopher Michel Foucault put it, to "normalize" oneself to the mass mindset.

To be Immortal-minded is live to the fullest and as one chooses, recognizing limitless possibilities.

To be mortal-minded is to expect and accept death as prescribed by the myriad belief systems known to the mundane.

To be Immortal-minded is to be open to the idea that death does not have to be inevitable.

The *Sanguinomicon* series is aimed at helping you achieve Zhep'r, a transformative process that extends to every facet of your being. The first step of Zhep'r is the evolution from a mortal-minded perspective to one that is Immortally-minded. Let Us begin . . .

Chapter 10

DAYSIDE INITIATION

The Argument: As the true method of knowldge is experiment the true faculty of knowing must be the faculty which experiences.
—William Blake, "All Religions Are One"

Within "Liber Elorath: The Vampyre Prospectus," We learned about the elementary concepts of Strigoi Vii through a general outline of the Strigoi Vii Mysteries. Here in "Coming Forth by Day," We will begin to directly apply those foundations. We shall do so by forging, through the Principles of the Dayside, an applicable functionality in the Corporeal world of the five senses. These Principles, their applications, and testimonials are detailed in this text. By testing and embracing these concepts, you will establish yourself firmly in the rational, material world we call the Dayside. Many occult systems absolutely ignore this concept and jump directly into the esoteric mysteries. Such an approach caters to individuals looking for quick fixes and, in practice, yields few or no results. Just as a student seeking to become a surgeon must first learn basic human anatomy and physiology, so must you build a strong Corporeal foundation before moving on to higher Strigoi Vii Mysteries.

With these practical foundations, you will have the platform from which to firmly launch yourself into the Higher Mysteries from a Strigoi Vii perspective. You should always be mindful of the basic foundations you will learn here. Even if you have mastered these Principles already, it is empowering to review them on a consistent basis and re-experience them from your advancing perspective. Return to these Dayside principles during times when you find the Nightside overwhelms your perceptions. Doing so will root and ground you, and then you may resume your Nightside activities with balance and renewed vigor. Without this balance, there is no duality; thus you cannot live within the Twilight of reality.

The following is an overview of the basic concepts of the Dayside Principles. You will find a detailed description and practical applications in the following chapters of this book.

The Dayside Principles

First Principle: The Cult of One involves establishing an Immortal-minded perspective and an inwardly empowered ego. Embrace your essentially self-sufficient and solitary nature. Understand and empower your will. Embrace a love of life and take steps to realize your dreams as attainable realities. Be able to forgive yourself for past trespasses and look toward a future where you fulfill all possibilities and dreams.

Second Principle: Material Mastery is a lifestyle in which you are the master of your material world. Money is not the goal but a useful tool—use it to your advantage. Achieve individual material independence, regardless of if you are in a committed relationship or not. Forge a strong sense of self-reliance in regard to financial matters.

Third Principle: Corporeal Immortality is to make your personal Corporeal Sanctum, the Temple of the Self, a healthy and vibrant foundation. Strive for both personal vitality and longevity. Be always mindful of your own self-preservation and avoid threats to your Corporeal well-being. Establish a personal legacy that will continue to live on and provide you with energy beyond your physical existence. Create works such as music, art, dance, and literature that will help build and contribute to mundane and Vampyre cultures.

Fourth Principle: Personal Glamour is to become socially empowered. Master your body language, physical appearance, presence, expressions, and the way you subtly communicate. The result will be immensely rewarding relationships with lovers, business associates, friends, mortal family, and Strigoi Vii Family.

Fifth Principle: Empowering the Quest begins with supporting the Family Quest to reach out to other members of the Family. Discover creative ways in which you can further enhance the experience of the Mysteries amongst the Sanguinarium. The ultimate goal of this Principle is to simply introduce an individual to Strigoi Vii without mentioning anything other than suggesting discretely that they read *Sanguinomicon* or refer them to the Sanguinarium website. Remember, answering questions defeats the purpose of the Quest and violates the individual's own ability to make his own educated opinion. Any other steps are in violation of the Black Veil principles of the Quest and Secrets.

On a personal level, this principle begins with a tradition known as *Gifting*. Gifting refers to giving a copy of the *Sanguinomicon* to a likely Seeker. You may choose to present your personal copy to a Seeker with whom you are close, or obtain them a new copy. Gifting is a tool of unity, energy flow, and exchange amongst Strigoi Vii. This generosity offers an individual the ability to fuel their own gratitude, enhances the Quest, and maintains a positive flow of energy. Gifting is only one example of empowering the Quest of Family and is elaborated on, along with many others, in chapter 16, "The Quest of Family."

In your exploration of the Jahira Mystery, begin to learn from the archetypal primal examples in this world. Consider the perspective of the noble and majestic rulers of the wild, such as the lion, shark, wolf, hawk, and eagle. As the Jahira formally embraces and Awakens to their Nature, their worldview shifts from mortal to Immortalist, from human to Vampyre. This can be called "Predatory Spirituality." This is a choice and requires consistent reflection, effort, and action on the part of the Strigoi Vii.

Realize that only results matter in your journey of Zhep'r. Personally confirmed knowledge, or *Gnosis,* as discussed in the Prospectus, is achieved through actions, effort, and results—not empty words, belief, or faith. As a Jahira, begin to loosen your grasp on the mortal-minded slave bonds of poverty, mental suppression, and depression. No Vampyre should ever be a member of the downtrodden proletariat! Be an objective skeptic. Always test and confirm all experiences in life for yourself.

Never force another to acquiesce to your perspectives. Invite them to open, respectful discussion, and, if they are Family and ready, they will come to their own understanding. If you speak with reason and demonstrate results, they may choose to agree. Always respect everyone else's right to have free will and to hold their own opinions.

Let logic and reason rule and guide you in your journey through the Strigoi Vii Mysteries. Take nothing on faith or blind belief! Tangible results of your experiments in Strigoi Vii can manifest as if you experienced them through the five senses.

Observe your actions and how they affect the mortal-minded. Learn to act to your advantage around them. Walk proudly upright, speak in slow clear tones, and gently or sternly look others directly in the eye when talking to them. You will command their respect through simple techniques, because it is the nature of most people to be followers. Thus, always present yourself as a leader and embrace your own noble nature. In turn, always treat all sentient beings with respect and regard. Appreciate the power of a long and healthy life, happiness, pleasure, and personal power. Be confident in your ability to secure all these things.

Uphold and abide by the common sense and logic of the Black Veil principles at all times, without exception. When you feel you have come to agreement with the Mystery of Jahira, make the *Jahira Ascension Rite,* and proudly walk through the Gates of the Dayside of your own free will.

Seek out other members of the Family through the Quest if you need guidance and encouragement. However, do not drain them by imposing mental slave bonds on them. This journey is *your own*—no one else can tread your path or tell you exactly how to proceed. Embrace your Blood and realize your potential. It is a solitary journey through Zhep'r, and only you can take the initiative. Yet it is the most important journey you will ever take. In the book *The Teachings of Don Juan: A Yaqui Way of Knowledge,* Carlos Castaneda writes that any true path must have a heart. The path of Zhep'r *is* the heart of the Strigoi Vii.

Zhep'r is the metamorphosis of the Ascended Self, combined with the foundation of a spiritual Awakening to and awareness of the perspective of the Strigoi Vii. It is necessary to understand and realize the many truths which come with Vampyric transformation. Once the Seeker achieves and maintains a high state of Zhep'r through initiative and action, the individual Living Vampire can be prepared to defeat the Second Death of the Self. The Mysteries are both the keys and the map—a system to facilitate this transformation.

Take your time and only proceed when you are ready. However, realize that there is a limit to the mortal coil. The opportunity is before you at this very moment! *Carpe noctem* and *carpe diem!* Do not lose Zhep'r by endless procrastination, for you only have one opportunity for success in this short mortal life. This is your chance to seize what is rightfully in your Blood. These things should be established firmly before taking on the challenges within the Third Mystery of Calmae.

A good book is the precious life-blood of a master spirit,
embalmed and treasured up on purpose to a life beyond life.
—John Milton, *Aeropagitica*

The Grimoire is the core tool of the Jahira. The term is often associated with ancient (sometimes diabolical) books of magick. The Strigoi Vii grimoire is a journal of personal practices and a spiritual diary of Zhep'r. Any notebook or journal can serve as a grimoire. However, many Strigoi Vii like to recognize the importance of their grimoire by customizing their book with leather covers, decorations, magickal signs, or similar embellishments. Each grimoire should be customized and attuned to the individual. Some even wish to keep their grimoire online in a secure server for ease of access and security purposes. However, a physical book is always more personal and intimate.

that way of inspiration
is always open,

and open to everyone;
it acts as go-between, interpreter,

it explains symbols of the past
in to-day's imagery,

it merges the distant future
with most distant antiquity,

states economically
in a simple dream-equation

the most profound philosophy . . . .
—H. D., "The Walls Do Not Fall"

The Dayside Initiation, also known as the *Jahira Ascension,* comes to an individual once they have Come forth by Day to their own personal satisfaction. Only perform this rite if you are in agreement with and have tested and validated the Strigoi Vii Dayside Mysteries. At the core of this ritual is reaffirmation of the Principle of the Black Veil and the Dayside Principles. If you are willing to abide by these principles and critically examine the Mysteries, you will be ready to perform the Rite of Jahira.

The ritual is simple. It is preferably performed during a Dark Moon phase when the moon is not visible in the night sky. Find a private place, such as a secluded spot in the wilderness or a personal room, free from intrusion and interruption. Place a mirror at eye level on the western wall, on the ground, or in some other convenient place. If indoors, light some candles, close the curtains to block out all outside light, and turn off phones and other electronic devices. You may wish to play some music and light your favorite incense for ambience. When your space is prepared, spend some time in meditation and self-reflection and focus strongly on your intention in performing this ritual. At the stroke of midnight look directly into your own eyes in the mirror and recite the following Oath:

THE DAYSIDE OATH

I speak beyond the Gates of this World. Ancestors, I come before You in pure love and sincerity.

I, [Sobriquet], come into this sacred Sanctum of my own free will, to stand before my Nightside Family, in love and loyalty, with the full intent of Initiating myself into the Mystery of the Dayside. I seek entrance through the Gates of Day into the Circle of Jahira.

I vow to test and explore the Strigoi Vii Mysteries from an objective perspective.

I vow to uphold the principles of the Black Veil and the Five Dayside Principles as my foundation, sword, and shield.

(Take your Legacy Ankh in your hand and place it over your heart.)

I place this symbol of Our Family and Mysteries above my heart to formally (re)consecrate it. I vow to honor and keep the Secrets of Our Family.

Thus, I now declare I have Come forth by Day as [Family or Nightside name] of the Strigoi Vii.

If you wish to have this Ascension further validated, you may request to perform it during a Sanguine Mass before a MoRoii, Azraelle, or Magister. You can also perform the rite with a Strigoi Vii or Black Swan partner present. If you would like your Ascension formally recognized by the Family and the Sanguinarium, you may submit a written testimonial to the Synod.

Chapter 11

THE EVOLVING HUMAN

*What a piece of work is a man! how noble in reason! how
infinite in faculty! in form and moving, how express and
admirable! in action, how like an angel! in apprehension, how
like a god! the beauty of the world! the paragon of animals!*
—William Shakespeare, *Hamlet*

The Living Vampire is a transhumanist, or one who seeks to transcend
the current human state. Advancing technologies and medical science
have provided many new Corporeal opportunities for life extension.
Yet this is just one aspect of several levels of advancement toward Immortality. Since the Mysteries are a series of keys to unlock potential
for Zhep'r, one must begin to think like the Immortals and move beyond the limiting conditionings of the mundane.

On the Corporeal level, the Strigoi Vii is absolutely physically and
genetically identical to any other human being. The difference begins in
the subtle world, or the Ethereal and Astral bodies, where Our "Blood"
truly exists. This Blood only gives one the *potential* for Zhep'r. It is not
a promise or guarantee! Initiative, will, and discipline are required in
order to realize your potential and ignite this Dark Flame.

First and foremost, the Living Vampire is a lover of life, finding
opportunity for Zhep'r in all of life's beautiful facets. We are far from
the eternally damned and spiritually agonized creatures of darkness

that many mortals believe Us to be. Continue to disregard the Hollywood conception of the vampire! The Immortal looks beyond mortal-minded society and to the laws of nature for the truest lessons.

Even within the established structure of civilization, survival of the fittest still persists. Those with the greatest talents and aptitude generally prosper, while the weak and ignorant often despair and die. Modern philosophers call this social Darwinism. Complete and indiscriminating equality is a mortal-minded construct. Darwin's theory of evolution states that those living beings with particular advantages will prosper and pass their strengths on to their offspring. So is it in the human world and civilization, no matter how altruistic and inclusive one wishes to be. While the Strigoi Vii would never condone discrimination or prejudice, We also refuse to blindly claim that all people are "the same" and shut our eyes to the talents and strengths of exceptional individuals. If everything were created equal, how could anything be extraordinary? We recognize that We have the potential to evolve from a mortal-minded to an Immortal-minded state and celebrate Our nature. We are the true kings and queens of Our own individual and personal realities! This is how We truly Live life.

The Immortal-minded individual, realizing the responsibility of their Blood, reduces risk and distractions that interfere with their Zhep'r. The Immortal-minded strive to surround themselves with others who inspire Zhep'r, choosing their associates from both the Family and the outstanding mortal-minded. As all actions are exchanges of energy, you will receive personal energies from all those with whom you interact. If you wish to be inspired as an artist, associate with other gifted artists. If you want to become a successful business owner, open a business in a location where your product is in demand. As part of overcoming a drug habit, end your associations with people who abuse drugs. Avoid those who sustain their own bad luck and unhappiness, as they will only transmit their misery to you. This process may be difficult if such people are friends or members of your social circle, yet you must end these destructive relationships if you truly wish to increase your Zhep'r. Moreover, you will discover that association with positive, like-minded individuals will have significant constructive results in the Corporeal realm.

This is not to say that you must disassociate with all but other Family members, as many cultlike religions and spiritual paths mandate. Strigoi Vii is not a cult and does not encourage you to discard important interpersonal relationships! However, We *are* encouraging you to surround yourself with people who bring vibrancy and joy to your life, who augment your talents, provide perspective, and edify you. Do not waste your time with the terminally miserable or depressed. Surround yourself with those who love you and love life.

Energy is the currency of Immortals. We see that the whole world is ripe for enjoyment. There is life and love in everything, ranging from a quiet dinner at home with a loved one to participation in an exciting mountain-climbing expedition to the success of earning a university degree. Above all, the Immortal-minded path is one of conservation. We celebrate life in all its many aspects and do not waste energies or physical resources. Those of the Blood are not destroyers! Life is about creation and the rising flow of energies.

The Immortal subscribes to the rules of courtesy and chivalry. We always strive to be ladies and gentlemen! Whenever possible, We show respect and consideration to all those around Us, including the mortal-minded, as well as Family members. Even if We dislike an individual, We will be civil in their presence and politely avoid future contact unless they serve a positive purpose in Our lives. Being Strigoi Vii brings with it a significant responsibility. If We are to be the rulers of Our own worlds, We must recognize the obligations associated with that role. Just as any reputable head of state would seek to always be above reproach in their behavior, so must We. The True Vampyre does not get angry at those who are not in agreement with their perspective, for those who are not of the Family will never completely understand Our ways. Also, the True Vampyre never argues with those who do not agree with the truth, nor will We sermonize. Doing so is simply a waste of energy.

The Living Vampire honors their history and has a deep appreciation of their spiritual heritage; holding their Strigoi Vii Family in utmost esteem, yet respecting other obligations. Corporeal commitments, including those to the mortal-minded, are not to be disregarded. Our Blood does not constitute a carte blanche to be disrespectful or irresponsible. Since We seek to embrace the next steps in human evolution, We must embrace the associated accountability. We must never disregard or hold in contempt those who are not capable of Zhep'r. The Strigoi Vii is not haughty.

The Immortal-minded seeks self-deification and self-divinity. Thus, We worship no beings save Ourselves. We revere and honor the Strigoi Morte as the mortal-minded in the Chinese or Native American traditions would revere an ancestor. However, We do not worship or pander to Them. We approach Them with an attitude of mutual respect and reverence. We choose to recognize Our own potential godhood and personal divinity! For example, a member of a Christian church may live in fear of committing "sins" against the code of their religion and timidly bow their head before their god, praying for favors and deliverance. We as Strigoi Vii proudly celebrate Our Selves and Our Strigoi Morte Ancestors and draw strength and dignity from Our Blood.

The Immortal develops a strong sense of patience and seeks to maintain a long-term perspective rather than an impulsive short-term perspective. We embrace the immediacy of each day, yet recognize the importance of future planning. We accept the ancient Roman poet Horace's dictum *carpe diem,* or "seize the day," as a core philosophy. However, We do not seize the day due to a fear of imminent death! The Strigoi Vii knows they have the opportunity for Immortality, yet simultaneously recognizes the unique importance of each single moment.

The Immortal-minded Vampyre rejects new-age superstitions and blind faith in favor of occult knowledge that produces tangible results. The rest of the world now calls some of these revealed magickal secrets "science." Unfortunately, much of new-age doctrine is no more than pop psychology for people seeking a quick fix. The True Vampyre critically examines all modes of thought and chooses to ascribe only to those which further Zhep'r.

The Vampyre knows the Corporeal body is their temple and physical center. The health and maintenance of the physical body affects all other layers of the Self. The Strigoi Vii Vampyre seeks to maintain their physical health, and pursues Corporeal Immortality and evolution through technology and other means. We never disregard the tangible world and Our place in it. We would never seek to mortify Our flesh if it costs Us a sacred flow of energy! This is why, for example, so many Strigoi Vii avoid extreme body modification like cuttings and implants. This is because such modifications change the flow of energy within the body, and a Vampyre must attune to these changes. However, Strigoi Vii are individualistic and unique, each on their own path. Some Strigoi Vii do embrace body modification and related practices in order to further their own personal expression or for specific focuses of energy. However, from a Dayside perspective, extreme modification of one's physical body can potentially serve as a detriment when entering certain professions or forming particular relationships. As pragmatists, Strigoi Vii seek to maintain Our Selves in a way that does not limit Us on any level.

I am of a sect by myself . . .
—Thomas Jefferson

My mind is my church.
—Thomas Paine

The Cult of One is the Dayside Principle at the core of the Evolving Human. For Zhep'r to truly take root, one begins inwardly with Mastery of the Self. The Strigoi Vii must embrace their Vampyre nature as a Cult of One. The Strigoi Vii realizes that the Self must be the center of their individual world, and they prioritize above all else what matters most to the Self. Becoming a Cult of One does not mean focusing on an egotistical, self-centered perspective. Instead, it involves embracing individuality, self-sufficiency, and absolute mastery of the Self.

The concept of "selfhood" appears in many world religions, philosophies, and sciences. In his famous "Allegory of the Cave," Plato spoke of the discovery of Self and truth as similar to a chained prisoner being released from a miserable, dreamlike cave into the pragmatic light of the sun. The Western Cartesian Self is organized around rationality and the intellect. Eastern practices such as Buddhism sometimes speak of seemingly "losing" the Self in union with those of others or with the energies of the universe. Psychologically speaking, both Freud and Jung discussed the psyche and the components of the personality. In contemporary postmodern thought, there is a trend toward dismissing the "essential" Cartesian Self and perceiving one's Self as being no more than a collection of experiences and memories. These comprise only a very few examples of historical and contemporary conceptions of the Self. A fundamentally important part of the Strigoi Vii evolution of Zhep'r is to come to a personal and validated understanding of your own True Vampyric Self.

So many members of mortal-minded cults and some Legacies become yes-men to their leaders, both mundane and spiritual. Strigoi Vii validate their own experiences individually. They approach life, spirituality, and philosophy as a scientist would approach a promising yet untested theory. In effect, the Strigoi Vii are in agreement with any group that shares Our perspective and not in agreement with any organization, no matter their name or claims, that is not interested in questioning and validating its own teachings.

This individualism is at the core of Our nature. We of the Family are by nature very convivial yet coincidently independent. The vast majority of Strigoi Vii are solitary and have no interest in using the Family as a social clique. Even fewer participate in Quorums and Moots. Many prefer to walk this path alone as solitary individuals, finding agreement with the Mysteries that they have validated themselves. Realizing this element of Our nature is one of the many steps in Coming forth by Day.

One of the most intriguing characteristics that differentiates the Immortal-minded from the average mundane is the capacity for independent thought and action. The mortal-minded generally operate on a metaphorical frequency of zero, unable to connect or operate, essentially set to "off." Like those trapped in the Matrix or the world of *Fight Club,* the vast majority of those who embrace the mundane perspective are virtually incapable of independent thought on a consistent basis. They shut off their brains by watching television, immersing themselves in useless and time-consuming activities, or succumbing to peer pressure and the constraints of the "normal." They are essentially playing an endless game of follow-the-leader. As stated in the philosophy of Ayn Rand, most people worship the principle of "we," where the greater good is always more important than the individual. They are thus locked into a current of needless self-sacrifice. Pop culture refers to this as the "cubicle" or "lemming" mentality. When we capitalize the word *We,* it refers to Our ideological agreement and differentiates the mortal-minded and Immortal-minded perspectives.

The Strigoi Vii thinks differently from the mortal-minded. They operate on a frequency of one, where the individual comes first. They revel in their individuality and find power in solitude. However, Strigoi Vii do not cause harm to others due to blind egotism. They reverse this thought and, instead of being brainwashed followers, realize that there is power in numbers as well as solitude. To the Vampyre, *1* and the sacred *I* are one and the same thing! Unlike the mortal-minded, the Living Vampire acknowledges that *all* sentient actions are selfish and serve the *I,* be it volunteering for a community service project or helping someone in need. These are certainly worthwhile and laudable actions, but it is completely unrealistic to claim the good Samaritan or volunteer worker does not benefit the *I* in some manner by their charitable actions. There is no purely selfless act!

We are approaching the close of the Piscean Age, the fourth aeon of the humanity's current evolution. The Piscean era of "self-sacrifice" and "virgin purity" dawns from the non-Gnostic Judeo-Christian mindset. However, throughout history, a select few have come into agreement with or have achieved similar perspectives to Our Current. They have kept the Dark Flame alight in the blackness of the Piscean Age. The coming aeon, the age that Our Family eagerly anticipates, is dawning. Some call it the Age of Aquarius. Magus Aleister Crowley called it the Age of Horus. It will be an Age of the Self, where individual divinity and secular rationalism will be celebrated.

In the Age of Horus, the love between the mundane world and Vampyres will deepen. As of this printing, the Strigoi Vii see this love epitomized by the mass popularity of vampire-themed books, films such as *Twilight* and *Underworld,* and television programs such as *True Blood.* Bram Stoker's *Dracula* and Anne Rice's more contemporary vampires have seduced countless readers. The world has moved from fearing Us to embracing Us in all levels of their culture. Just compare the archaic, grisly, Eastern European vampire legends to the current popularity of media images like the vampire Lestat. Our Glamour has never seen such great success!

You might think that joining or coming into agreement with a movement like the Sanguinarium, or labeling yourself Strigoi Vii, is subscribing to the herd mentality. Actually it is quite the opposite. Unlike a cult, the Sanguinarium is truly a "think tank" where you, as a member of an international network of like-minded individuals, can utilize Our resources and find inspiration to further your Zhep'r and Self. The Mysteries and the Sanguinarium are simply tools to unlock what is in your Blood. They are not cult dogma designed for the purpose of control. Strigoi Vii are independent, critically minded, inquisitive individuals. When We choose to associate with each other in a group setting, We do so on a footing of respect and equality.

In conclusion, what do you get if you add zero a thousand times? You get zero. What do you get when you add one a thousand times? A spiritual nation of a thousand independently thinking individuals who share a common agreement and an individual pride in their collective heritage.

You might have been a sparkle of clear sand.
You, who remember for a twinkling instant

All things, or what you think all things to be,
Whose cries consume you, or whose joys
Hoist you to heaven, such a heaven as you will:
You might have been a dream dreamed in a dream
By some one dreaming of God and dreamed by God.
You might indeed have been a God, a star,
A world of stars and Gods, a web of time;
You might have been the word that breathed the world.
—Conrad Aiken, "Preludes for Memnon"

To be a ruler of the Self is the Strigoi Vii will. In the process of Awakening, We admit Our differences from others. Indeed, many Strigoi Vii may even realize this before their Awakening. Before We have the ability to ignite the Dark Flame of the Vampyric transformation of Zhep'r, We must first begin to adopt the perspective of rulers of Our own lives from an Immortal-minded perspective. In order to achieve this, you must embrace the reason and logic within Our Blood. Look deep into the mirror, meet your Dragon, and explore the labyrinth of the Mysteries in order to discover those hidden truths. The Strigoi Vii Mysteries are simply a reminder of what you already know. All you must do is remember and embrace it!

The cornerstone of Strigoi Vii philosophy begins with thinking like a majestic and noble ruler of the Self. This ideology is forged by developing a no-nonsense perspective and building a solid foundation in the material world. The Corporeal world is composed of matter and energy, and only through mastery of this layer of reality can the Strigoi Vii truly be prepared to explore the more subtle realms that lie beyond the mirror.

The philosophy of the Living Vampire is an active mastery of one's own life, not the passive victim mentality lying within the hearts of most people who blindly stumble through life. The Strigoi Vii is in love with life and sees the beauty in all things. The only true enemy of the Strigoi Vii is the absolute death of the Self, or one's own personality. The "ruler of the Self" mentality ignites the Strigoi Vii's love and passion for life. Strigoi Vii seek only the best in personal mastery of their finances, mental and physical health, pleasure, and success in any of their interests and endeavors. The True Vampyre will not waste energy with frivolous and wasteful behavior or individuals. They place their own physical and mental well-being as the top Corporeal priority in their life.

All Strigoi Vii naturally exhibit a strong sense of individuality and independence. However, at the same time, the Living Vampire can be social by nature, exhibiting a strong love for pleasure and all that gives life flavor. The interests of the Strigoi Vii may include soirées, literature, cinema, theater, travel, sports, bon-faire, music, and dance, to name just a few. Even with this inherent love for such indulgences, the Strigoi Vii realizes the most rewarding experience remains personal Zhep'r. The Vampyre never sees failure as anything more than a lesson and challenge about how to reapproach an issue and then obtain success. The Strigoi Vii embraces all different facets of life, both positive and negative, and does not seek to be placated by false and simpleminded notions. Life is the ultimate experience, and, being grounded in reality, the Strigoi Vii is fully aware that the heaven or hell the mortal-minded population perceives is simply self-created. As long as the True Vampyre is still alive, they will stop at nothing to get the most out of each and every moment. The final Second Death is truly the only destroyer of the Self.

The Vampyre dances through life, never taking slights and offences personally, and is adaptable in their ways. Strigoi Vii often strive to be neutral and noncommittal so they have many options to be flexible in their actions.

The Vampyre is a model and symbol of chivalry. They often employ, in their personal Glamour, forms of etiquette that are not common to the era in which they live. They are thus masters of seduction and elegance and are sensible hedonists, never belittling themselves with base or unrefined behaviors. By employing the Glamour, the Vampyre always seeks to be thoughtful to others and rejects senseless and indiscriminate behavior, whilst still gratifying their own desires.

The Strigoi Vii is extremely proud and graceful and displays deep love and pride in their heritage, ancestry, and Family. They show an absolute level of respect, helpfulness, and courtesy when it comes to interacting with other members of the Family, both Awakened and un-Awakened. Additionally, a Strigoi Vii extends this courtesy to other deserving persons, whom We call Black Swans. Strigoi Vii always employ good manners and respect in all social dealings, Immortal and mundane. Our bond with others of Our Blood does not mean We are rude to those not of Our Family.

Many mortals possess an externally gratified ego, always seeking approval and attention from others of their kind. The Strigoi Vii naturally embraces an inwardly empowered ego. Self-satisfaction without the necessity of others' approval is a strong character trait of True Strigoi Vii. For the Strigoi Vii, performing, or what the mortal-minded would consider "getting attention," is simply a means of stimulating an audience to freely send precious life energy toward them. Unlike the mortal-minded, the Strigoi Vii do not seek to inflate their own ego and importance through such actions. The Strigoi Vii moves forward in a world where they are their own god. Only they, and no one else, can truly judge and satisfy themselves.

The spirit of the Living Vampire is strong. Strigoi Vii are beings of pure life and love. They walk through each and every moment strong and revitalized once they come to this Awakening. Right before them there is energy for the taking, both physical and subtle. This is the living testament of the Strigoi Vii embracing the Self.

> *With great power there must also come—great responsibility!*
> —Stan Lee, *Amazing Fantasy,* no. 15

Immortal morality is different from the mundane perceptions of the mortal-minded. It is a path only for a few, and the unprepared and un-thoughtful who attempt it will often be disappointed in their failures.

The average, spiritually un-Awakened mortal-minded, who are known to Us by their Gnostic name of *hyle,* often harbor the strong misconception that they are ultimately superior to all else. Most people only see the life of their own species as of any value and will slaughter and torture animals for food, sport, pleasure, and unnecessary scientific and medical experiments. The Strigoi Vii do not lower themselves to such views and actions, preferring that such horrid acts be on the bloody hands of others. We only end life when necessary for survival or defense, not for pleasure. Thus a True Vampyre would never physically harm a person or animal needlessly. In fact, quite a number of Strigoi Vii adopt this philosophy in their personal lives as vegetarians or even vegans.

The Living Vampire realizes that the transfer of energies is a reality of life. However, the Vampyre, who is ever more civilized, never seeks to torture their "prey." The Vampyre gathers and harvests life as expressed in their passion for all living things, never being destructive or wasteful. We perceive all living creatures with the knowledge that they are there for Our survival, and thereby deserve Our respect.

However, the Strigoi Vii does not sacrifice their well-being or Self for others without extreme need. The concept of martyrdom is deeply rooted in mortal-minded morality. Most mortal-minded ultimately believe that sacrificing oneself is the highest and greatest possible act. Just consider the story of Jesus from the Christian perspective, who "died for the sins" of all other humans, or suicide bombers who are willing to die for their religious beliefs. To the Strigoi Vii, the sacred *I* supersedes an abstract and fallible religious faith, as well as the anonymous and unappreciative masses. If Jesus' sacrifice had truly worked under the terms of Christian dogma, there would be much less sin and suffering in the world. Despite the terrorist attacks of suicide bombers, the beliefs and ideologies of their sponsoring groups or nations are not widely established. Even contemporary popular culture, such as the books and movies in the Harry Potter series, pass along the mortal-minded message that self-sacrifice is necessary for the greater good.

We, as Strigoi Vii, understand that ultimately most self-sacrifice potentially can limit or destroy the Self, and rarely, if ever, actually benefits some theoretical "greater good." As We worship only the Self, so do We refuse to destroy that Self, no matter what mortal-minded morality might prescribe. It is certainly worthy to help others, but much mortal-minded behavior of this sort stems not from altruism or true love of others, but from conditioning and selfishness. Mortal-minded sacrifice truly fosters an empty sense of false superiority, for the "martyr" can consider themselves better than others on account of their sacrifice. However, would not true superiority consist of taking pride in one's Self? Instead of throwing one's life or livelihood away in a dramatic gesture, would it not be much better and wiser to live thoughtfully, respectfully, completely, and in a manner that benefits the Self? Thus does one show respect to others as well as love of the Self.

Chapter 12
AWAKENING YOUR DRAGON

Now the serpent was more subtil than any beast of the field . . .
—Genesis 3:1

To Awaken the Dragon means to rise up and make Communion with the Divine Self. This is the most essential action of Zhep'r, save only the Arts of Vampyrism and the circuit of Communion with the Strigoi Morte. This chapter will delve into several simple exercises and philosophies geared toward beginning this Communion with the Divine Self. Put aside your fear, acknowledge your desire, strengthen your will, and embrace the Journey!

The only thing we have to fear is fear itself.
—Franklin D. Roosevelt

Fear is the most limiting barrier for most mortals. Mortal fears are nearly endless: fear of death, poverty, solitude, career failure—every hyle suffers from at least one such debilitating dread. For the majority of the mortal-minded, mastering fear is nearly impossible. However, those of the Current are evolved humans who must overcome this most basic of obstacles. We do not mean, however, that the Strigoi Vii should recklessly and dangerously "face" or overcome their fears.

Often the mortal-minded seek to ignore very real problems by bluntly denying their phobias (often coarsely called "being a man"), which usually means embracing an even more closed-minded ideology. This is a patriarchal, mortal-minded route that most often leads to failure. As seen through the Dragon's Eyes, overcoming fear involves rejecting the concept of linear Immortality (the mortal-minded perspective) and embracing the perception of timelessness (the Immortal-minded perspective).

Space and time as experienced from the Corporeal perspective are illusions. In his theory of special relativity, Albert Einstein showed that our perceptions of space and time depend on our position as an observer. An observer moving with great speed will perceive time differently from a stationary observer. A clock moving at accelerated speed runs "slow" compared to a nonmoving clock. Quantum physics shows that the results of an experiment depend on who is watching—the presence of an observer affects the outcome. From the Corporeal perspective, reality is relative. Begin to disassociate from the mortal-minded perspective and embrace that of an Immortal. You need to realize that you are only an observer, sitting on the Throne of Your Dragon. Thus your experience is personal to you, and, moreover, does not determine your True Self. Your body, home, belongings, pets, job, writings, and so on are not you; they are only Corporeal possessions of your own personal core Self, or your Dragon. They are not the true Self and are separate and distinct. To be Immortal-minded, you must begin from the perspective of the Dragon. Here is the very first step of true disassociation and Zhep'r.

Once you can taste the experience of timelessness, fear becomes another extension of the Corporeal world, which, being relative, can be viewed from different perspectives. Begin with the exercise known as *Throning*. This powerful tool of Awakening Your Dragon allows you to sit on the Throne of Your Self. The Dragon does not truly exist in the ordinary reality, even with a Corporeal counterpart of your Dragon's Throne. We cannot invoke, evoke, or talk to it, because it is Us; that from which all experience is observed. Your Dragon is essentially your perceptive Self, the observer, the part of your consciousness that *is* and sees. We cannot observe it, because who then would be making the observation? That would be like asking your eyeball to look at itself. We also cannot contemplate it, because once again, who would be doing the contemplation? To further understand this concept, We employ the tool of Throning.

Where is your consciousness? As a very simple exercise, close your eyes for a moment and think of something important to you, such as a favorite book or a treasured memento. Visualize it as clearly as you can. Where does this "thinking" take place, and where do you "see" the image? Do you visualize with your arm or your stomach? Obviously not—you visualize with your mind, and the mental image is "located" in the forehead, right behind the eyes and between the temples. This is where your Throne is situated.

Applying Throning

Stand or sit about a meter away from a mirror hanging at eye level. Your back should be straight, and you should be comfortable but in no danger of falling asleep. We suggest sitting in a wooden straight-backed chair, if possible. Once ready, stare directly into your own eyes in the mirror. Many find this exercise disconcerting after a few moments, but try not to break contact. Attempt to gaze into the Throne behind your eyes by looking through your pupils and through the mirror. Try doing this for five minutes to begin, and then add another five when you are ready. As you master this discipline, all sounds, lights, and experiences around you will begin to fade away. You will be sitting on your personal Throne. Your sense of time and space will also be lost. You will be the only being in existence, for your Throne is timeless. Your sense of time and space will merge with this expansion of your awareness, as your sense of Self surpasses the limitations of ordinary awareness. While looking from the Dragon's Throne, all may be possible.

Throning is the first of many techniques Strigoi Vii use to disassociate from the mortal-minded viewpoint and embrace an Immortal-minded perspective. With this basic exercise, you will be able to realize that your fears are illusions and merely barriers of suppression placed on your consciousness. With this realization, you will then be able to release your Self to explore existence on a profound level. Future exercises in the *Sanguinomicon* will add to your personal empowerment. Therefore, it is highly recommended that you practice Throning frequently. It is an excellent exercise to perform before retiring for bed.

Most people want things like a candle-flame, flickering, shifting. You, on the other hand, want like a forest fire.
—spoken by Desire in *The Sandman: Endless Nights* by Neil Gaiman

Desire is one of the most basic emotions, the deep-rooted feeling of want and need. In order to fuel your will, you must consciously reach into your Self and evoke the desire for the specific goal or action you would like to achieve. Desire is the tinder that lights the fire of motivation. For the mortal-minded masses, desire is a weak thing that centers on the need for basic survival and distractions. Most of the mortal-minded desire unearned wealth, complete job security, a cutting-edge home entertainment center, the newest video game console, and other such prosaic and often unattainable goals. Magus Aleister Crowley said that magick is "the art and science of causing change in accordance with the will." The majority of the mortal-minded eschew magick because their will is not forged to produce change. Their desire is mundane and lukewarm. Desire is the directed *fire* that fuels intent and will. Thus the Strigoi Vii has the desire and will to achieve their birthright as magickians and sculptors of change.

I am. I think. I will . . . What must I say be-
sides? These are the words. This is the answer.
—Ayn Rand, *Anthem*

The Dragon's will is an essential companion to the Self. Without will, no deed is accomplished, no end is achieved, no desire is fulfilled, and no idea sees realization. Will is the motive force necessary to change states from *being* to *doing*. When will is absent, We have only the dormant, inactive state of being—not the actualized, active, progressive state of achieving. Enter will, and the observer becomes the performer. Will enables us to bridge the gap between the intangible and the Corporeal, to bring thoughts into action and plans to fulfillment.

We hear this word *will* spoken often: the will to survive, great strength of will, lack of willpower. But what does it mean?

Will is not to be confused with desire. Desire can be an immobile thing. If left to its own devices, a desire will never fulfill itself. It is but an idea, a thought. A car without gasoline will not run on its own, and without a given direction it cannot reach any destination.

Will = Desire + Energy + Goal

Contrary to many people's assumptions, the will is not a set force, something one is born with that can never be changed. It would be a convenient excuse to say one was simply not born with willpower, but such is untrue and an excuse for laziness. The will can grow and become more potent and, inversely, diminish with disuse. The will can be strengthened by a variety of methods.

The training of professional athletes is a notable example of techniques that strengthen the will. The athlete in training does not seek to become what they are told they must be, but rather strives to overcome their limitations and turn their own potential ability into real ability. An athlete may receive guidance and advice from coaches, training programs, and other athletes, but ultimately their evolution is a personal one.

It is the same for the Vampyre. While there are proven methods that will help you achieve Zhep'r, you can only be shown the door to the Mysteries. Only your own effort will lead you to accomplishment. Desire is essential, but it is not enough. For every goal desired there is some price to be paid to achieve it, and you must be willing to follow through on your intentions! Dissociate your Dragon's will from the imposed will of others. Frequently partake of actions that allow you to ride your Dragon's will and strengthen the reigns of that will. Use the Dragon's will, and any goal can be achieved as long as you fuel it with enough desire and life.

Practical Application: Strengthening the Will

One of the greatest indicators of a weakened will is an inclination toward procrastination and stagnation. One of the greatest methods to strengthen the will is to overcome procrastination. Begin with small tasks. These small tasks, like pebbles, are easy to overlook, but if left alone will gradually accumulate into a mountain of unproductivity. Here is a very simple exercise to increase productivity and strengthen your will.

Take a few index cards or sticky notes and write on them the following words, in very large, readable handwriting: DO IT NOW. (And yes, do this exercise right now!) Take these cards and put them in visible places around your house or office: in the kitchen, by the computer screen, next to doors, in proximity to tasks and projects that you frequently shirk—perhaps by the garbage can or laundry basket. Also place a few next to the television, if you have one, or in any area of the house or office to which you might "escape." Now, follow the advice you have given yourself. Whenever there is a small task to be done, do it immediately, whether it is something you avoid or not. Even though they are not large endeavors, timely performance of these small tasks can greatly strengthen the will. Any bodybuilder will tell you it is not the weight on the bar that builds strong muscles; it is the repetition of exercises. Such is the same with will. Repetition of small exercises of your will builds its character and ensures its strength.

It is rarely lack of ability that hinders one from successful achievement. It is a lack of will.

There she sees a damsel bright,
Dressed in a silken robe of white,
That shadowy in the moonlight shone:
The neck that made that white robe wan,
Her stately neck, and arms were bare;
Her blue-veined feet unsandaled were
And wildly glittered here and there
The gems entangled in her hair.
—Samuel Taylor Coleridge, "Christabel"

Psychodrama is like the symbol of the Dragon. We use the vampire as Our overall archetype in the Dayside—powerful, primal, beastly yet civilized, romantic and beautiful, Immortal, a lover of life, more than human, and, most of all, a magician and a true sorcerer.

We use this archetype not only as a role model but as part of a powerful tool called *psychodrama*. We can pick the elements of this Immortal persona we find most empowering and place them into our vision. We then use that for empowerment.

This is why We relate to the concept of the vampire mythology in the modern incarnation. Many of Us have embraced this archetype and identified with it for Our entire lives. We love the power, romance, sensuality, strength, and Immortality it represents. This is Our tool, Our role model. When We put on a pair of fangs, it empowers Us. That is why so many, including Our cousins from other Legacies, come to Our Fangsmiths. The Glamour at its most basic levels is an example of this psychodrama. We then further it with symbolism in ritual and Our personal lifestyles. We Rise to the occasion with this power.

Application and Ritual: The Primal Howl

Find a secure room where you will not be observed or interrupted. Stand before a mirror, put your fangs on, begin to Throne, and then growl and tap into your primal nature. Ride your Dragon! Envision being the wolf, great cat, or hawk on the hunt. Physically growl and make animal sounds. As in the previous exercise, you may initially find this awkward. However, even if you feel embarrassed, persist! Your discomfort is a product of childish conditioning. You will eventually begin to feel your connection with these empowering totems.

When the opportunity arises, run through the woods naked, enacting the personalities of these animals. Paint yourself and wear a mask, as theatrics are powerful tools of the psychodrama! Do this alone at first, and then, if possible, join others of the Family. Leap through the air like a wolf, throw your arms up like a bear, break free of your mortal bonds, and you will begin to Awaken Your Dragon!

One common ritual in the Gotham Halo, created by the late D'Drennan, is the *Gotham Howl*. This is a basic ritual embraced by the Family and members of the community. It releases Our primal nature and honors the psychodrama which sets Us free and unites the Family. During this ritual, all participants throw back their heads and howl like wolves. We suggest you experiment with this ritual, whether it be in solitude or with a Quorum. As you howl, you will feel the fire of the Dragon surging within you.

Chapter 13

EMPOWERING YOUR PERSONAL GLAMOUR

*I am the source of the Glamour, the great seduction within
Our Blood, unleashed upon the mortal world. The Glamour is
a natural tool that has elevated select members of Our Family
to godhood and crafted mortal civilization itself. You might
have called this a magick spell. You may know the Glamour by an often illusionary and romantic attraction, or, most
commonly, an alluring fascination within yourself. Tap into
your Blood. Utilize your potential. Become the Glamour.*
—Words of a Dragon, channeled by
Madame X and Father Sebastiaan

Once you have a concept of the nature of the Glamour, you can use
the provided exercises to experience it firsthand. The Outer Glamour
will not be discussed in depth here. We now move beyond the basics.
It is essential to realize that the Glamour is not as simple as watching
a vampire movie, wearing black clothes, and speaking with a cliché
faux Romanian accent. It is much more than this. Within this chapter,
you will discover several practical exercises and examples of applying psychology and neuro-linguistic programming (NLP). The Greater
Glamour is a seduction of those around you that will help you get the
results you desire in life.

The Glamour is not intended for just simple ego gratification,
for this is a waste of time and energy. The Glamour should be used

to further your Self and control your life. Such powers must be employed with the specific and greater intent of empowering your Self. It is below the Strigoi Vii to mock or abuse the weak-minded. This is considered unacceptable abuse, like a young boy torturing a helpless puppy. Strigoi Vii are above such games! Those who use such power for the wrong purpose will lose the attentions of the Strigoi Morte. Such individuals are not worthy of Zhep'r.

The Glamour is a set of applied skills and, like Zhep'r, must always be rehearsed and practiced, even when one has reached a level of Mastery. There is no end to the study of the Glamour—like Zhep'r, it is an ongoing path.

Before you employ the Glamour, begin by visualizing your intentions and proposed applications. The Glamour is used for noble personal causes. Some examples include making subtle connections for tapping energies in the Art of Vampyrism, securing a raise or better position at your job, courtship through seduction and attraction of a mate, sealing a long sought-after business deal, improving one's stage presence, furthering relationships with friends and family, and so on. As you can see, there are endless applications of this advanced Glamour in all spheres of life, from business, entertainment, and performance to personal relationships and more. Mastering the Glamour can make one's life more enjoyable. It can be a fuel for Zhep'r at its finest!

First and foremost, you should study and read. Peruse books on body language, seduction, hypnotism, self-improvement, and psychology. Look to historical examples of applications of the Glamour. Robert Greene, the author of *The Art of Seduction, The 48 Laws of Power,* and *The 33 Strategies of War,* provides countless historical examples and applications of the Glamour. His books are extremely popular amongst those of the Family. Machiavelli's *The Prince* is also a classic text on how to employ the Glamour to gain power.

It is essential at this point to understand the difference between the Outer Glamour and the Inner Glamour. The Inner Glamour is less overt and communicates itself subconsciously through behavior and subtle cues. The Inner Glamour as employed by the Strigoi Vii does not always scream *I am a Vampyre* through visual aspects of clothing and action. Rather, employing the Greater Glamour techniques sends others the direct message that you are a powerful and evolved being, drawing them strongly to you.

The Lesser Glamour includes "shock tactic" modes of dress and behavior. Fledglings will often express their Awakening by rebelling against the masses. They may assume traditional punk or gothic garb, get several piercings, and employ dramatic and extreme makeup and hair colors. This is an easy way to get attention and stand out from others. Many of those with the Dark Flame come from the underground subcultures and communities, due to their Promethean creative and curious nature. However, the outré appearances often adopted by members of these cultures can be limiting, as they inhibit the individual's ability to "codeshift" within the Corporeal world. Those of Us who are innovators in subcultures often choose to present Ourselves in a manner so that we can blend in with the mundane world, such as by choosing tattoos that can be covered if necessary.

It is true that the more "dramatic" professions such as rock musician, body modification artist (tattooist or piercer), or entertainer can be extremely seductive to many of the mundane world. Strigoi Vii who follow such lifestyles have the associated freedom to consistently assume extreme appearances. However, even such individuals often find it challenging to employ all of the aspects of the Greater Glamour on a complete level. For example, if you have extensive piercings and tattoos, as well as outlandishly colored hair and all-black attire, you will most likely find it somewhat difficult to successfully apply for a large bank loan or an upscale apartment rental. The Vampyre must be able to be a chameleon and relate to those within the mundane world in many different spheres.

As part of mastering the Greater Glamour, look in the mirror and practice your expressions as if you were a public speaker. Be mindful of your physical appearance: exercise to maintain a healthy and attractive physical body, dress with care, and smile and speak with a powerful and controlled voice. Practice every day! Some of Us are already talented in these areas, whilst others must practice more. Such rehearsals are employed by the most successful business-men and leaders.

The Glamour is about achieving desired reactions from others. Test and experiment; observe and learn what works best for you. Keep notes in your grimoire and trade applications of the Glamour with other Strigoi Vii. The most important goal is to improve your experiences in life.

Remember, your personal Glamour is your own! Employ it, and you can increase the power of your personal relationships and have a much more fulfilling life. Try the following exercises and applications. There is no better time to begin than now.

The Vampyre Presence

This is a simple exercise to influence the minds of others to your will. It combines several techniques of psychology and presence. Like most techniques of the Glamour, it will take time to master; however, it is a simple combination of methods, and it will certainly gain the desired results if employed properly.

Begin with personal physical awareness. When interacting with others, make sure your posture is perfect and your back straight. Look directly into their eyes and speak slowly, subtly mimicking their blinking patterns. Speak in a calming voice and focus on the use of true statements such as "It is Friday morning" or "The library will close in an hour so we need to be there soon." Study the individual's physical gestures and discreetly mimic them; for example, if the person to whom you are speaking often rubs their chin, do the same. They will unconsciously acknowledge the similarity and become more comfortable and open in your Presence.

The Vampyre Presence combines several NLP techniques called "pacing." Watch as a calming and agreeable effect comes over the individual with whom you are interacting. Practice the entire exercise or break it up into individual applications. Do not be discouraged if you do not get results at first. It may take repeated practice for some, and it will be completely natural for others.

The Vampyre chameleon is distinct from the neophyte Vampyre who often comes to the Mysteries with the image of the cape-wearing, fanged, gothic Hollywood vampire in their mind. They are often very surprised to discover that the reality of Strigoi Vii can be much more than this stereotyped image. This image is fun for the neophyte, for Halloween, or even as a fetish or at special events, but in reality it has limited application for the Greater Glamour. The Adept of Strigoi Vii is a true chameleon. They can "codeshift," or meld, into the communities in which they function, ready to employ the Greater Glamour to obtain Prana and further their own needs and goals.

With the opening of one's "Vampyre eyes," the neophyte will find there are members of the Family in almost every possible position in society, from bus drivers to professional athletes to lawyers and professors and doctors. We are everywhere! For the Magister this is no surprise, as We assume many different roles throughout mundane society.

As the Strigoi Vii grows in Zhep'r, they will find themselves less conditioned by the Glamour and have more understanding of their own Self. Thus they shall gain the freedom to explore their own unique self-expression balanced with the Greater Glamour. We are not shallow individuals who claim to "transcend" ordinary society yet ultimately conform to the rules of a subculture just as codified as any mainstream clique. We are an evolved and unique species of individuals.

It is true that Strigoi Vii are often eccentric, with many, but not all, possessing a love of body arts and unique accoutrements such as Victorian fashions or antique jewelry. Such accessories can be a form of subtle communication between Strigoi Vii. Know where you are and what works for you, depending on the situation. For example, Freemasons in the United States wear "badges" such as rings or pins. However, the Freemasons of the United Kingdom only communicate through body language and preexisting knowledge of their brothers. There are no hard and fast rules, only techniques of personal empowerment!

Vampyres should be able to express themselves on an aesthetic level but not intimidate the outside world or appear foolish. Rather, We should communicate who We are through subtlety, self-control, and power—elements of the Greater Glamour.

Three Basic Modes of Strigoi Vii Dress (Garb)

Mundane garb is the chameleon skin that you wear in the mundane world, or the "normal clothes" that allow the Strigoi Vii to blend in at work, school, and in public. Mundane attire can also be excellent for walking unnoticed amongst the mortal-minded. It can allow the Strigoi Vii to subtly practice the Art of Vampyrism without attracting attention. For those living in large Halos, it is sometimes acceptable to openly mix elements of courtly attire with mundane garb on a daily basis, depending on the atmosphere and open-mindedness of the area.

Courtly garb is formal dress for a masque ball, banquet, or a Noir Haven. This usually includes masks, as well as elements of steampunk, fetish, historical, medieval, or classic gothic attire. Courtly attire is considered "dressing up" and is extremely enjoyable to wear when appropriate. Strigoi Vii often express their personal tastes through such attire. Fangs are an excellent addition to courtly garb, as noted in "The Vampyre Prospectus."

Temple garb is used within the intimate confines of a Quorum or ritual. This often includes full ritual robes and masks, which are specifically dedicated to the ritual. One can even consider being Nightklad (completely nude for the purposes of ritual) as being dressed in temple attire! Those of the three Currents often wear garb which communicates the role or Current they are assuming for the evening. For example, a Mradu could wear military-style attire such as the armor of a samurai, elements of a medieval knight's plate mail, or the uniform of a Prussian soldier. Kitra often drape themselves in the raiment of a Romani ("gypsy"), burlesque performer, or belly dancer. A Ramkht could wear scholarly or priestly robes.

Aesthetic empowerment of the Vampyre Brother, or *Frater,* involves truly embracing the Current of Mithu, the embodiment of the masculine element of Our nature. Aesthetics can be a powerful psychodramatic tool for the Vampyre Frater. Mithu, in general, have a more compact set of options than the Vampyre Witch when employing the aesthetic elements of the Glamour. One of the most effective presentations for the male Vampyre is a black-on-black or dark-colored suit and tie, which speaks of sophistication and dominance and thus commands respect.

CEOs and politicians wear suits of basic colors in order to project dominance in public meetings and business affairs. Politicians will often wear simple accessories such as a lapel pin in the shape of their national flag to show their patriotism. Similarly, the Mithu may bear the Legacy Ankh or glyphic lapel pin or cufflinks with dashing black leather gloves or other striking accessories from contemporary and past ages. These accessories will act as *zymys,* or masculine-empowered lures, to draw the curiosity of others and communicate one's position within the Family.

Fraters Mithu, see how the mundane will perceive you when you are dressed in a well-pressed, all-black suit. It is quite a powerful statement, and people will see and respond to you differently. From this foundation, go and explore what works for you, the individual. There are a hundred other applications that can further the Self.

The Vampyre Witch is truly the embodiment of the feminine element of the Strigoi Vii nature, known as Kalistree (the name is partially derived from the Currents of Lilith and Kali, the Sumerian/Hebrew goddess of the night and feminine empowerment and the Hindu goddess of death and power, respectively). The Kalistree is a True Vampyre Witch. She should present Herself as a powerful Dragon Goddess. Her feminine power can and should be used to great advantage. Women, historically, have often been considered weaker and gentler than men.

This is a misogynistic myth! The Vampyre Witch is beautiful and powerful! She can use such patriarchal stereotypes to ensnare men with Her Glamour, as Circe ensnared Odysseus.

The Kalistree may employ contemporary sexual stimuli in a natural yet empowered way, without appearing crude or coarse. When one thinks of a courtesan or geisha, they may think of a refined, educated, and powerful goddess whom mundane men worship and women fantasize about resembling. The Vampyre Witch can manipulate and seduce both genders through simply triggering instinctual responses, then further empower Herself with more advanced techniques based on this foundation. The Kalistree will sometimes sabotage Herself and make the mistake of trying to cater to an ideal (often unrealistic and unattainable) self-image, rather than paying attention to the responses of others. She will then end up intimidating Her targets and will become frustrated as to why She cannot provoke the intended reaction. If the Vampyre Witch wishes to seduce an individual who has specific tastes, She should determine what pleases them, either through asking questions or observation, and respond accordingly. No matter what Her physical appearance, the Kalistree should embrace Her natural charms and talents—then strike!

Consider, for example, Cleopatra or Marilyn Monroe, who were physically not exceptionally attractive. Cleopatra was small in stature and plain of face, and Marilyn Monroe would wear approximately a size 12 or 14 dress today! However, both women learned to use the powers of seduction, body language, fantasy, and imagery to gain the responses they desired. Cleopatra seduced and controlled two of the most powerful men in history, and Marilyn Monroe became an international sex symbol. These results speak for themselves. Today these powerful women are worshipped as goddesses, and nearly everyone in the world knows their names.

Re-examining traditional gender roles and markers can be very powerful for both the Mithu and the Kalistree. We live in a society comprised of many different sexual orientations and predilections. A good example is a dandy, or someone who takes on the characteristics and mannerisms commonly associated with the opposite gender. This can, as well, be a powerful tool of manipulation or seduction. For example, the contemporary movie star Johnny Depp presented a feminine appearance in the *Pirates of the Caribbean* movies. He wore eyeliner and jewelry, and behaved in a sexually ambiguous manner. Consequently, both men and women consider him a sex symbol. The great actress Marlene Dietrich sometimes wore men's tuxedos to parties, and people of both genders were enamored of her. Many, but not all, drag queens employ the feminine aesthetic in a glamorous way, and much of women's corporate power attire takes its keys from formal male suits. Mithu and Kalistree should never forget the power of each other's aesthetics, and adopt them themselves when appropriate.

For the purposes of Strigoi Vii workings, We pull energy toward Ourselves. This is why Vampyres often wear black more than any other color, sometimes complementing it with crimson, purple, or silver. On a purely Corporeal level, black clothing is quite often seen by the mundane as striking and distinguished.

Summation

Whether Vampyre Knight or Witch, embrace your Self and your personal tools of empowerment. The so-called mating game exists at the foundation of society. For animals, "sexual selection" is simple—the strongest members of any species strive to mate with the strongest of the opposite sex in order to ensure superior offspring and the survival of the species. For humans, it is much more complicated. Although inherent genetically programmed responses still exist, "strongest" means something very different for wolves, for example, from what it means for humans. Human beings are attracted to each other based on appearance, intelligence, charisma, wealth, and numerous other factors. From the Strigoi Vii perspective, the Vampyric Witch's feminine power often comes through aesthetic seduction and control, while dominance and authority may be effective for the male Living Vampire. However, with the many complexities of modern society, the Kalistree and Mithu should carefully examine and dance within the many available gender and sexual roles when employing the Glamour to their greatest advantage. Watch and experiment, verify and learn, find out what works for you, and then enjoy the results!

Chapter 14
MASTERY OF THE MORTAL COIL

*Rich and poor are states of mind and conditioning. The Strigoi
Vii thinks rich and masters their own material world instead
of being its victim. When a Strigoi Vii is monetarily broke, that
is not the same as being poor. It is only a temporary state.*
—Father Sebastiaan, inspired by the book *Rich Dad, Poor Dad*

For the Strigoi Vii, money is a vessel of energy and a tool of power.
From the Dayside perspective, We seek mastery of Our material world
and avoid being a slave to it as so many are. To the Strigoi Vii, money
is simply a tool, just as a paintbrush is the tool an artist uses to create
a great masterpiece.

The contemporary drive toward commodification in society is seen
clearly in the fact that most people are seduced by and obsessed with
material comforts instead of mastering themselves. The majority of
the mortal-minded population lives in a complacent world. Throughout history, they served as disciples of the world's religions and as
unthinking subjects of monarchy. Today, they are lulled into a form of
mental slavery through mass media tools such as television and video
games and expensive "toys" with little use value, such as overpriced
cell phones and costly clothing.

The Strigoi Vii sees money as just another tool and will not be
blindly seduced by such symbols of slavery! Instead, the Strigoi Vii

thinks as a master of their money, which they see only as an instrument for personal evolution.

The individual nobility of the Blood can be most easily witnessed through this Principle. Those of the Family do not see money as "the root of all evil." So many mortal-minded work their entire lives for a faceless corporate Egregore, world government, or an impersonal university hoping for a high salary, basic health benefits, and investment package. Most of these people will one day find a pink slip in their mailbox or be "let go" in some corporate downsizing plan. Even if they avoid these near inevitabilities, they will be slaves to "assets" such as a home or to credit card debts. The combination of contemporary corporate globalization and rampant consumerism means that most mortal-minded find themselves in a never-ending cycle of debt and dissatisfaction. They make choices based on what they are brainwashed into *believing* they want, not what actually *fulfills* them.

The Strigoi Vii applies money practically to increase their experiences and satisfy their curiosity about life. Why should the Strigoi Vii Vampyre spend $100,000 to purchase a fast sports car when they can rent it for an afternoon for $1,000 and enjoy it just as much? They appreciate the experience to its fullest, and then spend the other $99,000 on a lasting and more important investment, such as traveling the world or obtaining a university education. In the end, which is more permanent?

For those truly of Our Current, experience and knowledge are valued above money or any material item. Cars, fancy clothing, houses, computers, and all physical items will expire. The Strigoi Vii see the value in these items, yet do not become slaves to them. They seek to make an investment in themselves, enriching their own lives through travel, education, developing their musical and artistic skills, or any other discipline that focuses on creation, not consumption!

Of course, material items, such as the security and comfort of a private personal Sanctum or investment in a practical car for transport or a piece of real estate that will eventually make more profit, are within the concept of the Vampyre's material mastery.

Physical items are not you! Spend your money and wealth on your Self and invest not in external obsessions that are simply going to decompose or be destroyed. Would you not rather have those things that are of true value to an Immortal?

Chapter 15
CORPOREAL IMMORTALITY

And the will therein lieth, which dieth not. Who knoweth the
mysteries of the will, with its vigor? For [it] is but a great
will pervading all things by nature of its intentness. Man
doth not yield himself to the angels, nor unto death ut-
terly, save only through the weakness of [a] feeble will.
—Joseph Glanville, quoted in "Ligeia" by Edgar Allan Poe

According to the *Miriam-Webster Dictionary,* the word *immortality* is defined as a state of unyielding existence. Achievement of this state is at
the core of Strigoi Vii Zhep'r. From the mortal-minded perspective,
this may seem to be completely impossible. However, certain forms
of potential Corporeal Immortality will be explored here. The Higher
Mysteries explore the realities of Nightside Immortality, which cannot
be understood without first mastering the Dayside perspective.

Immortality has been the dream of humanity ever since their first
contemplation of the mortality of the soul. For the most part, it is
completely out of their grasp. The vast majority of religions claim to
grant Immortality and everlasting life if their followers adhere to a
particular set of principles. However, these are not solid guarantees,
as there is no way to actually prove religious faith and bring it into
the realm of knowledge. Faith and belief, the cornerstones of human
religion, still imply the lack of tangible or verifiable evidence, the opposite of Gnosis.

Listed here are three basic possibilities of Corporeal Immortality: posterity, production of offspring, and science.

Posterity consists of branding yourself into the collective societal consciousness so that you are never forgotten. Your actions, image, words, or creations continue on and survive for many future generations. Examples of those who have achieved posterity include writers, artists, musicians, actors, war heroes, religious leaders, politicians, and inventors whose deeds and names live on today.

Even the wealthy who do not have such talents or skills to define themselves can "buy" their way into Corporeal but not spiritual Nightside Immortality by donating huge sums of money to museums, universities, or commercial ventures that then bear their name. Rockefeller Center in New York City, named after the millionaire Nelson Rockefeller, is an example of this sort of legacy Immortality.

If you just mention and remember names such as Jesus, Queen Elizabeth, Confucius, Alexander the Great, Sappho, George Washington, Leonardo Da Vinci, and so on, you will be contributing to their Corporeal Immortality and posterity. The drive for power and desire to leave a mark is inherited by a select few of the teeming masses of humanity. This is identical to the true spark of Our Current. Many try and few truly Ascend to Immortality.

In nature, there may be as many as eleven to twenty unborn sharks in their amniotic sac. The fledgling sharks will follow Darwin's law of survival of the fittest, turning on one another for sustenance, until only one is born. It is not unknown for a human fetus to absorb or "devour" its twin in the womb. Both the god of Abraham and Mother Nature are indiscriminate and oftentimes cruel for the sake of survival. The mortal-minded worship anyone who shows dominance and power to survive. Even if they cannot achieve it themselves, they will follow and attach themselves, like groupies, to that legacy.

Their main motivation is survival of the Self. Why else would Virginia Woolf have written so many great works of literature, including her own memoirs? Or would Elvis have sought after fame so desperately?

For example, Rembrandt, who has become a common name in text-books and art classes, has been dead for hundreds of years. Yet through his numerous self-portraits, we continue to know his face and image.

No matter what your accomplishments, your branding in the public memory creates an indelible "cult of personality." However, this imprint becomes its own entity. Is it still you? Does the legacy of Sylvia Plath, the so-called suicide poet, for example, represent her actual life and body of work?

Offspring is another path to Corporeal Immortality and is why humans have such a strong desire to mate and reproduce. The production of offspring is about survival of one's genes. The sexual drive of courtship and reproduction is one of the most dominant of all human instincts. Having children guarantees that one's genes will continue from one generation to the next. For example, many modern parents wish for their children to surpass their own achievements and have better lives than they had. Socially, the dominant parents have left their mark on the next generation, often in ways they never expected. This is a natural trait amongst all species. The bottom line is first, personal survival, and then, survival of the species. This is expressed in the mundane world as well, as many cultures revere their ancestors, such as the Chinese and Native Americans and practitioners of African syncretistic religions, such as Santeria, Yoruba, Candomble, and Voudoun.

Many different cultures even practice rituals to honor their ancestors. However, by honoring and venerating their ancestors, they are essentially worshipping themselves as members of such an exalted family line. Moreover, these people think that perhaps if they keep the memory of their ancestors alive, their children will do the same for them after they are dead! Visit any large cemetery, and you will see the massive, elaborate monuments designed to show the glory of both the deceased and the family that raised such mausoleums.

Science today, unlike any other time in known history, is showing signs of the possibility of extended life or even Immortality. The mapping of the human genome, the potential of cryonics, and the discovery that aging is indeed a genetically programmed process are some examples of groundbreaking science in the area of life extension.

You may ask, "What can I do right now?"

The first and most obvious thing is to do your best to reach a point of good health. Use common sense. If you are an addicted smoker, simply quit immediately, for obvious reasons. Avoid drinking alcohol to excess. Drink a great deal of water (at least eight to ten eight-ounce glasses per day) in order to remain hydrated. Exercise daily. Other suggestions include reducing your consumption of, or completely eliminating, refined sugars and processed foods. Avoid fast foods! Move to more organic items, and eschew food that is filled with steroids and chemicals. Eat a balanced amount of protein and green vegetables. Of course, if you live in a country such as the United States that does not have socialized health care, and you do not have health insurance, obtain it as soon as possible. Critically examine the popular diets of today, as many are fads that may actually be harmful to your health. This is primarily not about your appearance. It is about your personal health and keeping your body intact and strong for a long life. Healthy weight and body type for one person might not be the same as for another.

Consider the preservation of your physical body or DNA. The most affordable process is to take a cotton swab, wipe it inside your mouth, and put it in a well-sealed, heavy-duty plastic bag in the freezer. This will preserve your DNA. You can also purchase DNA preservation kits. More advanced techniques include making arrangements with a cryonics or mummification facility. Some examples include the Cryonics Institute in Clinton Township, Michigan, and the Alcor Life Extension Foundation in Scottsdale, Arizona; or Summum in Salt Lake City, Utah, for mummification. These can be easily found on the web through your favorite search engine. When contacting these organizations, do not mention that you are a Vampyre, for these ways of burial are often unpopular amongst mortal-minded society, and a public connection between Vampyres and cryonics or mummification would not serve Our Glamour or their business relations. (Please always be respectful of the interests of others, especially when involved in business relations with them.)

Even though science does not offer a solution to the puzzle of mortality at the present time, the speed at which new thresholds are broken show us that in the not-too-distant future the science of medicine will be able to do far more for us than now. Thus, We should seek to preserve Our Corporeal bodies and genetic material in anticipation of that time.

What is the primary difference between a mundane person and someone who has the sign of the Current of Elorath and thus potential for Zhep'r? The masses love death. They welcome it, often coming up with a multitude of reasons and excuses as to why they wish to expire. They cling to false hopes that they will be reborn into another body or enter an afterlife as themselves. However, there is no guarantee their personality will remain intact. Due to the law of conservation of energy, after the Second Death your energies will be recycled as a drop of water in the ocean. Is the soul recycled just like the energy and matter in your Corporeal body? No one living can say for sure. Why gamble on a mere improvable chance of Immortality?

As famous World War II general Erwin Rommel once said, "I never gamble—I only take risks. A risk I can calculate. Gambles are completely random." For the life-loving Strigoi Vii, this gambling of "faith" is ludicrous. A Vampyre will not base their choices, for example, on a gospel that carries no proof other than badly translated two thousand-year-old scriptures written from third-person viewpoints. Basically, if you have not validated something for your own Self, it is a gamble. Be wise and rational in your decisions and preparations for your extended future.

Chapter 16
THE QUEST OF FAMILY

I have been and still am a seeker . . . I have be-
gun to listen to the teachings my blood whispers to
me. My story . . . has the taste of . . . dreams—like
the lives of all who stop deceiving themselves.
—Hermann Hesse, *Demian*

Our Awakening can happen in many ways, from reading an enlighten-
ing book to meeting an inspiring individual from a similar esoteric system to having a Vampyre tap one's energy. Whatever the trigger, age of
the individual, or how much experience they have, during Awakening
they can only trust their instincts and the bits of information they have
gathered. In the beginning, the process is as passionate and turbulent
as falling in love, but with the passing of time we acquire a deeper understanding of and personal obligation to Our Blood and Family. The
un-Awakened may have the hardware for Zhep'r within their potential, but do they have the software of knowledge? The purpose of the
Quest of Family is to "distribute the software" to those who are "compatible" with it. The goal of Our great Quest of Family is to discover
and welcome Our Sorors and Fraters.

Many will hear the *Calling* within their hearts and seek out the
Family on their own through a variety of means. These range from
attending Our public events to trying to seek out Our discreet interna-

tional gatherings to meeting others of the Family on the Internet. However, there are still many who have not yet become aware of their potential.

The Quest of Family exists simply to provide an opportunity for Seekers to become aware of the tools for Zhep'r. The Strigoi Vii should not degrade the Family and the Quest by trying to forcefully convert, manipulate, or preach as do most mortal-minded cults and many religions. Strigoi Vii is not a closed-minded fundamentalist religion that seeks to brainwash individuals. Free will and the ability to come unforced are amongst the highest of all Strigoi Vii ethics and a sign of the potential. This is how We show respect for all of Our Family and other Awakened traditions.

Together We have built the Sanguinarium as a philosophical and spiritual movement to further the preservation and prosperity of the Current of Elorath. The Sanguinarium is a metaphorical Sanctum for Seekers, Initiates, Black Swans, and Elder Strigoi Vii alike. There is a bewildering array of organizations, societies, websites, and books claiming to know the "truth" about vampires. This can be confusing. These do not perceive the path of the Vampyre as We do. It is often hard to see through the propaganda and disinformation about what is Strigoi Vii tradition and Family and what is not. However, the True members of the Family will find Us of their own free will, if the Family Quest is performed properly. Some elements of the Glamour can also be a part of Our Quest of Family.

Identifying Seekers

Many Seekers know they are different from other people and may explore a variety of lifestyles and spiritual paths. They most often find their way to the gothic, vampire, occult, Satanist, or neopagan communities, which intersect with the more public levels of the Family. When Seekers finally make the choice to come to the Family, they are often already dissatisfied and feeling a sense of loss or frustration.

Often they have begun to build a strong foundation by having spent the time to genuinely test and experiment with other systems. Sometimes their nature is right in front of them and, like a "closeted" homosexual or fetishist, they are filled with relief and pleasure upon discovering there are others like themselves.

Seekers are most often quite easy to recognize. They show a passionate and genuine curiosity by asking questions, being willing to challenge their beliefs, attending gatherings, and educating themselves. They will radiate the Dark Flame to others of the Family.

Be aware while pursuing the Quest of Family that *only* specifically appointed agents of the Synod are qualified to speak to the media or perform interviews regarding the Current, OSV, the Strigoi Vii Mysteries, and the Sanguinarium. These individuals have been Initiated into the Synod and are properly trained in dealing with the mundane world and communicating Our ideals. Do not become overzealous in your pursuit of the Family Quest and thus place yourself and the Family in a compromising position!

When you see the Radiance in a potential, you must be circumspect, mysterious, and respectful. Play into the Seeker's curiosity and their awareness of their inherent difference from the rest of the world. However, Awakening can often be a challenging and confusing time, when the potential will question their spiritual and philosophical perspectives. Let them lead themselves, and just spark the fire to show them the way along their own path.

Do not be disappointed if a *Nasarim,* or potential, who shows a strong Radiance does not hear the Calling. Many will come to the Family on their own. They may read the *Sanguinomicon* and take days, months, or even years before actually taking the first steps of Zhep'r. Nature, as always, will cull out the weak and unfit so the strongest will have the best chance of survival.

It may be heartbreaking for the Immortal-minded to watch a loved one knowingly face the Second Death. It is their choice and not Ours. We first must concern Ourselves with Our own individual Self and look to others who are passionate about the path of Zhep'r to surround and inspire Us. Never forget that, in time, the pain of loss does fade. In most cases, we can apply the old proverb "Time heals all wounds," especially since we welcome Immortality!

A warning: It can be difficult to perform a mission like the Quest of Family without becoming overzealous. Be calm, discreet, and respectful. We are *not* a cult, and such a collective mentality does not benefit the prosperity and preservation of Our Family. Dogma only becomes dogma if it is forced. Realize that others, even if you perceive them as Family, may not be in agreement with you. Do not argue; let them believe whatever they like. They should come into agreement of their own free will through observation and personal validation, not because they are persuaded or coerced.

Remember, Strigoi Vii is not about mindless followers. We seek those who are beautiful of mind and spirit; the cunning and talented individuals who truly relate to Our Mysteries. Do not apply the Quest indiscriminately to everyone you meet. Be patient, observe, determine if the Radiance is true, and then apply the techniques of the Quest of Family. Many of those who try to create a group of followers do so out of a deep-rooted sense of inadequacy and a need to be worshipped and adored. We are not a cult, and we are not interested in "recruiting" followers! We focus on independent, self-chosen like-mindedness and bonds of unity. Binding people together through desperation or intimidation is a mortal-minded trait and will only promote mortal-minded structures and hierarchies. Remember that only teachings and knowledge can live forever.

There are many ways to further the Quest of Family without violating the Strigoi Vii Black Veil, degrading the Quest of Family, or compromising your own personal privacy. These may be employed by any supporter, Initiate, or Black Swan to further and support the Current and the Family Quest with integrity and discretion.

Read the *Sanguinomicon*: This is the first suggestion to make to a Seeker or anyone who is curious. Let them read it and make up their own mind. Never try to explain its contents through exposition or enthusiastic discussion. Allow a seeker to ask educated and informed questions on their own. The *Sanguinomicon* was designed to clearly explain the elementary concepts of Our Mysteries without revealing too much. This allows the individual to be presented with a common foundation and make their own choice.

When a Seeker asks about Strigoi Vii or the Sanguinarium and has not made the effort to at least read a book, they honestly are not interested, sincere, or ready. Let the *Sanguinomicon* explain for you. Do not expend your energy or weaken Our Mysteries by revealing too much verbally. We all have a foundation from this book. Reading is an internal experience, while listening is an external one, and thus not as intimate and personal.

Why do you think that reading is so often prohibited in science fiction and dystopian tales such as *Fahrenheit 451* or *1984*? The written word holds power and is a tool of transformation. Do not seek to transform others; let them transform themselves. Let the Seeker read, explore, and determine what works for them. If they then still have the Calling and a strong Radiance, they will come to Us of their own free will and with a strong foundation of self-sufficiency through dynamic and independent thought.

Place the book in your personal library or on your coffee table where it can be subtly visible to guests who you feel might have the Radiance. Put official *Sanguinomicon* links and banners on your email signatures. If you are mysterious and tactful, it will strengthen the Glamour for you and the entire Family. If you are pushy or sensationalistic, you will simply weaken Us all. Remember, everyone loves secrets, and We are an Open Secret hidden in plain sight! We are only there for those who are truly Curious.

Quest Cards: Another practical technique is to use the Quest cards, which are about the size of a business card and have *Sanguinomicon.com* or *StrigoiVii.org* printed on one side and "Are you Curious?" on the other. There are predesigned Quest cards available on the Synod-endorsed

Strigoi Vii websites. You can subtly pass these cards out to Nasarim in a social environment like a nightclub or a coffee house, or even post them on bulletin boards in occult shops, libraries, or esoteric bookstores. You might mail the card to someone or place one in a book in your local bookstore or library that might be of interest to Seekers. One powerful technique is to have another member of the Family send the card to a friend in the mail so as not to reveal your identity and to stay within the mystery of the Glamour.

Internet Banners and Signatures: When pursuing the Quest on the Internet, you can provide a link to a sanctioned Strigoi Vii website or where to find *Sanguinomicon* online by using one of the endorsed banners on your personal or business website or community pages. You can also put one of the Family Quest endorsements in the signature of your emails and profiles, such as "Are you curious? Sanctum of the Living Vampire: *StrigoiVii.org.*"

Gifting: You can provide a Seeker you know personally with a copy of the *Sanguinomicon* as a gift. This places the knowledge within their hands in a gracious gesture without imposing. If they are curious, they will read it on their own terms. You can even have it sent anonymously, which is less of an obligation and further leaves a sense of wonder.

Heritage Copies are personally owned copies of the *Sanguinomicon* that are passed from a Strigoi Vii to a worthy Seeker. This is generally only done for those to who you are close. If there is someone in your life who you feel has the Radiance, and you would like to present them with the *Sanguinomicon,* consider passing on your own copy to them as a gift. This is a very personal and familial experience that can be extremely rewarding, especially since you have consecrated the book. Please use discretion when revealing your Vampyre nature, especially if it is to a loved one. Once revealed, what you say can never be undisclosed.

Remember that doing anything beyond these recommended techniques can easily violate the secret Principle of the Strigoi Vii Black

Veil, and doing so will only be working against the Current. Never speak of the Strigoi Vii Mysteries with anyone who has not taken the time to read the *Sanguinomicon*. Being willing to read and ponder a text on one's own shows maturity and responsibility. Those who are open-minded will make an effort to understand Us, even if they are not of the Current. Anyone who is not truly interested cannot even begin to comprehend Our Mysteries, and speaking to them will be a waste of energy on both sides.

We have no need to defend Our Mysteries or force them on others. If someone is not of the Current, they will never fully understand Our ways, as they cannot personally experience them. We must let the conditioning of the Glamour work its course. If, out of a dozen Seekers who read *Sanguinomicon,* only one feels the Calling and Awakens, then so be it. We are not concerned with sheer numbers, only with making contact with others of Our Blood.

Some Testimonials of the Results of the Quest of Family

The following are examples of applications of the Family Quest and its results. These quotes are based on real-life testimonials of Family members. Their identities are kept confidential to protect their privacy. Many of these may seem familiar to you, as it may be the Quest has affected your life and brought you to reading this book.

> Many years ago, I was in Europe on a business trip. I had previously encountered an individual over the Internet who I felt had the Radiance and who had read the *Sanguinomicon*. When I was in his country, I took the opportunity to have a drink with him. During the conversation, he realized he was with Family. Today he is a Magister and has served on the Synod. (Frater S.)

> For many years, I kept the secret of being Strigoi Vii from my wife. She knew I was into Vampyrism; however, she only knew

about the social level of Our world. She asked about the subject, and I replied, "The book is on my altar. Read it when you are ready." After a year, she read the book and began to ask questions. I told her to go to the Sanguinarium. Today she is actively involved in the Family. (Mr. E.)

I received the Sanguinarium business card back in 1997 at the Anne Rice Ball in New Orleans. One day, almost ten years later, I saw a vampire documentary on A&E and remembered the majestic individual who gave me that card. Now I am enjoying Zhep'r and challenging my beliefs, as I know I am Family. (Soror L.)

During an outing at a local gothic gathering, I noticed a lovely girl in a Victorian dress wearing fangs and a Legacy Ankh. I had never met her before or seen her in the local community. She was screaming the Radiance, and I approached her. After spending a few days with her, I gave her a copy of [The Vampyre Sanguinomicon] as a gift. She read it, questioned it, and became a Seeker. Now she has solved more of the Mysteries than I thought I could ever achieve. (Soror T.)

Beyond the Basics

Introducing someone who you feel has the Radiance to the principles of Strigoi Vii is only one part of the Family Quest, but there is danger in going too far. Too many groups and individuals distract themselves from their core purpose by trying to reinvent the wheel, write another "definitive" book on Vampyrism, or start another order, clan, or coven. The purpose of the Quest is connecting with others of the Family, not glorifying oneself. Seeking personal notoriety by repeating actions and not complementing them, or trying to redo things that already exist is a waste of energy and time. Rather, bring *unique* and *new* tangible ideas to the table—new ideas, new customs, fresh perspectives, new visions, and new rituals. Remember, the modernist poet Ezra Pound always urged his fellows to "Make it new!" instead of copying and regurgitating already-existing ideas and artforms.

Here are some further suggestions on how to further the Family Quest, contribute to the Sanguinarium movement, and strengthen Our Current. In all cases, be sure to consult with the Synod if there is any danger of copyright or intellectual-property infringement. The Sanguinarium was born of a collective of ideas and inspirations. Expand on this with courtesy and honor! The following is a list of suggestions for inspiring Strigoi Vii to further the Quest of Family.

- Help organize a Moot, Quorum, or gathering in your local area. Be aware that group ritual Communion should only be led by an Initiate who has completed at least the MoRoii Ordeal. However, you certainly can take the initiative to contact one of these individuals, suggest your idea, and assist them as a Deacon.
- Create a burlesque or performance art troupe using Strigoi Vii concepts and aesthetics.
- Further the art of Strigoi Vii dance by choreographing a Strigoi Vii–specific dance piece.
- Create Strigoi Vii poetry or prose.
- Offer to assist the Synod by translating the *Sanguinomicon* into other languages. Please make sure you are qualified to undertake such a project and get proper permission from the Synod so as not to violate copyrights.
- Encourage or sponsor the creation of Strigoi Vii music, poetry, or visual art.
- Organize Kulls and discussion circles on esotericism and Strigoi Vii.
- Open a Noir Haven if there is not one in your Halo or coordinate a Vampyre Ball. (Be cordial and make sure you do not conflict with other local events. Too many times, local groups and event coordinators do not coordinate, leading to divisiveness and unneeded competition. Try to compromise if events seem to conflict, or help lead others to compromise.

This is often a point of conflict in Halos, even with non-Family-coordinated similar events.)

- Host an art gallery or viewing of Strigoi Vii artwork.
- Write a supplemental and complementary text to expand on the Mysteries or give your perspective on Strigoi Vii and submit it to the Synod.
- Write a review of a book that will inspire other members of the Family.
- Compose music for meditation or ritual.
- Start a Strigoi Vii–oriented band or record label.
- Contribute to the Strigoi Vii presence at Burning Man or similar events.
- Open a Strigoi Vii–friendly bar or restaurant.
- Magicians can use Strigoi Vii Glamour techniques in their performances.
- Belly dancers can add Strigoi Vii elements to their performances.
- Design clothing or robes for ritual and Strigoi Vii fashion.
- Develop or create a system of martial arts for the Mradu.
- Breed capable Strigoi Vii familiars and companions, such as cats or dogs.
- Design handcrafted jewelry or artifacts with Strigoi Vii glyphs and symbolism.
- Create Strigoi Vii–specific candles or incense for use in ritual.
- Explore an ancient location or potential sacred space and write about your experiences. Share such sacred places by taking others to them.
- Offer Strigoi Vii and Black Swans special services or discounts if you own a business. For example, you might offer discounted admission to your Noir Haven for a Vampire Ball for those wearing an ankh or fangs.
- If you are a fashion or pinup model, include subtle Strigoi Vii aesthetics in your images.
- Create leather book bindings for personal grimoires.

- Create food or drink recipes of interest to the Family.
- Ask your local esoteric shop or bookstore to carry the *Sanguinomicon*.
- Submit an article for the *Vampyre Almanac*.
- Open an online store or storefront offering Strigoi Vii merchandise and services.
- Tattoo artists can offer specially designed tattoos, including Strigoi Vii glyphs, symbolism, or the Legacy Ankh.

A warning: Attempting to rewrite the *Sanguinomicon* for one's own personal or communal group use, or misappropriating or misrepresenting it in whole or in part, constitutes plagiarism. Also, it is counterproductive to Our Family unity and to the Current of Elorath and Sanguinarium movement. Attempting to replace the Legacy Ankh with another symbol is unscrupulous and undignified. The Legacy Ankh is the original symbol of the Sanguinarium and the Strigoi Vii. The Synod has copyrighted and trademarked this symbol to protect it from misuse. Personal use of the Legacy Ankh for purposes such as artwork is permitted; however, whenever in doubt, contact the Synod for direction. Our symbols and teachings must be used legally and ethically, with the intent of uniting and furthering Our Family. Misuse and violations will not be tolerated.

In the end, the Quest of Family is simply to suggest and direct individuals to read *Sanguinomicon* as their starting point.

Chapter 17
VAMPYRE SENSUALITY

We are not sexual as much as sensual.
—Magister Dimitrius

*How much passion there is in you! It is that I feel
in you. I do not feel the savant, the revealer, the observer. When I am with you, it is the blood I sense.*
—*Henry and June,* Anaïs Nin

Vampyres are most often, by nature, deeply romantic and sensual.
This, combined with their love of life and awareness of the subtle levels of reality, brings to them a unique perspective on sexuality and
intimate relationships. Sexuality is seen as a sacred act, as it involves
an exchange of energies. The Glamour, sexuality, and courtship are
sensual art forms for those who are part of the Current.

From the Dayside perspective of Strigoi Vii philosophy, the
Vampyre is a libertine in the truest sense. The Vampyre libertine is
far removed from the mass-media concept of libertines as sex-crazed,
irresponsible, and hedonistic individuals. From the perspective of the
Strigoi Vii, libertines advocate sexual freedom of the individual, whilst
not imposing their values on others. Sexual freedom comes with a
balanced respect for the free will of others and does not impose limits
on the individual. If the individual finds homosexuality or bisexuality

their nature, then it is their right; if they wish for heterosexual monogamy, then that is their choice as well, as long as it is true to their nature. Since We are responsible hedonists, there is no limit to Strigoi Vii sexuality as long as it is pursued safely and sanely, with the mutual consent of all involved. The True Vampyre seeks to be aware of their core primal nature, and if they feel empowered by expressing their fetishes, they should explore such desires without personal limits.

Elegance is most important to the Strigoi Vii, yet forwardness, as long as it is respectful, is absolutely embraced. Some even humorously refer to going out on the town as a "hunt," yet they never forget their True Nature. True Vampyres will often find simple mundane sexuality limiting and uninteresting. The mundane world might assume painful sadomasochism and fetishistic bloodletting to be associated with those who adhere to what they would call a "Vampyric philosophy." However, this is yet another distortion perpetuated by mortal-minded society. The Strigoi Vii's sense of the arousing and the sensual is often associated with erotic symbolism, literature and poetry, aromatherapy, stimulating dance, feather play, masks and costumes, music, role-playing, and romance. The erotic predilections of the Strigoi Vii are often far more sophisticated than those found in "normal" pornographic films and magazines. The Strigoi Vii is playful, subtle, and seductive. Since the Strigoi Vii nature is often highly sexual, those who choose to embrace their sexual side will not shy away from practices or professions such as burlesque dancing or high-class erotic consultation. The Strigoi Vii Witch is often drawn to the artistically erotic burlesque striptease or belly dancer archetype.

Dominance and submission are mere games and roles of power exchange, which the Strigoi Vii may enjoy. While the Strigoi Vii is far too individualistic to truly submit their Self to any other, role-playing in this manner, with full understanding that it is merely a game of pleasure, can be liberating and highly enjoyable.

As mentioned in "The Vampyre Prospectus," romantic chivalry is also a part of the Strigoi Vii sexuality for both ladies and gentlemen. The Mithu find the ethics of the chevalier, Renaissance man, and

Victorian gentleman to be powerful role models that often appeal to women. Yet the Strigoi Vii Knight is by no means limited to any seductive archetype, and He may deliberately pursue any number of romantic images. The Mithu may assume the character of a maverick rebel as embodied in the image of the rock star, cowboy, or pirate, whilst always seeking to maintain the deeper romantic and sensual undertones. These values are not simply limited to courtship between Strigoi Vii Ladies and Gentleman. They also extend beyond Vampyre sensuality into codes of honor on how to deal with mortals, family, lovers, colleagues, and friends.

Many of the Strigoi Vii Kalistree also maintain a sensual and highly sexual Vampyre Presence. Lovers of the arts of seduction, the accomplished Kalistree embraces Her sexual and sensual nature, no matter what Her physical body type. The True Vampyre Witch knows that the beauty myth disseminated by mortal society is no more than an artificial system of patriarchal control. True feminine sexuality and sensuality encompass far more aesthetics than an unrealistic and prohibitive "Barbie doll" image. The Kalistree taps into Her own personal natural Dragon sensuality in courtship and seduction. Kalistree maintain standards of honor and chivalry as do the Mithu. Strigoi Vii Ladies are far from dainty and submissive; they are often referred to as "Spartan women"! In a relationship, She demands active equality from Her consort, whether male or female, and forms partnerships based on mutual respect.

Strigoi Vii prefer to address their lovers with discreet titles such as *partner, lover, companion,* or the more formal *consort.* Many of them reject mundane terms like *boyfriend and girlfriend* or *husband and wife.* The Strigoi Vii often finds the mundane terms quite limiting. As the mortal-minded conception of heterosexual courtship and marriage derives from a system of male ownership of women, many Strigoi Vii find following it puts up conditioned barriers to their individualistic sexual freedom. This is why many Strigoi Vii, in terminology and intent, take inspiration from the forms of homosexual partnerships.

Experimentation in polygamy or multi-individual relationships is not uncommon amongst the Strigoi Vii. However, this is not to say that all or even most Strigoi Vii engage in such practices! The realities and complexities of such couplings often cause irreconcilable difficulties for the Strigoi Vii. Some Strigoi Vii choose to engage in such practices only in very limited or short-term instances. Many Strigoi Vii also enjoy the deep intimacy found in one-on-one monogamous relationships.

Strigoi Vii sexuality *absolutely* does *not* involve rape, child molestation, underage sex, sexual relations with animals, or any other form of sex that violates free will or takes advantage of those who are too immature or unfit to give consent. Strigoi Vii philosophy on all levels calls for personal responsibility. No Strigoi Vii should ever manipulate or take advantage of another, whether physically, mentally, emotionally, or sexually. Should a Strigoi Vii become enamored of a minor, they must wait for the individual to mature. Aside from the obvious legal repercussions of a sexual relationship with a minor, patience and self-control are core Immortal virtues.

The Living Vampire seeks to be true to their Self. It only defeats the Self to ignore one's natural sexual preferences and desires. It is mortal-minded to lie to oneself. A great number of mundane religions encourage one to deny their natural instincts and conform to one standard of sexual behavior. With the reality of different sexual preferences among humans, there can be no uniform system that can be applied to all. For the Strigoi Vii, personal sexuality is accepted as a natural part of life and not ignored.

The Strigoi Vii employs the sensual side of the Glamour as a tool of courtship and seduction. This must be done carefully, as the Glamour must used for a specific purpose, not to fulfill a weak or damaged ego. Far too many unscrupulous individuals employ Strigoi Vii Glamour techniques to seduce Seekers or demand sexual favors for knowledge. This is a horrid abuse of Our Glamour! The Glamour is much better applied ethically to the mortal-minded, as they love Us and are often freely drawn to those of the Current through both the Outer and Inner Glamour. Knowledge of psychology and body language is an empowering tool and must be used responsibly. There is an enormous difference between employing such tools in order to further Our ethical Art of Vampyrism, and using them to control a fellow Strigoi Vii! A comprehension of responsible Immortal- and mortal-minded sexuality is a major component of Zhep'r.

Many, but not all, Strigoi Vii love BDSM (bondage/discipline/sadomasochism) and dominance and submission; however, they see such behaviors from a different perspective from the mortal-minded. They may view themselves as "SM artists" and often embrace the ritualistic aspects of BDSM practices. Due to their strong sense of Self, some Strigoi Vii prefer to use the terms *active* (the person performing or directing the activities) and *passive* (the person who is receiving or the focus of the experience), rather than terms such as *dominant* and *submissive.*

Of course, it is plain common sense that all individuals educate and inform themselves before engaging in any form of sensual or sexual play. There are many good sex and BDSM manuals available that detail the necessary precautions, from the use of a "safe word" to the proper and safe way to employ restraints, toys, and tools.

Flogging is the practice of striking another in order to provoke a sexual and sensual reaction, whether it be with a paddle, a scourge (a whiplike instrument comprised of multiple strands), or the bare hand. Flogging is a concept often associated with harsh beatings and rough play by the mortal-minded. However, flogging is a highly sensual exercise for those of the Family and does not involve torture or bodily mutilation. Many Strigoi Vii view flogging as an erotic performance and massage and do not perceive it in terms of dominance and submission.

However, some Strigoi Vii prefer a much more forceful and intense experience. They see flogging as an exciting tool to push their personal limits. This ritual is known as *scourging* and is not to be done by the inexperienced or timid. It is often used as a ritualistic behavior for testing the limits amongst Mradu.

Bondage involves the physical restraint of another. It may include ropes, cords, handcuffs, or other restraining items. Often the active partner will sensually bind the passive partner. Again, amongst the mortal-minded, this is often seen as a show of dominance. The Strigoi Vii may employ it as a way to experiment with power roles and to enhance physical sensations. As with all such practices, bondage should never endanger the physical well-being of the subject.

"The Hunt" is a process of flirtatious courting and seduction that is often a joy for the Strigoi Vii, be it with a donor, potential lover within the Family, or simply for the purpose of tapping Ambient energies (which is often called Safari). This courtship is often called the Hunt amongst members of the Family. One tradition amongst the Kalistree is to gather a group of like-minded Witches for a "night on the town," during which the Kalistree will tap the Ambient energy they draw to themselves by employing aspects of attractive dress, flirtation, and the Strigoi Vii Glamour. Of course the Mithu do the same.

Red Magick is a form of sexual magick practiced by the Strigoi Vii, inspired by Eastern sexual techniques and linked to Tantric sex. Red Magick involves the denial or delay of sexual release. The sexual energies are then focused into fueling artistic or other creative or magickal endeavors. To practice Red Magick, one might stimulate oneself to the verge of release and then stop and focus on calming oneself. This rise and calming of energies can build up an immense amount of interior energy within the individual to the point of intense empowerment. It is thus an excellent way to raise energy for intense applications such as healing. However, be aware that prolonged sexual frustration is deleterious to the individual. The Strigoi Vii do not seek to mortify or deny their sexual urges or fulfillment. Thus, Red Magick should only be employed in specific and necessary instances, not on a constant basis.

Tantra and Sex Magick are part of the Nightside of the Strigoi Vii Mysteries. They involve a deep mastery of energy work and manipulation and are of high interest to the more sexual Strigoi Vii Vampyres. Tantra and Sex Magick are employed by Strigoi Vii who seek to experience their pleasure and desire on every level. Kitra, by the nature of their attunements and practices within the Current of the Trinity, are often especially attracted to these practices.

At this point, We cannot fully explain the practices of Tantra and Sex Magick, as many of the details of how and why Strigoi Vii energy work can aid in sexuality are beyond the scope of this book. However, We can introduce the ritual of Chakra Kissing. Chakra Kissing occurs when two lovers kneel face-to-face and physically place their chakra points as close together as possible. They then meditate on the physical and energetic contact and feel their personal energies flowing through each other through their chakra centers. This is an enormously arousing experience and one with which the Jahira should experiment, if possible. Breathing exercises, self-stimulation, and other topics are also relevant to the Nightside of Strigoi Vii philosophy and will be discussed in the more advanced books of the *Sanguinomicon*.

Do not think that any of these above definitions, terms, or examples are absolute. They are mere observations regarding general Strigoi Vii sexuality and sensuality. Each of Us is unique on all levels! We must all put aside guilt for past "mistakes" or lack of conformity and have the courage to embrace Our True Self.

Chapter 18
BEGINNING VAMPYRISM

[Feeding] is no ordinary act . . . It is the experience of another's life for certain . . . It is again and again a celebration of that experience; because for vampires that is the ultimate experience.
—Anne Rice, *Interview with the Vampire*

Within "Liber Elorath: Vampyre Prospectus," We explored the overall concept of the Art of Vampyrism and how it is used within the Strigoi Vii Mysteries. Here in "Liber Jahira: Coming Forth by Day," We will begin to apply the most elementary application of drawing in and receiving energy, which We call the Ambient Art of Vampyrism. The reason We are exploring the Ambient Art of Vampyrism at the Dayside level is because it is the most basic and tangible method used by those who practice Vampyrism. The more advanced forms of the Art of Vampyrism will be dealt with in the higher-level Mysteries, due to the complexity of their applications and the knowledge required by the practitioner. In brief, the Ambient Art of Vampyrism makes use of the fact that large groups of people release their excess life force into a vaporous cloud. The Vampyre can then tap this released Ambient energy and utilize it for the purposes of sating their spiritual hunger for life and increasing their Zhep'r.

All living things contain and radiate life force, best known to the Strigoi Vii by the Sanskrit name *Prana*. There are many other names for this vital life energy, from *Ka* in Khem (Ancient Egypt), *Ki* in Japanese martial arts, and *Chi* in traditional Chinese medicine. Essentially, reality is comprised of a wide spectrum of types and frequencies of energies, from physical matter and energy in the Corporeal realm to the dream energies of the Astral realm. Prana exists on the Ethereal plane and is made up of auras, chakras, and meridians. Prana is the essential "energy of life." Ambient Prana is "sweated" out or "radiated" by the subtle body of all living beings and thus may be absorbed or harvested by the Strigoi Vii.

As mentioned in "The Vampyre Prospectus," Strigoi Vii gravitate toward professions in which they are the center of focus. It is not uncommon to find Us working as actors, politicians, tour guides, professors, or religious leaders! In such professions, the Strigoi Vii is the center of energy and attention, so they can forge subtle energetic links and tap the collective energy of the crowd without ever revealing their true identity. Ambient Vampyrism also allows the fledgling Vampyre to avoid drawing too deeply from one individual, by spreading their focus and attention across many people, harvesting a bit of Prana from each.

Be aware that every living being naturally draws energy on this level. For example, the audience at an exciting blockbuster movie will leave the theater happy and animated. This is because each of them has unconsciously absorbed a little bit of the communal energy radiated by the other members of the audience. However, the Living Vampire absorbs energy far more subtly and gracefully, with a focused conscious intent. Learning how to be aware of and control this process lays the foundation for all Our other Arts of Vampyrism.

In order to tap Ambient energies, try to begin to sense energy. This can be simply done by breathing deeply and paying attention to your environment. It is not at all uncommon for Strigoi Vii to find themselves naturally sensitive to the quality of energy around them. Start by consciously opening your awareness to the subtle layers of the Corporeal world, and try to intuit the collective mentality of people around you. Feel the "vibes," and allow the energy in the atmosphere to coalesce about you. At this point, straighten your spine, tighten your stomach, and meditate on your solar plexus; breathe in deeply, feeling the vaporlike energy flow into you. Visualization is a powerful tool that can help you in this process. As you breathe in, visualize the energy as shining, silver white, vaporous strands flowing into your solar plexus. You can also sit on the side of a crowd and, by deeply breathing in, slowly call forth the energy. You are essentially making yourself the focus for the energy in the vicinity, just as a magnet will attract nearby iron filings. Sit back and feel the energy penetrating your skin and flowing throughout your body.

Test this form of the Art of Vampyrism whenever there is a large gathering of mundanes in a specific mindset or focused on a specific intent. Recommended places for practicing Ambient Vampyrism include museums, shopping malls, sports events, concerts, public transportation, churches, nightclubs, busy streets, schools, or parks. Famous locales such as Times Square in New York or Piccadilly Circus in London are excellent places to experience massive amounts of Ambient energy. Innumerable mortal-minded tourists flock to these places, all energetically excited and exhilarated by the experience.

If you are lucky enough to have a profession or talent that brings you into contact with large numbers of mundanes, seize the opportunity! Be you a salesperson, bartender, customer service representative, or teacher, you are already interacting unconsciously with Ambient energy. During your next workday, try consciously tapping into the energy that constantly surrounds you.

When practicing Ambient tapping, We recommend you meditate before beginning so to center your own energies. Also, it is usually helpful to dress in mundane garb. You are not trying to draw attention to yourself—you are trying to blend in to the crowd like a chameleon to better to partake of the Ambient energy. Be aware you may be doing this naturally already and not even know it. The difference between unconscious and conscious tapping is intent. Once you are Awakened to your True intent, bask in the energy!

Many of those new to Strigoi Vii, or coming from other Legacies to explore Our techniques, may say to themselves, "I hate crowds! I can't do that!" Many of us are very solitary, so this is a common response. However, be aware that Ambient tapping does not involve actually interacting with these crowds. Simply stand unnoticed within or near them, and let the energy flow into and nourish you.

While this may seem obvious, always remember that the Strigoi Vii needs to consume both Corporeal and Ethereal energy. In other words, Vampyric tapping is not a substitute for physical eating! It is only in folklore that vampires are able to survive without eating. Since all levels of the body are connected, the Vampyric urge may sometimes manifest as physical hunger. Similarly, Ambient tapping may forestall physical hunger for a short time. However, it is necessary that you keep your body healthy on all its levels.

As the Strigoi Vii learns to manipulate this harvested energy, they will be able to change the very shape of reality around them, as detailed in the Higher Mysteries of Strigoi Vii. However, the main purpose in obtaining Prana is to fuel Zhep'r by exchanging it with the Strigoi Morte in Communion for *Sorra* (more highly refined energy). This concept and its application will be explained in "Coming Forth by Night."

Filtering and Shielding: These are protective and cleansing techniques that are of great use to the Strigoi Vii when employing the Art of Vampyrism. Most energy has levels of quality, or "flavors," from negative to favorable. In reality, Prana is simply the pure fuel of life. There is no need to actually filter or shield from it, as it permeates all things and is transferred with every interaction. There is no such thing as negative energy—this would simply be an absence of energy. There is, however, "negatively charged" energy. Emotions from the Astral level of reality can become attached to Ethereal energy. It is these that must be filtered and blocked. For example, consider two people having a violent argument. They will release a great deal of energy into the atmosphere, but that energy will be "colored" by their anger and frustration. Any Strigoi Vii attempting to tap that energy will most likely sense the negative emotions of the people who have released it. However, be aware that you need only block the negative Astral attachments—the energy in itself is still energy. It may "taste bad," but it will still fulfill the same purpose as more "positively flavored" energy.

Blocking such Astral attachments can be very challenging for the Jahira. If you sense the quality of Ambient energy you are tapping has a negative feel, simply break contact. Stop allowing the energy to enter into you. This is the technique of "shielding," as you are shielding yourself from the unwanted energy. The flow of Prana can be controlled through breathing techniques. These are quite similar to the techniques found in Pranayama yoga. Simply stop breathing in the energy, hold your breath for a moment, and then push it out. This simple technique can be used to block these "negative energies." You may find it helpful to visualize a shield or protective bubble around yourself. When shielding, many Strigoi Vii like to visualize themselves behind a thick wall or surrounded by an iridescent "force field" that the energy cannot penetrate.

Filtering is a more advanced technique that will be discussed in full in higher-level teachings. It is much more effective than shielding, for while shielding involves simply blocking or stopping the tapping of energies, filtering involves choosing which energies are drawn to you and absorbed in your subtle body. As an analogy, you might think of passing water through a carbon filter in order to remove any dirt or impurities. Filtering is a technique beyond the abilities of most Jahira.

Many Jahira prefer to avoid the whole problem of "negative energy" altogether by tapping energy only in positive environments. It should not be hard to distinguish which locales will yield positively and negatively charged energy. As an illustration, the energy on a commuter train early Monday morning will be "colored" with the exhaustion, stress, and malaise of workers beginning a long workweek. Conversely, the energy of the crowd at a ball game where the home team has won a championship will be jubilant and celebratory. You should experiment to determine which environments yield the most favorable energy for you.

The Energy Ball: This is a basic energy-work technique with which you should work to control energies. A visual reference that could serve as an example is a "raver" at a club, twirling glowsticks in their hands. In a darkened room, your eye will trace the moving glowsticks as spheres or waves of light around the dancer's body and hands. It may be helpful to visualize a similar image when performing this exercise.

Begin the exercise by simply cupping your hands into a ball. Envision all of your body's energies focused in your hands. Breathe slowly in and out to control the energy flow. Close your eyes and let the energy grow. Visualize this collected energy as a glowing mass within and around your hands. Move your hands to "shape" the energy ball. Experiment often to determine how you experience the energy collected between your hands. Many Strigoi Vii will feel a sensation of heat, pressure, or tingling in their palms. For group work, an energy ball can be passed around like a "hot potato," with each participant contributing their own energy. You should also perform this exercise after you have tapped Ambient energy and see how the absorbed Prana affects your results.

It is not our intent to relist the variety of techniques available to the Living Vampire that are enumerated elsewhere. There are already many excellent books on the subject, which can be found in the suggested reading section of the bibliography. Books on yoga and Reiki will also be extremely useful to the Strigoi Vii. This short chapter simply touches on the most elementary form of the Art of Vampyrism. The next book, "Liber Calmae: Coming Forth by Night," will discuss intermediate applications of the Art of Vampyrism.

Summation

The foundations of the Dayside are all but forgotten in too many esoteric systems. The path of Strigoi Vii realizes the necessity of a strong Corporeal foundation, as We have discussed here in "Liber Jahira." Your Corporeal body is the Temple of the Self. The Jahira must maintain a healthy and vibrant Corporeal Self and master the Dayside Principles before entering the magickal Nightside of the Strigoi Vii.

Remember that the True Strigoi Vii is sincere, focused, and dedicated. The Living Vampire loves life and the Self and follows their own path of personal evolution and Gnosis. Return often to the contents of this book and never cease practicing, testing, and experimenting with Our Mysteries. You must develop your own mastery and understanding of your True Nature. This book is a key and a gate to your own evolution.

You have taken the first step toward Immortality of the Self. . . .

> *I celebrate myself, and sing myself . . .*
> —Walt Whitman, "Song of Myself"

Book III

LIBER CALMAE

COMING FORTH BY NIGHT

Chapter 10

NIGHTSIDE INITIATION

I heard the sounds of sorrow and delight,
The manifold soft chimes,
That fill the haunted chambers of the Night
Like some old poet's rhymes.
From the cool cisterns of the midnight air
My spirit drank repose;
The fountain of perpetual peace flows there,—
From those deep cisterns flows.
—Henry Wadsworth Longfellow, "Hymn to the Night"

Welcome to "Liber Calmae: Coming Forth by Night." In "The Vampyre Prospectus," We explored the elementary concepts of the Strigoi Vii Legacy and the Sanguinarium movement. Within "Coming Forth by Day," We explored the foundations of the Dayside and the functional principles of the Strigoi Vii Mysteries, philosophy, and traditions. In this current book, We move into the Nightside, the supernatural and magickal world of the Living Vampire. As before, you should enter into these Mysteries freely and of your own will, with an open mind free of stereotypes and blind belief. Continue to cast aside your residual mortal-minded perceptions in order to be able to truly understand and experience the full results of these Mysteries.

Breaking Free of Belief

We know the majority of the average mundane world is locked into a confining and limiting system of belief. A useful film analogy is that of the humans still willingly "plugged into" the Matrix. Recall that one of the villains of the first movie in the trilogy decided to return to the false virtual world instead of dealing with true reality. Many of the mortal-minded are virtually inexperienced and un-Awakened to the universe beyond what they experience through their five senses. According to Gnostic scripture, hyle accept only what they choose to see and are easily herded into a slave mentality. In contemporary society, this brainwashed and slavelike mentality is created by factors such as cutthroat capitalism and consumerism, oligarchies, legal and illegal drugs, and many organized religions. Being awakened to Zhep'r is to metaphorically open your "vampyre eyes," to see beyond these barriers and continue the Great Work of the Self on an independent and enlightened individual and collective level.

Yet, amongst the masses there are those who are different; they are the Awakened. The True Vampyre carries a Promethean spark, or the "Dark Flame," within their Self. An important aspect of this Dark Flame is the potential to embrace the Immortal-minded perspective. Fully awakened Strigoi Vii and Our spiritual cousins are within this Awakened minority. Such individuals strive for and require independent, critical thought and question the nature of the reality in which they live. These Awakened individuals have the potential for personal evolution and spiritual transformation. Throughout history, genuine mystics, yogis, prophets, saints, and others who touched spiritual and philosophical evolution showed similar potential. They were able to experience the subtle worlds beyond the Corporeal realm of the five senses. However, there are many other fraudulent individuals who claim supernatural powers and are only con artists and charlatans.

We encourage you to explore *all* possibilities for evolution, including systems beyond the Strigoi Vii Mysteries. *Never* limit yourself! Be wise enough to sift through the masses of available information. Do not lose focus. If you are a True Vampyre in the Strigoi Vii perspective, you will always eventually come home to the Sanguinarium and know that you are Family. We Strigoi Vii recognize each other. Our Radiance is unique. It is Our energy signature, which makes each of Us a part of Our Promethean Blood, known as the Current of Elorath.

Obviously, if you are reading this far into the *Sanguinomicon,* you are either extremely curious about Strigoi Vii or drawn to Our Current. You are most likely one of those individuals who are aware of the differences between themselves, mundanes, and Others. Perhaps you have sensed this difference from an early age, feeling disconnected from or misunderstood by those around you. Alternately, you may be recently Awakened to your True Nature. Strigoi Vii are unique, unconventional, and often very solitary. There are no absolute "guidelines" for Strigoi Vii evolution. The aspiring Calmae should develop and refine their individual potential with confidence and tenacity.

Rejecting mundane belief systems and shifting from the mortal-minded to the Immortal perspective are the key challenges of those seeking to Come forth by Night.

Throughout history, the mundane world has always feared what it does not understand. This is where Our Nightside truly begins. Due to the Glamour, many of Our number may have been mistaken for nocturnal beasts and magickal beings of ages past, such as the werewolf, vampire, nephilim, or changeling. Born between two worlds, We have the potential to Ascend beyond the restraints of Corporeal perceptions.

The mundane often greet this difference with fear and misunderstanding. We have come to understand and utilize their fear on a more subtle level, forging a balance and equilibrium that benefits both Ourselves and the mortal-minded. Humanity evolved to benefit from the symbiotic relationship with Our Ancestors, and many vampire myths reflect this relationship. We have incorporated mortal-minded fear into Our Glamour, and in recent years this fear has turned into a seductive, multidimensional construct that has sincerely aided Our Glamour. Just compare the horrendous revenants of Eastern European folklore to the glamour of Anne Rice's vampires! Our Ancestors have evolved, and the Promethean Currents have set ablaze an indefinable yet unmistakable mark of creation, innovation, and discovery.

Be aware that many with the potential for Zhep'r, due to a failure of will, voluntarily remain in the bonds of oppression that have held the masses in a mental prison for so long. Religion, faith and belief, mind-numbing drugs, chemical and artificial additives, and multimedia "entertainment" are just a few examples of the conditioning that must be broken in order to experience Zhep'r. Most mortal-minded individuals resort to such props in order to numb their senses and forget the inevitable cycle of death that is their fate. The aspiring Calmae should fully embrace the opportunity of their own Immortality and reject mortal denial. You cannot let yourself be lulled into or continue to be bound by complacency. Break free and enjoy the pleasures of Zhep'r!

Science or Myth? Black or White Magick?

Throughout the ages, mortals have responded to the unknown with fear. It is often said that yesterday's magic becomes tomorrow's science. When Galileo first spoke of the Earth revolving around the sun, he was forced to renounce his claims, as they were considered blasphemy! Many of those burned as witches and sorcerers during the Middle Ages in Europe were in reality scientists, visionaries, skilled healers, and midwives. Various classic works of literature, such as James Joyce's *Ulysses* and J. D. Salinger's *Catcher in the Rye,* were banned upon their initial publication for being too "shocking" or "inappropriate." When looking deeply at great manifestations in art, architecture, philosophy, science, music, or performance, you directly witness the inspirations of the Awakened tribes and the spark of Prometheus.

We of the Family do not limit Ourselves to the perceptions of "black" and "white" magic or good and evil. Many mortals may choose to categorize us as "black magicians." Yet, in his own time, Galileo was considered a sorcerer! Recall the legend of Faust. Many of the un-Awakened simply cannot accept that brilliance or great wisdom can be achieved without blasphemy or "deals with the devil." We, as Strigoi Vii, inherently know better! We refuse to let changeable mundane standards limit Us. To further genuine Zhep'r in your mind and heart, come to accept your *true* freedom from the slave bonds of the mundane world and experience Awakening—you hold the potential in your Blood!

As Strigoi Vii, be aware of the grain of truth in every metaphor. Such vigilance is especially necessary when exploring the Nightside. We are not just creatures of darkness. The vampire who must skulk in the shadows and cannot survive in the sunlight is a creation of Hollywood and nothing more. Many of Us simply enjoy the quiet of the night so that We may avoid the endless hum of mundane world. We might choose to live like the nocturnal predators We revere, and embrace the night due to Our connection with the unknown. Some of Us also find Communion more efficient at night. However, We are not pandering to the contemporary occult and gothic mentality that associates the night with all things forbidding and "spooky." Many of Us are also equally drawn to the light of day.

Why, then, bother with the distinction of the "Nightside"? Darkness is a powerful symbol. Since the beginning of time, humankind's collective unconscious has identified the night as representing that which is hidden and mysterious. The un-Awakened cannot pierce the Corporeal or symbolic darkness, so they populate it with monsters and demons, exclaiming, "Here there be dragons!" To Plato, the sun was the light of reason that dispelled the shadows of ignorance and delusion. Even psychologist Carl Jung viewed the "shadow" as the aspect of the human psyche that is secret, repressed, and *verboten*.

For the True Vampyre, darkness and the night are powerful psychological tools. However, the Strigoi Vii Master is truly free of all limiting associations and knows, indeed, that the light is no less powerful than the dark. Nevertheless, the evolving Vampyre may find they are more easily able to let go of mortal constraints under the midnight sky. We never scorn to use the tools at Our disposal! Although part of building Zhep'r is seeing through the veil of illusion, another essential part is recognizing the power of symbols and archetypes.

The Nightside, simply, symbolizes all in Our nature that is hidden from the light of un-Awakened eyes. To explore your Nightside is to take the first steps on a journey of exploration of your own soul. The true Calmae must be able to stare unflinchingly into the depths of the black mirror and embrace what they see there.

Zhep'r

Igniting Zhep'r comes when you sincerely endeavor to pursue your own path of Zhep'r. However, keep the following in mind: the True Strigoi Vii wisely never proselytizes, argues, or tries to convert others to Our Mysteries. An individualistic and solitary nature is a major characteristic of the Blood, and We must always allow nature to take its course. Those Strigoi Vii just beginning their journey should learn to take the initiative and manage their own distractions. Thus is the never-ending experience of Zhep'r individually and independently enhanced and furthered.

The Family is not like any organization, political party, church, temple, or occult lodge you have yet encountered. The Strigoi Vii Family cannot be "joined" in the mundane sense. You cannot "purchase" the true understanding of Initiation. It is a process that begins with a shift from the mortal-minded perspective of the prisoner to the Immortal-minded perspective of the ruler of the Self. It is a profound autonomous journey of Selfhood.

The True Vampyre lives by the laws and hierarchy set forth by nature, in which the strongest and most fit shall survive and thrive. Yet We of the Family are not in competition with each other or with the mortal-minded. We are in competition with the individual We each see when We gaze into the mirror: Our True Self. While the path of Strigoi Vii is a path for the individual, be aware that your Sorors and Fraters of the Family are your teachers, students, and fellows.

Be loyal to the Quest of Family, uphold the principles of the Black Veil and your Blood, and you will always be loyal to the Family and the Self! In the end, you are your only judge. Only you must judge and live with the consequences of your actions.

Raising Zhep'r can be achieved once you have realized the principles of the Mystery of night and established mastery of your Dayside. You are now ready to make the next step of pursuing your Nightside Zhep'r!

The core of raising one's Zhep'r in the Nightside is Communion with the Strigoi Morte, in which you give an Offering of Prana to the Strigoi Morte, and They return a gift of the highly refined energy We call Sorrra, which advances your personal Zhep'r. Coming to realization of this is a significant challenge, as the Strigoi Morte only grant Zhep'r to those They deem worthy of Their gift.

Spending time in Sanctums such as Quorums and the Sanguinarium, where you are free to be exclusively in the company of members of the Family, is a valuable opportunity if you are able and choose to embrace it. This environment, whether it be a small or large gathering, provides more than just an opportunity for socialization. It is a forum for teaching and advisement and is a powerful way of furthering your own Zhep'r. What better way is there to reinforce and be exposed to new ideas than teaching and aiding others in Zhep'r? Of course, do not break the Principles of the Black Veil by speaking of the core Mysteries to those individuals who have not had the opportunity to read the appropriate section of the *Sanguinomicon* and reflect on its contents. If you can inspire them to further their experiences or direct them to validation, you both will benefit. Most of all, encourage others to ask questions. This will be more beneficial than forcing the information on them. Of course, advising others beyond your means and level of experience is not wise. The Calmae, while honing their own skills as inspirators within the family, should not attempt to advise Strigoi Vii beyond the Jahira level.

Many mortal cults and religions discourage spending time with your mortal family if they are not in agreement with your path. More than once We have heard the grumblings of Satanists, Wiccans, pagans, or occultists who say members of their family "do not approve of their path" or try to convert or "save" them. We find humor in the fact that those of fundamentalist religions and cults are jailed by their own faith and beliefs. Those strong in their faith should be appreciated for their offerings to the Ancestors! If your mortal family cannot accept your nature as Strigoi Vii, wisdom dictates you are better to "agree to disagree" with them and still appreciate them for the benefits they may bring to your life. You may choose to simply listen to them and enjoy their ramblings while you tap their energies to fulfill your thirst for Prana! If the negativity of those with whom you are speaking becomes overwhelming, simply disengage or walk away. If you are in a situation where you must cohabit with a hostile mortal-minded family member, practice discretion and recognize their limited perspective. Being a discreet individual, you have no need to be flashy about your nature. Secrecy is a far more powerful tool.

Enjoy your time with mortals, and love your family. Live and let live! Do not be emotionally injured by their personal choices. A bond with birth family can be extremely fulfilling and can indeed help further your Zhep'r. Do not neglect your mortal family over petty differences of opinion. You never need justify to those not of the Blood your personal spiritual views nor reveal your True Nature as Strigoi Vii. The legally protected freedom of religion in many countries allows you to maintain your own spiritual perspective. Even should you not live in a country where this freedom is your legal right, it is always and forever your *personal* right. Employ and embrace this freedom, and remind others of your rights when you they try to confront you in disagreement.

There are many inhibitions to Zhep'r. One of the most significant is dying before you reach the level of evolution to defeat the Second Death. Violating the common sense of the Principles of the Black Veil is an obvious way to inhibit and limit your evolution. Feeding into the melodrama and politics of asarai is another roadblock. Prospectii and Jahira commonly fall into this trap. At the Calmae level, it is important to learn to practice discrimination and maturity and form strong associations with those persons who will further your Zhep'r.

Relying on belief and faith before personally experiencing results is a common error of the mundane! Test and validate everything in the

Mysteries for yourself. You are the only one who can judge the validity of your path and your results on it. Experiment and personally determine what is true on your own. This is a solitary Quest which, once begun, is as important as eating or drinking. The Path of the Mysteries is not a system of threat and punishment. The only "punishment" for feeding into distractions will be less attention and Recoiling from the Strigoi Morte in Communion. The more you deviate from the path of Zhep'r, the more likely you are to be deprived of the chance for Immortality. This is where focus and inward sincerity are best applied.

The Nightside Initiation (Calmae Initiation Rite)

This is an Initiation into the Nightside of the Strigoi Vii Mysteries. For some Strigoi Vii, this is the most challenging Initiation of all and requires dedication, patience, and willpower. Of course, the Calmae Initiation is only for those who have made the Jahira Ascension and have read "Coming Forth by Day" as well as "Coming Forth by Night." The following steps are the traditional method of formal Ascension from Jahira to Calmae within the Strigoi Vii Mysteries.

Practice the Surjaah. This is a personal ritual for Calmae Seekers and Initiates. It should be performed every morning in order to prepare oneself for the day's achievements of Zhep'r. It involves several phases, which include a mix of yoga, meditation, grounding, physical exercise, and mental planning for long-term and short-term Dayside goals. The Surjaah should take about twenty to forty minutes per day and is divided into three separate parts as detailed below. It is recommended that the aspiring Calmae adopt the Surjaah as a regular part of their daily morning routine.

First, you should, upon awakening from sleep, sit quietly in a comfortable position. If possible, the lotus position may be assumed. You should spend five to ten minutes meditating and grounding yourself. Adopt a slow, steady breath during this step and focus on pushing all negative thoughts away with the exhalation of the breath. Focus on and think about personal Dayside goals. If you are skilled in yoga, specific poses may be utilized during this step to help facilitate concentration.

After the first step is completed, you should initiate a program of positive physical exercise. Any standard workout routine will suffice; however, We suggest trying aerobics, Pilates, dance, various martial arts, or some such system that does not unduly strain the physical body yet helps build strength and endurance. There are many excellent workout DVDs and books available for inspiration.

Third, and finally, you should rest in a comfortable position (perhaps the lotus position), and concentrate on your goals for the day. Focus on how you may apply the Dayside Principles and work toward furthering Zhep'r through them. You should then concentrate on long-term goals and plan how you shall apply your will toward Dayside mastery. You should then spend a few minutes meditating on your Nightside goals and allow the energy of Prana and the Current to flow freely through you.

This simple exercise should be done every day. It is of prime importance in the evolution of Zhep'r and will help establish a short- and long-term set of objectives and goals. You should feel free to customize it according to your own needs and tastes. When going to rest for the evening, meditate on the Surjaah for the next day, so that one day leads to the next with the bridge of the night in between.

Obtain the Tools of the Calmae. At this level of Ascension, tools are powerful elements of psychodrama. However, be clear in regard to what is solid fantasy and tangible reality, as these regalia are only useful tools and not essential requirements. Thus, if you wish and are able, procure a quality black robe, attractive mask, personal grimoire, ar'thana (black-hilted ritual blade), chalice, wand, and speculum (black mirror that acts as a portal to the subtle world). Many of these items can be obtained at occult or new-age shops. Internet websites, including online auction sites, are also useful sources. Check within the "Bizarre Bazaar" section of the Current of Elorath message boards for more information on where to find some of these items. Collecting these tools is a meaningful and personal process. Of course, if you possess the skills, personally crafting some or all of these items means they will be more attuned and precious to you. It is a ritual unto itself and mentally prepares you for the next step in evolution.

Practice the Art of Vampyrism. Take an afternoon or evening to engorge yourself on Prana. Setting aside a time for nothing else but tapping energy is a powerful personal ritual. Do this alone if you can, as the presence of another Vampyre can be distracting. Going alone allows you to completely focus on your intent and experiences. The Art of Vampyrism should be performed consciously every day, or as often as possible. When you feel you have personally verified and experienced the flow of Prana and learned to draw energy to your own satisfaction, you may attempt the Communion with first the Strigoi Morte, then your Dragon, and, finally, Elorath directly.

Perform the Sanguine Mass. This is the essential aspect of the Calmae Ascension, which should be completed alone many times. Results must be achieved before even considering entering group ritual. Communion is the most sacred of all Strigoi Vii acts. Be warned that only truly experienced individuals should enter group Communion; the inexperienced individual will taint the experience for all present or simply become a source of energy for another's Offering. The Sanguine Mass (provided later in this text) is a formulated ritual containing a set of tools, steps, and systems that are proven to yield results for many Strigoi Vii.

Many Strigoi Vii agree it is best to memorize the standard rituals as presented later in this book. However, as ritual is a highly personal experience, feel free to modify them and experiment with different formulations. Not everyone is expert with the same exact formulae or elements of ritual. Most of Us do not participate in group ritual, so being flexible within your own ritual format is a powerful solitary tool.

Do not get discouraged if you do not achieve immediate success in Communion ritual. The Ancestors will judge you on your potential and the sincerity, quality, and quantity of your Offering. Some Initiates have had to perform Communion at least a dozen times before achieving a successful Recoiling, whilst others received it the first time. Some even received Recoiling subtly over a period of time after the actual ritual. Every experience is different, and you should not judge your own ritual results by those of others. Also, do not be overzealous and delude yourself that you have obtained ritual results if you have not! Communion is a deeply sacred and hallowed aspect of Our Mysteries that requires time and dedication to master.

You are only truly Calmae and have "Come forth by Night" if you have successfully received a True Recoiling. Be patient, sincere, and dedicated to your goal. Do not give up after the first few unsuccessful attempts, as often the results are cumulative and contribute to a successful Communion days, weeks, or even months afterward. True Strigoi Vii know this reality!

Perform the Oath of Calmae (Nightside Oath). This is very important as a personal tool and marker of Ascension. It is a sincere communication and testimonial to the Ancestors that the Seeker is beyond the stage of testing and is exploring the Dayside and Nightside Mysteries. This Oath must be spoken in ritual during Communion, after an Offering of Prana has been made to the Strigoi Morte. As in the Jahira exercise of "Throning," the Initiate should look directly into their own eyes through a mirror, preferably set at eye level. Of course, if desired, active members of the Family can request an Azraelle or Magister or other Strigoi Vii be present within a formal Quorum to observe their Oath of Calmae. Sharing this experience before the Sorors and Fraters whom you honor and respect can be an empowering and rewarding experience. As with the Oath of Jahira, you may submit a written testimonial of your Oath of Calmae to the Synod if you wish it to be formally recognized by the Family and the Sanguinarium.

THE NIGHTSIDE OATH

Ancestors, hear me now!

I, [Sobriquet], come into this Sanctum of my own free will, to stand before my Sorors and Fraters, in love and loyalty, with the full intent of reaffirming my Jahira Oath and entering into the Nightside of the Strigoi Vii.

This Ascension is my testimonial to the reality of the Nightside and the existence of the Ethereal realm of reality.

I have been touched by the Ancestors in sacred Communion, and in my heart know I stand here proudly amongst Family!

I vow to become a shield in defense of the Family.

I vow to be a sword to protect from the enemies of Our Family.

I vow to be a pillar of strength, passing on the Mysteries of Strigoi Vii to those who hear the Calling of Our Quest.

Does anyone oppose my Ascension? Speak here and now!

Thus, I now declare myself Calmae [Nightside name] of the Strigoi Vii.

Chapter 20
BEYOND THE MIRROR

How do you know but ev'ry Bird that cuts the airy way,
Is an immense world of delight, clos'd by your senses five?
—William Blake, "The Marriage of Heaven and Hell"

For the vast majority of mortal-minded humans, the only world they have truly experienced is the physical world of what they can see, touch, hear, taste, and smell. They call this "reality." We call this Corporeal layer of reality *Maiiah,* adapted from the Hindu term *maya,* or "illusion." This physical or "solid" world is merely an illusion covering multiple subtle layers of reality. These layers are often called *realms* or *planes* in various esoteric systems. The Living Vampire and other Awakened beings see beyond the Maiiah and seek a more diverse personal and spiritual worldview. Those of the Current have the potential to Awaken as lucid dreamers within the dreamworld and thus experience and interact with subtler layers, realms, and planes of existence such as the Ethereal and Astral realms.

These more subtle layers of reality intersect and coexist with the physical world and are akin to the different dimensions of perception. Consider the familiar fable of the blind men attempting to describe an elephant. Each man perceived but one aspect of the elephant, and each one had a different theory about the elephant's nature. The man who seized the trunk was certain the elephant was like a snake. The man who touched the tusk thought the elephant must be like a spear. The one who felt the side was convinced the elephant was like a massive wall. None were correct, yet none were wholly wrong. All the dimensions of their perceptions were required to form a picture of the truth. This ability to see the larger picture of reality is known as the Awakening.

We Strigoi Vii and Our Awakened cousins have the potential to see beyond the limitations of the Maiiah from a unique perspective. Many mortal-minded psychics, witches, and magicians obtain results in their occult endeavors yet miss the grander equilibrium of Twilight and thus become ungrounded and lost in the Nightside. Most remain truly un-Awakened to their limitless potential, as they are only able to solve half of the equation of reality. Even if they can detect layers of reality beyond the Maiiah, many remain bound by restricting belief and faith. They do not take the necessary steps or possess the vision to obtain Ascension to True Immortality of the Self. Many will make excuses for going to their deaths without a solid guarantee of Immortality or rebirth.

The mortal-minded thus fall into the trap of faith and belief. They provide a variety of pretexts for their willingness to die, claiming their souls will ascend to a dubious afterlife or that Immortality is "unnatural" according to the boundaries of mortal-minded ethics. Like the prisoners in Plato's cave, these individuals choose to be blinded to the broader perspectives of reality. They accept what is presented to them by "gurus" and spiritual leaders as pure fact, without any solid proof or evidence. Thus, the vast majority of the mortal-minded are seduced by beliefs and religions that lull the masses into complacency. The True Vampyre must strive to be different. See the world as your science lab, experiment with everything, and come into agreement for yourself! Validation may take time, but patience is truly an Immortal virtue.

Having a genuine love for life, members of the Family are willing to strive for Zhep'r, fully embrace the complete nature of reality, and take the necessary steps to solidify their own Immortality. This is the most difficult challenge of Zhep'r. We deeply resent the Second Death and consider it Our only true enemy. Those who deny their own evolution, from a lack of spiritual confidence, pure weakness, or a simple love of self-destruction, face what We call the death of the Self, or the Second Death. Only the truly Awakened amongst Us who embrace their heritage will experience Immortality of the Self.

Evolving and continuing to build Zhep'r is the true agenda of all Strigoi Vii. As Our personal Zhep'r grows, We experience the associated evolution of Our perceptions, thus laying the foundation for Our transformation from the mortal-minded perspective to that of the Immortal. Few have potential for genuine and complete Zhep'r, as only those willing to discipline and apply themselves will be able to achieve Communion with the Strigoi Morte.

Mortal scientists and artists may catch glimpses of the deeper nature of the ultimate reality at this stage in mortal spiritual and scientific evolution. Yet many such perspectives have been known to those of the Family and other Awakened beings throughout the aeons. The rise of modern physics, such as relativity and quantum and chaos theory, as well as the contemporary popularity of science fiction, only confirms what We already know. Consider the scientific notion that there are several dimensions to our universe. For example, physicist Albert Einstein spoke of "multidimensional space," which must be defined by more mathematical variables than those of the three-dimensional space that our senses normally perceive. Some physicists currently believe that the fully descriptive structure of the universe may contain more than twenty dimensions! This is an example of mundane science becoming increasingly aware of the subtle levels of reality. Einstein published his theory of spatial relativity in the early twentieth century. H. G. Wells, widely considered the first science fiction writer, published many of his famous tales in the late nineteenth and early twentieth centuries. As humanity evolves, We evolve as well, and the ultimate realities become validated in the Dayside. As the Promethean Awakenings filter through the collective human consciousness, We benefit. The mortal-minded may believe they discover new truths, but they are only beginning to discover what many of Us already understand.

The multiple layers of reality are not alien to Us. They are all an intrinsic part of the world that We inhabit. These layers constantly interact with each other. All living beings exist simultaneously on these different levels. You have already, perhaps unknowingly, experienced these different levels. For example, with every thought, emotion, or memory, you are interacting with the Astral realm. When you breathe or work with *Chi* or *Ki* (as energy is called in martial arts), you are carrying with you the life force of the Ethereal realm. At the time of this writing, mortal sciences have explored the Corporeal but only touched on the Ethereal and Astral layers of reality. The layer of most interest to the prospective Calmae, as explored in this book, is the Ethereal Nightside.

Strigoi Vii define the basic geography of reality as consisting of five layers, which are most often called *realms* or *planes.* Each has its own characteristics, density, and frequencies of energy. As We know, the scientific law of conservation of energy states that energy is never destroyed, only transformed. Energy comes in many forms, such as heat energy, atomic energy, and potential energy. It may also function at different intensities and frequencies. The Corporeal world is made up of specific frequencies of energy and is denser and less flexible than the higher realms. According to the Outer Mysteries, what might be possible in one layer of reality may not be possible in another. For example, shape-shifting is generally impossible in the physical world; however, it is completely possible to shape and transform Ethereal matter through the application of energetic will.

The Hindus believe that the veil of the maya must be penetrated in order to achieve *moksha,* or liberation from the cycle of death and rebirth, which is Our ultimate goal in defeating the Second Death. Ego-consciousness, or *ahamkar,* is one of the forces that binds the unenlightened to the maya. In Strigoi Vii terms, ahamkar could be seen as another expression of the externally gratified ego that is fixated on a mortal mindset.

Be aware that a complete description of these layers is extremely difficult to understand without firsthand experience. Hinduism, Buddhism, and other religions and philosophical systems have concepts similar to the Maiiah and present a well-considered depiction of the geography of reality. However, most religions and spiritual paths involve prescriptions for enlightenment that involve Corporeal deprivation and varying levels of asceticism, including the proposed elimination of the individual Self. We understand that existence is far more complex. All of reality is a dream or illusion, beginning with the Maiiah. The Awakened members of Our Family have the ability to be "lucid dreamers" within that illusion. However, the un-Awakened essentially live their lives as sleepwalkers. They allow themselves to be deluded and enslaved by illusions and can never Ascend to the great heights of understanding and enlightenment.

The Strigoi Vii does not see the Maiiah as something to be overcome, but rather as the first piece of the puzzle of reality that must be assembled in order to achieve Zhep'r. The Maiiah is the surface reality and Our first level of perception. The Strigoi Vii is able to shift their perceptions and thus have the potential to become aware of all the planes of existence. With such awareness comes a mastery of reality and a realization of the mortal constraints of perception. Thus does the Vampyre achieve the necessary freedom to move from one of the mortal-minded to an Immortal.

The layers of the reality and the Self, as defined within the Strigoi Vii Mysteries, are as follows.

The Corporeal, or the *Maiiah,* is the realm of the Dayside, physical matter, and the tangible reality experienced through the five senses. This is the world of the mortal-minded, where energy and matter are bound by the known laws of physics. For example, in the Corporeal realm it is impossible to transform or shape-shift into a bat, at least from the perspective of the Outer Mysteries. The Strigoi Vii Jahira Initiate focuses on this realm, as it is the most easily and commonly experienced. The Corporeal body is the physical body containing flesh, organs, and blood. The physical death is the First Death, and when the physical body dies, the other layers of the Self begin to break down.

The Ethereal is the realm of the Nightside, the mirror reflection of the physical world. It is the first layer beyond the mirror and is the focus of the Calmae. It is also the subtle framework on which the Corporeal realm is based. Sometimes known as *Chi, Ki,* or Prana, Ethereal energy is the level of pure life force. Personal Ethereal energy is analogous to the *Ka* of Egyptian mythology, which was understood to be the life force of a human being. In the ancient Egyptian Book of the Dead and other iconography, the Ka was often depicted as a ghostly double of the deceased person. Through advanced techniques, the Ethereal body can be manipulated and is the vessel for shape-shifting. One element of Ethereal energy is Our "Blood," which is of use for the Art of Vampyrism and in making Offerings to the Strigoi Morte. The death of the Ethereal body is the Second Death and may follow days or weeks after the death of the Corporeal body. Upon the Second Death, the Ethereal body shatters into countless fragments and is released into the universe and the cycles of creation, to be transformed and recycled in accordance with the Principle of conservation of energy. This is one of the reasons why the spiritual philosophy of Khem hinged on the process of mummification, which preserves the Corporeal body.

The Astral is the realm of the Twilight, which is the concrete consciousness, encompassing dreams, emotions, thoughts, and imagination. It is this realm on which the MoRoii focuses. The Astral body, closely related to the Ancient Egyptian concept of the *Ba,* is far less dense than the Corporeal and even the Ethereal body and is not bound by space and time. Therefore, the Astral body is the perfect vehicle for out-of-body experiences, telepathy, and what are considered by mortals to be "psychic powers." The Astral body is perhaps closest to the Egyptian concept of the soul, or the essential Cartesian Self. The death of the Astral body comes with the Second Death.

An understanding of these layers of reality is the basis for exploring the Nightside and is required for furthering Zhep'r. Collectively, the subtle reality begins with the Ethereal layer and ends with the Spirit layer (not detailed here and explained in Higher Mysteries) and is, at first, best perceived with a dark mirror, as will be discussed in later chapters of this text.

Between the physical world and the subtle layers of reality exists a frontier, which is a Shroud Between Worlds (SBW). To the un-Awakened with magickal potential and those Vampyres with limited Zhep'r, this is as strong as any physical hurdle and is most effectively traversed through meditation, altered states of consciousness, and ritual in sacred spaces or at certain times of the year. This limitation is only a perception conditioned in our minds due to the programming of the mundane world and can be overcome. Eventually, through the growth of Zhep'r, the Strigoi Vii will be able to achieve magickal results with a simple thought. It takes time and practice, but do not be deterred by this fact. Any destination is reached by a journey of many steps.

The foundation of Zhep'r is the tapping of radiated Prana from the Ethereal bodies of humans, which is then offered to the Strigoi Morte in exchange for higher energies. This simple circuit of Communion is the key to the evolution of the subtle body for the Strigoi Morte. The Prana of the Earth and lower animals and plants is generally not useful as an Offering in Communion. Due to its low frequency and energy level, it is of little use to the Strigoi Morte. The Ethereal energy of the human subtle body is the only energy of use to Us, with the exception of Sorrra from Our Ancestors.

If the Offering of Prana is strong enough and the Strigoi Vii is deemed worthy, they will receive a direct gift of highly refined energy from the Strigoi Morte. This energy will function as "fuel" to aid the Strigoi Vii in reinforcing and preserving their memories, experiences, and personality after the First Death and to help them avoid succumbing to the Second Death. This is analogous to the union of the Ba and Ka in Egyptian mythology and results in a state known as the "Shining Ones," or the *Akh*.

We see evidence of some understanding of these layers of reality in almost every ancient culture's mystic traditions, including Sumerian, Babylonian, Chinese, Assyrian, and Egyptian. The Egyptians knew of these patterns, and their entire religious system was devised to avoid the Final Death by preserving the patterns found in the *Khat* (Corporeal body), *Ka* (Ethereal body), and the *Ba* (Astral body). Their temples were designed for Communion with the Ascended beings and the Egregores that were godforms of the Ancient Egyptian pantheon.

Some may say the process of the Art of Vampyrism and Zhep'r is unnatural. The vast majority of the mortal-minded, who possess an externally focused ego, understand survival in terms of blind faith, religion, and belief. The Strigoi Vii has an inwardly empowered ego and places personal survival of the Self above all else. We focus on Our own Zhep'r and Our associated Immortality.

Chapter 21
THE ETHEREAL REALM

*[T]he radiant world [is] where one thought cuts through
another with clean edge, a world of moving energies 'mezzo
oscuro rade,' 'risplende in se perpetuale effecto,' magnet-
isms that take form, that are seen, or that border the visible, the matter of Dante's* Paradiso, *the glass under
water, the form that seems a form seen in the mirror . . .*
—Ezra Pound, "Mediaevalism and
Mediaevalism (Guido Cavalcanti)"

The Ancient Greeks used the term *Aither* to refer to the upper reaches
of the sky and the heavens, which they considered the pure air breathed
by the gods. The word is derived from the Indo-European root word
aith, meaning to burn or shine. Over time, the word was changed to
Ether or *Aether.* In mediaeval alchemy, the Aether was the fifth element,
or Quintessence, that was seen as being the key to the Philosopher's
Stone. It was often associated with the topmost point in the penta-
gram. Victorian occultists, notably Madam Blavatsky, viewed the Ether
as corresponding to Akasha (the fifth element in Hindu metaphysics).
Blavatsky saw Ether as being related to the Hindu concept of Prana,
or the life force of all living beings. In the nineteenth century, before
electromagnetic and quantum theory were fully understood, scientists
coined the term *luminiferous ether* to mistakenly describe a proposed

substance filling empty space, through which they thought electro-magnetic waves propagated.

The Calmae Mystery of Coming forth by Night focuses on working with the Ethereal plane, whilst the MoRoii Mystery deals exclusively with the Twilight perspective and Astral plane. Confusing the Ethereal and Astral levels of reality is a common mistake of the neophyte Strigoi Vii and occurs in multiple paradigms of occultism and vampyrism. Such confusion is perpetuated by the fact that many esoteric sources conflate the two. This is why in "Coming Forth by Night," We focus Our perspective on the Ethereal realm.

The Ethereal plane is the layer of reality which lies between the Astral and the Corporeal. It is the beginning of the subtle realms of reality. Energy is eternal but takes different forms in each layer of reality. The Ethereal realm is slightly less dense than the Corporeal. It cannot be perceived by the five senses; hence, the concepts of the "sixth sense" and seeing with the "Third Eye" refer to perception of this layer. If the Corporeal realm is that of solid energies (analogous to ice), the Ethereal realm is the place of liquid moving energies (analogous to water). Ethereal energy flows from and between all things, suffusing everything we know in the physical world with its eternal dance. The Ethereal is a realm of pure vital energy and life force on which the Strigoi Vii taps and draws. Strigoi Vii commonly call this Ethereal energy Prana. Living things, especially humans, are the prime generators of Pranic energy. Prana is produced by the body's natural functions and can be manipulated by breath and will. Ethereal energy is influenced by the moon, which creates tides in the Earth's Ethereal atmosphere. In accordance with the Gaia hypothesis, the Earth is itself a living being and thus possesses an Ethereal field as well.

The Ethereal body is strongly influenced by breath. Indeed the English word *spirit* is derived from the Latin *spiritus,* meaning "breath." The word *ruah* in Hebrew means "breath," "wind," "air," and "spirit" simultaneously. Many cultures have legends of vampires stealing not blood but breath from their victims. Echoes of these beliefs remain in the enduring legend that cats can kill infants by stealing their breath whilst they sleep. Prana may be seen as corresponding to Corporeal blood; thus the metaphor "the blood is the life" may be understood. While the Corporeal blood may be the living fluid of the physical body, Ethereal energy is truly the essential vitality of all living things.

The Ethereal body, or the *double,* is a mirror image of the Corporeal body that exists in the subtle realm. It has its own anatomy, which partially reflects the Corporeal body. Prana is analogous to blood, nadis to the arteries and veins, and the chakras to vital organs. Each type of being has its own anatomy. Some types of beings do not even possess a Corporeal body, so their existence begins in the Ethereal realm. Some entities have only chakras, whilst others have different paths of meridians and flavors of Prana. Strigoi Vii and many other vampiric beings, such as ethical psychic vampires and Kheprians, have subtle bodies very similar to those of humans, although different from each other. Of course, here We only focus on the subtle body of the "normal" human and the Strigoi Vii.

The subtle body is linked to the Corporeal in many ways, and due to this linkage, the subtle and the Corporeal body are causally joined. Breath and will are the most powerful tools of manipulating Prana and the flow of energy in the subtle body. Wounds in the Corporeal body will affect the Ethereal body, and, conversely, Ethereal wounds may manifest physically. Some Ethereal ailments can also affect Corporeal health; likewise, physical diseases can also weaken the Ethereal body. The Corporeal body is the material anchor within the universe and provides shape and form for the subtle body. Without this anchor and a conscious application of will, the subtle body will lose shape. That is why many seemingly "ghostly" beings and effects, which are remnants of mortals who have not faced the Second Death, do not hold their shape easily and are flexible like an amoeba. Practices such as Reiki and traditional Chinese medicine (TCM) specifically focus on treating the Ethereal body through its relation to the Corporeal body. With the growth of Zhep'r, the subtle body of the Strigoi Vii also evolves and grows stronger, eventually achieving a state where it is strong enough to exist and survive on its own without the Corporeal body. At this point, the Strigoi Vii is prepared to conquer the Second Death. This is why the un-Awakened Strigoi Vii will have an undeveloped Ethereal body, whilst the subtle bodies of advanced Strigoi Vii can be likened to what an un-Awakened individual would describe as an angelic being. Just as with the Corporeal Self, maintaining the health and strength of the Ethereal body requires exercise and persistence.

The Signature is the subtle equivalent of one's personal scent or fingerprints. Each person has their own unique Signature, whether they are Awakened to the subtle reality or not. This Signature leaves an imprint on all things the being touches and with which they interact. When a Strigoi Vii practices the Art of Vampyrism and taps the Prana from another being, the Signature can be sensed as a "flavor" or "taste."

Since each being has their own Signature, it can also be used to differentiate between types of energy, such as human Prana or Strigoi Morte Prana, or that of a dog or cat. After much experience in Communion, the Strigoi Vii can grow to identify Strigoi Morte from other subtle beings by identifying Their unique Signature.

All beings are drawn by and attracted to different Signatures. For example, some people may be drawn to certain individuals and repulsed by others. Compatible Signatures result in this experience of seemingly "knowing" or being attracted to another whom you have never previously met. Also, Signatures may even slightly change in regard to the being's moods or environment, while staying fundamentally the same at the core. The Signature is not only Ethereal; it contains elements of the Astral, such as emotions and mood.

The aura is the "radiated" energy and outer layer of the Ethereal body of living beings. The aura may be compared to light radiated from a light bulb or heat from the body. This outer shell of the aura is very flexible and layered. The aura is densest closest to the body and slowly becomes thinner and thinner as it radiates outward. On a surface level, the Art of Vampyrism depends on aural contact.

The aura is also a protective device that screens out harmful energies and welcomes beneficial ones. The subtle body is constantly interacting with the universe on all levels, cycling energy in and out through the aura. Auras often have specific shapes and colors, and those who are Awakened can perceive the mood, health, and nature of a being based on its aura. The aura of a Strigoi Vii generally appears radiant and bright, especially once their Ethereal metabolism is raised and they are full of energy. The aura can be changed and modified through will, and adept individuals can mask their own aura and Signature.

Tendrils are parts of the aura that can be created by the use of will and projected beyond the normal constraints of the subtle body. They begin as small filaments, akin to hairs on the arm, which can be controlled and extended by the will. Once extended like the arms of an octopus or the pseudopods of an amoeba, these tendrils can be used to touch others, defend oneself, and create links with other beings. Most importantly, tendrils are used in the Art of Vampyrism and are extended out at a distance in order to interact with the energy of other beings.

Tendrils are exclusively native to vampiric beings, and their presence can be easily used to identify those of vampiric nature. Other entities may possess the ability to form tendrils in a limited fashion if they are advanced in energy work; however, for the Vampyre, they are a natural and identifiable feature of the subtle body.

A hundred and one are the arteries of the heart,
one of them leads up to the crown of the head. Go-
ing upward through that, one becomes immortal.
—Chandogya Upanishad

Nadis are akin to veins and arteries and function as channels for the flow of vital energy through our subtle bodies. The term *nadis* comes from the root word *nad,* taken from the Sanskrit for "channel," "stream," or "flow." Nadis are equivalent to the meridians of traditional Chinese medicine, which are a main feature of practices such as acupuncture, acupressure, and qigong. Nadis intersect with the chakras and control the flow of Prana throughout the body. Practices such as Pranayama, breathing alternatively through the left and right nostrils, can help control and stimulate the flow of Prana.

Links are subtle connections to everything and everyone with which you have ever interacted. These links vary in strength and intensity. The Norse concept of the "Web of the Wyrd," or the cosmic linkage of the ebb and flow of energy and destiny, is analogous to Our understanding of links. Links are akin to strings of Ethereal energy through which Prana and Astral energies, such as emotions, flow. Links can be formed from physical contact, such as touching someone's personal possession or wearing someone else's clothing, sharing intimate experiences, or even drawing energy through the Art of Vampyrism. Links can also be created by nonphysical contact, such as emotional conversations over the phone or making eye contact with someone. Common experience often creates links.

For example, links that are formed and reinforced between lovers will allow emotional energies to flow between them, causing a feeling of "connection" even when physically separated. Thus, links are direct connections and channels to another being, place, or object. Links are excellent tools for employing the Art of Vampyrism and for tapping energies.

Within esoteric systems such as Voudoun, objects that are connected by links can affect another person at a distance. Most powerful links come from the physical body, such as hair, fingernails, or skin. These links can be used to draw energy even when the individual is not present, bypassing the illusion of space and time by functioning in the subtle world where these things have less meaning. Voodoo dolls, when created and used properly, are an example of such phenomena.

Links can be broken. However, the effort required to break a link depends on its strength. All living beings create links to those with whom they interact. The more frequent and intense the interactions, the stronger the links. For example, breaking a link with a casual work acquaintance would probably not require a great deal of energy. In contrast, breaking a link with a former lover would take a much larger effort. Within the Art of Vampyrism, links are easily formed by drawing energy directly from a specific donor. Drawing large amounts of energy creates very powerful links. This is why many Strigoi Vii prefer Ambient Vampyrism, as it does not cause direct or strong links.

Links are useful for empathy and telepathy. If two people have strong links with each other, such as often happens in the case of identical twins, they may be able to sense the pain or emotional state of the other. Two lovers who are deeply in love will possess a strong level of empathy for each other, creating heightened emotional states. However, it is sometimes necessary to break links. This may be accomplished through ritual or energy work. Be wary and careful in your intense interactions, since links of which you are unaware can be used against you. Sometimes links cause damage or subtle wounds, which must be healed and treated.

Chakras have been embraced by various belief systems, especially new-age and neopagan groups. They are an excellent beginning point for those seeking to increase perception and manipulation of their Ethereal bodies. They can also be used as a tool of focus in meditation. Strigoi Vii work with a series of chakras within the geography of the Ethereal body. The Hindu Tantric Shakta system practiced by the Theosophists is partially reflective of Our own. The Theosophists and other contemporary occult orders were largely responsible for introducing the system of chakras to the mundane world. The system of chakras employed by Strigoi Vii includes the following.

> *Crown* (AK)—Located at the top of the head, the Crown Chakra is the connection to the higher planes of existence beyond the Maiiah and to the Dragon (higher Self and intellect). This is the seat of the Immortal Self, free of the perceptions of time and space. It is the core of identity and the key to

self-actualization as a deity. It can be used for tapping energy in conjunction with Flight of the Succubus, as explained in Higher Mysteries, or for Astral projection when in meditation or deep sleep. In meditation it is used to communicate with one's Dragon. It is the seat of the will, balance, and wisdom.

Third Eye (AH)—Located right above and between the eyes, this chakra is the seat of perception and the "sixth sense," or the vision of the subtle levels of reality beyond the Corporeal, such as the Ethereal and Astral realms. Clairvoyance is seeing with the Third Eye. The Third Eye may be used for drawing in energy at a distance within the subtle world and is considered the "Eyes of the Throne." *Mal'acchio,* or the "Evil Eye," is a MoRoii-level form of Vampyrism and employs this chakra. In meditation, this chakra can be used in some forms of divination and for connecting to the consciousness of others. The Third Eye Chakra is related to the Elorathian aspect of Ramkht, the Oracle.

Throat (AY)—Located in the throat, this is the chakra of self-expression, power, voice, and creativity. To speak with the Throat Chakra's voice is to speak prophecy. When used in the Art of Vampyrism, the Throat Chakra facilitates contact via tendrils created by the seduction of the voice. For personal self-realization, the Throat Chakra may be utilized for vocal seduction and persuasion.

Heart (SA)—Located in the upper chest area, the Heart Chakra corresponds to emotional states and social identity and is focused on self-acceptance. This is the middle chakra of the seven employed by the Strigoi Vii. This chakra is used for feeding from Ambient energy at a distance within social environments. For personal meditation, the Heart Chakra relates to self-love, the balance of ego, and intelligence.

Solar Plexus (TA)—Located near the navel, this is often called the Center Chakra and is the core of the Self, as well as the seat of the Dark Flame. Here is where the difference between the mortal-minded human and the Immortal Vampyre begins. Self-empowerment is focused in the Solar Plexus Chakra. Focusing on this chakra aids in contemplation of the Self.

Sacral (AE)—Located near the pelvis and sexual organs, the Sacral Chakra deals with self-gratification, instincts, and sexuality. This chakra can be used as the link in cycling energy in Vampyre sex with another Strigoi Vii. It can also be employed for feeding as a "Succubus" or "Incubus," either through tactile contact involving actual intercourse or through sexual arousal without direct contact. In meditation, this chakra can be used for knowledge of one's emotions, prowess, and endurance. The Sacral Chakra is related to the Elorathian aspect of Kitra, the weaver.

Root (NE)—Located between the genitals and the rectum, the Root Chakra relates to the element of earth and is linked to the grounding of the Self and the Corporeal body. When tapping energy, this chakra is used for draining through tactile contact. It is useful in meditation in regard to setting goals and being grounded. The Root Chakra is related to the Elorathian aspect and Current of the Mradu, the warrior.

The Need is the necessity for the Strigoi Vii to tap and process large quantities of Prana, or human vital life force. This comes from the growth of Zhep'r and the high frequency of energy of the Strigoi Vii's subtle body. Think of the Vampyre subtle body as having the equivalent of a very active metabolism. Thus, it is beneficial to fulfill that metabolism by absorbing Prana. The Need is not analogous to psychic vampires who have an energy deficiency such as weakened chakras.

Our thirst for Prana is a different condition and is not a result of damage to the subtle body. It is an evolution and enhancement. The Need is intimately associated with the possibility of Immortality, for when the Strigoi Vii absorbs Prana during their Corporeal life, this absorbed energy allows the subtle body to maintain a high vibrational frequency and maintain cohesion, thus preventing the Second Death.

Many Strigoi Vii feel the Need as a sort of physical thirst or hunger for Prana and will instinctively seek out situations where they can obtain large amounts of Prana. As previously mentioned in the *Sanguinomicon,* the Need may sometimes be interpreted as Corporeal hunger or thirst, especially by un-Awakened Strigoi Vii. These un-Awakened individuals often subconsciously employ elements of the Art of Vampyrism even before their Awakening. Strigoi Vii who have Awakened to their nature become more consciously aware of their Need for Prana and tap energy on a very regular basis.

Of course, as the Strigoi Vii evolves in Zhep'r and becomes more practiced in Communion, their "reservoirs" of Prana increase. However, the entire process of Zhep'r requires Prana as fuel, so the Strigoi Vii will experience the Need to absorb energy at every step on their path of evolution. This Need is purely spiritual; however, since all layers of the body are connected, not fulfilling the Need to tap Prana can deleteriously affect the psychological and physical health of the Vampyre. The solution is practice, development, and mastery of the Arts of Vampyrism.

When a Strigoi Vii's Need for Prana is fulfilled, their aura will contain bright and vibrant colors, alive and radiant with the fire of life. In contrast, the psychic vampire will have a dark aura, often giving the impression of illness. The fact that We Need Prana in order to enhance and further Our evolution, not to fulfill any sort of deficiency, is the main difference between psychic vampires and Strigoi Vii.

Chapter 22
INTERMEDIATE VAMPYRISM

*[T]hink me not cruel because I obey the irresistible law of
my strength and weakness; if your dear heart is wounded, my
wild heart bleeds with yours. In the rapture . . . I live in your
warm life, and you shall die—die, sweetly die—into mine.
I cannot help it; as I draw near to you, you, in your turn,
will draw near to others, and learn the rapture of that cru-
elty, which yet is love; so, for a while, seek to know no more
of me and mine, but trust me with all your loving spirit.*
—Carmilla, *Joseph Sheridan Le Fanu*

"The Vampyre Prospectus" introduced you, the reader, to the Art of
Vampyrism from the Strigoi Vii perspective. In "Coming Forth by Day,"
We learned the most basic application of Our Art, known as Ambient
Vampyrism. Here, within "Coming Forth by Night," We move further
into intermediate levels of Our Art: *surface* and *deep* Vampyrism.

Since all living things exchange energy with every interaction,
these energy exchanges can be directly applied to the intermediate applications of Vampyrism. Mortal society is comprised of constant energy exchanges between individuals, ranging from casual eye contact
to a friendly conversation to intense sexual contact. Within the animal
kingdom, animals eat plants and other animals, and, near the culmina-
tion of the cycle, humans eat both animals and plants. This "food web"

is a never-ending exchange of energy, with humans seemingly sitting atop the hierarchy. Thus, humans produce the most refined form of Prana because they have taken in the life energies of all living things below them in the exchange cycle. Vampyrism is the act of obtaining this highly refined energy for the purposes of furthering Zhep'r and employing Nomaj, which is vibrational high magick or, simply, Strigoi Vii Sorcery.

To the mortal-minded, the Strigoi Vii practice of absorbing Prana may seem very much akin to traditional psychic vampirism; yet the Strigoi Vii do it with a different intent and purpose. The absorption of Prana enhances the subtle metabolism of the Strigoi Vii and fuels Zhep'r. It is also a necessary practice so that the Strigoi Vii may then offer forth the collected energies to the Strigoi Morte in Communion. During Communion, the Strigoi Vii receives a higher form of life force from the Strigoi Morte, which We call Sorrra. Practicing Communion is the primary manner of increasing Zhep'r. Also note that regularly taking in large amounts of Prana from humans promotes physical, emotional, and spiritual health in the Strigoi Vii.

Strigoi Vii enjoy a mutually beneficial, or symbiotic, relationship with the vast, teeming masses of humanity and take full advantage of the more than six billion donors on our planet. At first glance, it may seem that what a Vampyre does is unethical and harmful. To the contrary! The Immortal-minded simply has a different perspective than the mortal-minded. Mortal ethics are most often artificial constructs and are different from the laws of nature. Civilized morality is a synthetic construct, not a natural or inherent law. Consider how the accepted codes of conduct and morality have varied between historical periods and cultures. In truth, the ruling class almost always prescribes behavior in order to better control their subjects.

For example, the antiquated Western European constraints prohibiting anyone other than clergy from reading and interpreting scripture were merely a way to keep power in the hands of the church. Slavery was legal in the southern United States until the nineteenth century because the economy of the South depended heavily on slave labor. In Europe and America, women could not vote, own property, or work in most professions until relatively recently. These were primitive mortal-minded concepts that were eventually overcome as mortal-minded ethics evolved. In contrast, natural laws are pragmatic and innate. As Hermann Hesse wrote in *Steppenwolf,* "look at an animal, a cat, a dog, or a bird, or one of those beautiful great beasts in the zoo . . . . You can't help seeing that all of them are right. They're never in any embarrassment. They don't flatter and they don't intrude. They don't pretend. They are as they are, like stones or flowers or stars in the sky."

While the kingdom of nature is quite often "red in tooth and claw," its brutality is impersonal, unlike concentrated deliberate malice. The Calmae should look both to the positive elements of human civilization and the naturalism of the wild. The philosophy of the Strigoi Vii Art of Vampyrism achieves a harmonious balance between the two, embracing the best aspects of each.

With large amounts of Prana and concentrated will, the Strigoi Vii can raise their Ethereal metabolism. Due to their un-Awakened minds and the conditioning of the Glamour, the mortal-minded are mostly unaware of Our process of Vampyrism. The tales of "blood-drinking vampires" in literature and folklore are but echoes of the true Art of Vampyrism. We, as Strigoi Vii, are so subtle in Our Vampyrism that most humans never truly realize nor are harmed by Our intentions. In fact, they benefit from the process!

Interacting with and exchanging energy is something humans do every day. Vampyrism on the level needed for fueling Zhep'r requires effort and intent and, at higher levels, a significant energetic exchange. Purchasing an item with cash or credit represents an exchange of energies and creating links. Continual and prolonged contact between two humans often results in Ethereal bonds of familiarity, and thus produces links. Advanced Adepts of Vampyrism benefit significantly from learning how to consciously tap and draw out the energy of the human's life force through these links. The Vampyre then uses the acquired energy for their own purposes.

Maintaining large reservoirs of Prana aids the Strigoi Vii in dream recall, promotes physical health and emotional well-being, increases memory, improves vision and psychic awareness, and increases the ability to draw in and store larger amounts of Prana. It is also essential to Communion, as the collected energies are offered up to the Strigoi Morte. Drawing in this Pranic energy is the Art of Vampyrism. It is one of the most beneficial things a Strigoi Vii can do.

"Donors" are those from whom We draw energy through the Art of Vampyrism. From some donors, we only draw residual and excess energies; from others, We draw deeply and consensually. Either way, donors must never be harmed and always respected, as they are Our source and deserve Our regard.

The ethics of Vampyrism from an outsider's perspective might seem like a paradox, as the mortal-minded might consider us predators or parasites. While there are many things We can learn from predators, We are not truly analogous to the lion or the hawk. The Art of Vampyrism is not a brutal form of predation! It is a much more refined, elegant, and ethical system of energy acquisition. We are evolved beyond the beasts of the wild as well as what many vampire Legacies call "predatory spirituality."

The mortal-minded, in their blissfully distracted and comfortable lives, believe they sit at the top of the food chain. They are highly mistaken. The Strigoi Morte and the rest of the Ascended Masters are more highly evolved beings than humans and even the Strigoi Vii. They are also the supreme sentient beings with whom the Calmae is concerned. From the perspective of the average mundane, the Strigoi Morte may seem to be angelic or spiritual beings. From the perspective of the Vampyre, They are Our Elders, Sorors and Fraters, teachers, and parents. The Strigoi Vii do not worship such evolved beings but instead experience a student and mentor relationship with the Strigoi Morte.

As you progress in your journey of Zhep'r, it is important to fully understand that Vampyrism is an act which at first might seem morally difficult. Embracing your potential is one of the most challenging aspects of your own personal spiritual evolution. It is beneficial to overcome such mundane conditioning! The wolf preys on the deer and, in order to survive, humans eat animals such as cows and chickens and other living organisms such as plants. This process is part of the natural web of life, and no one would call it wrong or unethical. Even passionate vegetarians or vegans admit the necessity of eating plant matter in order to survive. Vampyrism is a much more evolved form of the same action, albeit one that is performed in a completely different way.

We, as Vampyres, have no need to physically kill Our "food" as predatory animals do. There is more to being a predator than simply surviving on the life energy of others. An essential element of the life for the predator is the hunt. The wolf does not ask the deer's permission to eat it. Most human ethics do not usually require a journey to the slaughterhouse to obtain the cow's consent before ordering a hamburger in a restaurant. One of the reasons why people living in countries such as the United States eat so much meat is because they are distanced from the process of obtaining it. They usually have never killed an animal for food or even witnessed such brutality acted out by another. Most people are desensitized by going to the supermarket and buying a nicely packed piece of meat from the butcher's counter. Similarly, it is highly unlikely that the mortal-minded would ask permission from an ear of corn before attending a summer picnic luncheon! We do not physically harm those mortals from whom We draw energy. This is one of the distinctions between the death-accepting mortal and the Vampyre. Nor are We as coldly and inexorably vicious as natural predators in the animal kingdom, such as the lion or the bird of prey. The Strigoi Vii takes a far more civilized and artful approach when performing the Art of Vampyrism. We fully admire and embrace the philosophy of the Native American hunters who would give thanks and praise before taking the life of their intended prey.

Many humans would say Vampyrism is theft. However, does not the human steal the life of a cow whenever they take a bite of hamburger? Vegetarians kill or harm plants for sustenance, which are also living beings. There is no creature in the world that does not survive due to consuming energy of other beings. Even plants absorb sunlight and the minerals of dead animals present in the soil and convert them to useable energy to fuel the plant's growth. However, unlike the actions of the mortal-minded meat eater, Vampyrism is far less harmful. We know it is actually beneficial to the health of the human.

Donating Corporeal blood is healthy because the loss of the donated blood forces the body to generate newer, healthier blood. The old blood then goes to serve the well-being of humans who are less healthy and in need of a transfusion. It is no different when the Strigoi Vii draws in human Prana. Tapping too much Prana from a mortal may cause minor and temporary damage, just as draining someone of too much blood will cause dizziness or weakness. Therefore, be careful not to draw too much Prana from one donor. There is an additional disadvantage to drawing too much energy from a single mortal; it may result in something commonly known as "sympathetic vampyrism." Any human whose Ethereal body has been too deeply drained of Prana will unconsciously seek to replenish it by taking it from another human's subtle body. This is not an actual evolution into Strigoi Vii, but rather a purely instinctual response of the subtle body. It is, in fact, a common cause of temporary traditional psychic vampirism and the myths of the vampires "bite" turning their victims into vampire minions.

From the Immortal-minded perspective, it is not an ethical violation to take energy from others. The wolf does not ask the rabbit or the lion ask the gazelle if they can eat them. However, the lion has the instinctual common sense to not overhunt their prey, as that lion's pride cannot survive without the herd of gazelle. These simple laws of the wild are examples of Vampyric ethics. We want mortals to multiply and live long, happy, and healthy lives, generating more Prana so we can both mutually further our respective evolution. The human race only truly benefits from a respectful coexistence between us.

Different frequencies of energy occur depending on the nature and source of the energy. A common misconception is that lower forms of Ethereal energy, such as that of plants and animals, are of a high-enough frequency to be useful to the Strigoi Vii. These low-grade energies cannot, by themselves, sustain the Vampyre. The low-frequency energies of the Earth, as well, are not enough to provide fuel for Zhep'r. When a Vampyre seeks to tap only these energies, it is like a carnivore trying to survive solely by consuming plants. The system of the carnivore is simply not constructed to endure in a healthy state without eating meat. Human Prana is the best and most potent form of Pranic energy of use to the Strigoi Vii.

Vampyric Cannibalism and Rape is the procedure of drawing energy from other Strigoi Vii, Awakened beings, or ethical psychic vampires without their knowledge and consent. These practices are extremely unethical. Tapping energy from those who are Awakened and/or have attained Zhep'r is equivalent to cannibalism. As an analogy, while humans consume lower animals, consuming human flesh for sustenance is one of the most universal and deep-rooted human taboos. It is also unethical to drain a donor to the point of temporary impairment, especially if the draining is severe enough to produce sympathetic vampyrism.

To the neophyte, it may *seem* like cannibalism when two Strigoi Vii exchange energy. However, energy exchanges between Strigoi Vii are for the purpose of cycling, not drawing on energy. This can be done in playful games, during ritual to amplify an Offering and raise more energy, between two Strigoi Vii as part of a healing, or for Vampyre sex and Tantric practices.

Surface Vampyrism occurs through direct physical contact or any form of social interaction. This form of Vampyrism may be simply accomplished through the application of intent and will. Since all living beings exchange energy and form links in this manner, it is a natural process that does not require consent, just directed intent. In surface Vampyrism, the Vampyre does not draw Pranic energy from below the surface of the aura and definitely not deeply and directly from the Ethereal double body. Any basic link can be utilized for surface Vampyrism, such as a simple touch, kiss on the cheek, handshake, discussion, or casual and "accidental" physical contact. Everyday social settings and interactions are forums for such indirect forms of the Art of Vampyrism. Surface Vampyrism is a simple surface draw of energy in order to satisfy the general and immediate needs of the Strigoi Vii and should be done discretely and subtly.

To understand the role of physical contact in surface Vampyrism, remember that any time your aura directly interacts with that of a donor, immediate Ethereal links are created between the two of you. Physical contact can create some of the strongest and most energetic links. However, even if you are at a distance and have a conversation with another individual without physical or even visual contact, links are formed. The more prolonged and interactive the contact, the more links are forged and, therefore, more energy can be drawn in.

Once contact is achieved, the Vampyre must simply focus their intent on using the tendrils to pierce the aura. These "Ethereal fangs" open the aura slightly, allowing the Vampyre to tap the subsequently freed Prana. To aid this process, you may wish to visualize shining tendrils or tubes connecting you and your donor, each tube filling with Prana, which you then draw toward yourself. You can inhale deeply and rhythmically or even clench your abdominal or sphincter muscles to facilitate the process.

Many of Us perform this type of Vampyrism instinctively, but like all arts, you must consciously and repeatedly practice in order to become a Master. When performing surface Vampyrism, make a silent statement to yourself regarding your specific intentions. This will solidify your intent and engage your will. Once the process is concluded, the Vampyre must extract their tendrils and break all links between themselves and the donor in order to prevent an unwanted reversal of energies. Many Strigoi Vii choose to visualize the tendrils "fading away" or slowly disengaging and dissolving.

Indirect surface Vampyrism should be a brief and shallow form of tapping. Take only a small amount of energy from each donor, and do this from as many donors as required to satisfy your needs. This is one example of why being in an urban setting can be beneficial for the Strigoi Vii. If you live amongst a large number of people, there is no lack of energy and no reason to ever tap too deeply from any one donor. As explained in "Liber Jahira," when you deeply absorb energy from the subtle body of another, you may likely also absorb their emotions and moods. Try instead to focus on directing the tendrils toward the shallower Ethereal layer, as you may suffer distasteful effects from absorbing another's emotional sensations. This process is part of the skill of filtering.

Deep Vampyrism is the process of penetrating deeply into a donor's subtle body, beyond the aura, and directly into the core of their Ethereal double. This is where the most concentrated Prana is located. Deep Vampyrism is a process that must only ever be performed with great caution and care and by those advanced Strigoi Vii who have mastered the process of tapping. It is a process too sophisticated for the Calmae. Deep Vampyrism can negatively and harmfully drain the donor and may quickly cause symptoms of sympathetic Vampyrism. Deep Vampyrism requires physical contact, and the longer it is maintained the more Prana can be drawn. Strigoi Vii Adepts who are skilled in this process, if they choose to practice it, will often develop a consensual and informed relationship with a specific donor before tapping them deeply.

When you cannot maintain a constant physical contact with a donor, it is possible to simply touch an individual as in surface Vampyrism and let the tendril root deeply into them. Once this is done, and if the Strigoi Vii is expert in the Art of Vampyrism, they can forge a strong link and draw deeply. However, this is not recommended, as many consider it Vampyric rape. It may also be extremely exhausting to the donor. Experience and practice with surface Vampyrism is required to master this technique. Also, if you were to practice this form of Vampyrism on a powerful and skilled Awakened being, they might be aware of what you are doing and fight back consciously or unconsciously. The Strigoi Vii makes sure to refine and develop ethical tactile Vampyrism, as it is subtle, respectful, and not harmful to the donor.

Direct Vampyrism without deep tapping is actually *beneficial* to the donor! When the link is established and the energy drawn from the donor, their subtle body interacts directly with that of the Vampyre, thus stimulating the donor's energetic system. This stimulation may cause a faster flow of Prana throughout their subtle body, thus cleansing them of stagnant energies and increasing the vibration of their subtle metabolism.

Direct Vampyrism can be best equated to many healing practices, such as "laying on of hands," energetic or therapeutic massage, and Reiki techniques. Studying and experimenting with these practices is a good way to master this form of Our Art of Vampyrism. You will also offer your donor pleasure and healing energy work whilst drawing on their energy.

Consecutive or repeated interactions may lead to a powerful bond between the Vampyre and their donor. In such a case, the two will form lasting links, which the Vampyre can then use to tap energy from the donor. This is similar to deep Vampyrism. Obviously, in such a case the Strigoi Vii must take care to not draw too much from their donor. We strongly advise that this form of the Art of Vampyrism be consensual.

Sensual Vampyrism is an aspect of both surface and deep Vampyrism and can include any combination of sexual elements, such as seduction, erotic stimulation, and Tantric techniques. Intercourse need not be part of sensual Vampyrism. Of course, because of the ethical implications of this form of Our Art of Vampyrism, the Strigoi Vii must obtain consent if physical contact is to take place. There are two main forms of sensual Vampyrism:

> *Surface Sensual Vampyrism* is used in intimate situations to stimulate the donor to release Prana. Sensual or erotic arousal creates an incredible amount of available energy. Surface sensual Vampyrism may include body massage, dance, masturbation, erotic performance, or a multitude of other situations. The most common technique is to sexually

arouse the donor into a state of heightened stimulation. Examples include a dancer doing a striptease, a burlesque performance, or even reading erotic poetry to a lover. Through these and many other techniques, energetic links are forged through which the donor is unconsciously Offering Prana. The Vampyre can then tap this energy.

Deep Sensual Vampyrism requires sexual intercourse and is a deeply penetrating form of interaction. This, of course, is an extremely intimate technique that should only be performed between two consenting adults. Deep sensual Vampyrism often involves stimulating the chakras and moving deeply into the subtle body of the donor, as during this process the subtle bodies of the Vampyre and donor are deeply and profoundly connected. This form of Vampyrism is often extremely empowering for both the Vampyre and their donor, as there is a direct flow of energy from the donor to the Vampyre. Deep sensual Vampyrism often produces a great deal of intense stimulation in the donor. This technique should only be attempted by the most skilled Strigoi Vii in the Arts of Vampyrism, as it requires great skill to filter the immense flood of Astral energetic residue that may be released by the process.

The Calmae should be aware that deep sensual Vampyrism and other forms of deep Vampyrism are only discussed here for informational purposes. These are techniques that require a large degree of practice and evolution in Zhep'r to master. The Calmae, at this point, should focus on practicing ethical and responsible surface Vampyrism.

Commencing is the equivalent of surface Vampyrism and the most elementary application of cycling. It involves a variety of techniques such as mutual erotic dance, energy wrestling, mutual performance, BDSM practices, martial arts sparring, or many other activities. The participants collectively create a "circuit" of energy between them, in which they both give and receive energy.

In summation, the Art of Vampyrism requires that you shift your ethics and perspectives from those of the mortal-minded to those of an Immortal. Immortal ethics are based on natural laws, the survival of the fittest, and a deep sense of personal responsibility. Remember, it is *only* the Prana We desire from the hyle, never their physical blood! Prana is the key to defeating the Second Death.

Consider deeply and wisely. Do you wish to experience the fullness of eternity as your Self, retaining your memories, free will, knowledge, and experiences? Or would you rather be "reincarnated" as a thousand disparate shards spread among a thousand new beings? Tapping Prana will fuel your Zhep'r and build your own Immortality.

Defeating the Second Death is genuine Immortality of the Self.

Choice is freedom.

The choice is yours.

You hold the tools this very second in your own hands.

Chapter 23
THE ANATOMY OF DEATH

That is not dead which can eternal lie,
And with strange aeons even death may die.
—H. P. Lovecraft, "The Nameless City"

For all living beings, life begins with the Divine Spark and continues outward to physical manifestation. Upon the First Death, or the death of the Corporeal body, the Ethereal body, being inextricably married to the Corporeal, begins to lose its pattern and shape. In most cases, the survival of the Ethereal body is aided by preservation of the Corporeal body. That is why the Ancient Egyptians were so concerned with preserving the physical body through mummification. We, as Strigoi Vii, realize this extreme possibility, and the health and preservation of the physical pattern is correspondingly important. Systems such as cryonics, DNA preservation, and the potential option of cloning are powerful advantages for the modern Vampyre.

The death of the Ethereal body, or the *Second Death,* occurs when the patterns anchored by the Corporeal body begin to lose density and cohesion. Regard the Corporeal body as a drinking glass. Imagine the glass being filled with water (the Ethereal body). When the glass is shattered, the water spills and will eventually be dispersed into the universe through evaporation. Similarly, when the Corporeal body deteriorates, the Ethereal body begins to decompose, very much like ice melting. This process usually takes days to weeks, depending on the strength of the individual's Ethereal body and their mental and spiritual health.

Since the Ethereal body is the vessel for the Astral, the Astral body is, in turn, jeopardized by the destruction of the Ethereal body. Remember that all levels of the Self are connected. Without the solid foundation of the Corporeal body and the Ethereal body, all dreams, memories, and experiences evaporate like water vapor. During the Second Death, the Astral body and its associated characteristics are dispersed across the universe as a thousand shattered crystal shards or disappear like a drop of water into the ocean. Rebirth or reincarnation beyond the Second Death cannot be validated by any spiritual path or religion beyond the assumption of belief and faith. We do not choose to gamble on an unproven theory. The aim of the Strigoi Vii is to avoid the Second Death and therefore achieve Immortality. Those consciously existing between the First and Second Death might thus be known as "Undead."

The separation that occurs between the First and Second Death is often the cause of near-death experiences (NDEs). NDEs involve a form of Astral projection during which the subtle senses of the individual are heightened. People who have experienced NDEs often report phenomena such as looking down on their Corporeal bodies from above, seeing bright lights or entities, and other Ethereal sensations. However, there is a strictly biological explanation for many of these experiences. The "bright light" reported by many individuals during an NDE is often just random neural firing in the optic nerve and brain. The peace and comfort commonly associated with such experiences is due to the release of chemicals and subtle substances that create a feeling of euphoria. Strigoi Vii are always very skeptical of all accounts of near-death experiences, as We know how unusual it is for mortals to be able to maintain the higher levels of their body beyond the death of the Corporeal.

Sometimes, however, a human's Ethereal and Astral energies will be caught between the First and Second Death due to a variety of circumstances. This occurs mainly due to Ethereal links, such as strong emotional ties to a specific place or person, which are maintained across levels of reality to the physical world. Violent or sudden deaths can forcefully separate the Ethereal body from the Corporeal, and the strong emotions of the individual involved will forge links to the specific location. These circumstances comprise much of what we know today as ghostly phenomena. However, such occurrences are quite rare, and a persistent Ethereal link is hardly a "ghost" in the commonly known sense of the word. Most of these links are little more than a semiconscious collection of emotions, like an accumulation of dust beneath a bed. Many cultures have rituals for releasing these clogged partial entities, such as exorcisms or funeral rites.

We Strigoi Vii wisely choose to master knowledge of the Anatomy of Death and to keep survival of the entire Self as the first and foremost goal in Our lives. As lovers of life, what other option could there be possibly be for Us?

> [B]ehold a new cycle of life and mortality. Your genius will
> not be allotted to you, but you will choose your genius;
> and let him who draws the first lot have the first choice,
> and the life which he chooses shall be his destiny. Virtue
> is free, and as a man honors or dishonors her he will have
> more or less of her; the responsibility is with the chooser.
> —Plato, *The Republic*

Reincarnation does not mean the same thing to the Strigoi Vii as it does to the mortal-minded. Mortals only detect a bare echo of the truth of Our reincarnation. Various forms of reincarnation in mortal-minded belief systems focus on the continuation of a "soul" rather than continuation of the Self. What, then, is a soul? It is not memory or experience or identity. Instead, the mortal-minded see it as a loosely defined concept that is closely affiliated with their idea of God.

Imagine, for a moment, waking up tomorrow morning in a completely unfamiliar house. You do not know your name or personal history. You have no idea if you have a family. Any occupation you might hold is also a mystery. You also have no sense of your personality—are you a weak or strong person? Do you take pride in your accomplishments (whatever they may be)? Are you physically abusive or charming to those close to you? Are you intelligent or mentally challenged? Imagine looking at your own face in a mirror and not recognizing a single feature, as if you were staring at a photograph of a stranger.

Now consider forgetting, absolutely, everything that ever mattered to you in your life—your parents, your profession, your lover, your hobbies, your children. Imagine passing the one whom you love best on the street and having absolutely no idea who they are.

Such is the mortal-minded conception of reincarnation. The mortal-minded individual who believes in reincarnation sees their rebirth as a moment of complete, ultimate forgetting. Their experiences, dreams, and ideals are completely shattered into millions of energetic shards and recycled throughout the universe. Their essential spark or "soul" has been transferred into a different body. They have become an entirely different person. Hindu doctrine maintains that humans can even be reincarnated as animals or insects! Mortals see themselves as helpless on a wheel of rebirth that inevitably grinds their consciousness through incarnation after incarnation. This is no more than an extension of a slave mentality. They cannot conceive of truly taking control of their own destiny and believe it to be ordained by chance or by higher forces that "punish" them for transgressions against some artificial moral or religious code.

In "Coming Forth by Day," We discussed Corporeal Immortality. Spiritual Immortality is Immortality of the entire Self, not just one portion of the Self. The myth of the undead, undying vampire derives from the truth of Our reincarnation and the prevention of the Second Death. We have no interest in rebirth as an endless process of memory loss. We value the treasures of experience and knowledge We have collected during this life! Why struggle toward Awakening and strive for spiritual evolution if all understanding and advancement will be lost upon the Second Death? Imagine having centuries to obtain experiences and knowledge to develop the Self.

Vampyre Immortality is one of the Mysteries of Strigoi Vii, and something the mortal-minded can rarely even begin to comprehend. As long as We can conquer the Second Death, We live forever in a timeless existence, free of the constraints of time and space.

Vampyre Immortality is to never forget, to break the cycle and to remember who you are. This is a True Awakening, and together We shall remember and not forget who We are.

Chapter 24
THE STRIGOI MORTE

Honor thy mother and father . . . so that your days
may be long and that it may go well with you . . .
—Deuteronomy 5:16

The Strigoi Morte are the spirit guides of the Strigoi Vii. They are often known within the Family as *Whisperers* or the *Ancestors* and are said to be Our disembodied Elders, Sorors, and Fraters who have conquered the Second Death and thus exist in subtle form. They are thought to have once been human and, through manifestation, can still influence the Corporeal Dayside world by such means as inspiration, visions, and possession. Once a True Vampyre is Awakened to the Current, the possibility of direct contact with and validation of the Strigoi Morte becomes possible.

In Romanian mythology, the Strigoi Vii were the Living Vampires, and the Strigoi Morte were the undead spirits who haunted the living. In actuality, some of these myths may derive from the partially Vampyric beings known as *Ethereal revenants*. Only the namesake is employed here, as Our True Strigoi Morte differ greatly from their mythological counterparts. The wisdom of the Strigoi Morte is said to survive throughout the aeons with the continuation of the consciousness in Their Divine Self. They are an essential part of the Current of Elorath and the Family. Our Mysteries state that They are the keepers of the ancient knowledge and secrets of True Immortality of the Self.

Mortals throughout history may have caught faint glimpses of the Strigoi Morte and possibly interpreted Them as angels, miracles, spirits, faeries, gods, and demons. From a spiritual and religious mortal-minded interpretation, the Strigoi Morte are on the same level as beings who have Ascended to a higher plane of spiritual existence. Mortal religions and spiritual paths speak of Ascended Masters such as the Great White Brotherhood, Secret Chiefs, or the Order of Blessed Souls. These Masters are individuals who have spiritually advanced beyond the Corporeal to a transcended state that many mortal-minded would call Buddhahood, sainthood, nirvana, or enlightenment.

More recently, such contact could be possibly interpreted by the mortal-minded as some of the sources of alien encounters. Occultist Aleister Crowley claimed to have made contact with a particular entity, known to him as Aiwas, who may indeed have been a Strigoi Morte. Crowley always claimed it was from Aiwas that he received *The Book of the Law.* Prior to his death, Crowley drew a picture of his visions of Aiwas, which looked quite similar to what new-agers and UFOlogists describe as a "grey," or an alien. Crowley created and led the occult organization known as the A∴A∴ (*Argentium Astrum,* or Silver Star) for the purpose of spreading Aiwas's teachings.

As Strigoi Vii, We use the potential of Our heritage to aspire to Ascend and join the Strigoi Morte in what humans consider eternity and the Mysteries consider timelessness. Through self-mastery and the esoteric technology of Zhep'r, the Strigoi Morte truly have achieved a conscious state not bound by space and time. They are Our catalyst for Zhep'r and Our guides through the Mirror Gates of Immortality.

The manner in which Native Americans and various Asian cultures honor their Corporeal ancestors is loosely analogous to Our respect for the Strigoi Morte. We see them as guides and inspirators. The Ancestors are said to have achieved a point in Zhep'r where They are able to maintain the Self at a point between the First and Second Death. Legends amongst the Family tell of some Vampyres who have been able to achieve this state during their Corporeal existence, and thus have easily made the transition to Strigoi Morte upon their First Death.

Many Strigoi Vii speak of finding the transition very challenging and even more ultimately have failed. Ascension to undeath and Immortality in a timeless state is the ultimate agenda of Zhep'r for the Strigoi Vii. Only thus may the Self pursue Zhep'r and continued evolution on grander levels of existence.

Although disembodied, the Strigoi Morte can theoretically manifest Corporeally if They so choose. They can assume physical form through possession of a human. This is known as "skin riding." A Strigoi Vii may perform the same process via Astral projection upon proper development of their Zhep'r. This is explored more thoroughly within the Higher Mysteries.

Many Strigoi Vii encounter the Ancestors throughout their entire lives, directly or indirectly. Some Strigoi Vii have reported experiencing whispers, hints, or inspirations that directed them to the archetype of the vampire or the Family. These Seekers have used such clues and tools to begin the foundations of Zhep'r. Many simply felt a general Calling of sorts and finally took their first steps on a path leading to the gates of the Sanguinarium. A great number of Strigoi Vii have said they came upon the Family and the Mysteries in ways that seemed oddly synchronistic or almost mystical. While the mortal-minded would say such experiences are simply blind coincidence, We know they may be the result of a Patron Strigoi Morte guiding the Seeker and creating circumstances to prepare them for their Awakening. The Strigoi Morte are a powerful element of Vampyre ritual and esoteric workings. They give guidance and inspiration not just to the Family but to individual Strigoi Vii. One Vampyre may not have just a single guide but a group of them, known as a *Pantheon.*

Before the Sanguinarium, the Family had highly intimate and solitary relationships with the Strigoi Morte. Many Strigoi Vii theorize that the Ancestors would even orchestrate the birth of a potential by arranging the union of humans possessing the "Vampyre gene" or implanting a piece of the Current during conception. The Strigoi Morte would then guide the chosen potential as they matured by taking the form of apparitions, spiritual guides, inspirators, or visions. As the

Nasarim grew older and began to realize their true potential, the Ancestor would formally reveal Themself and begin teaching the Mysteries to Their chosen student. Some Ancestors would even have several potentials, knowing only a few would truly Awaken and show promise for success within Zhep'r. Today, the Strigoi Morte not only guide individual Strigoi Vii, They also guide and inspire the entire Current of the Family as a whole.

One of the qualifications for advancing within the Central Mysteries is to personally validate the existence of the Strigoi Morte in ritual Communion. Learning of the Secrets of the Strigoi Morte is one of the key principles in experiencing Zhep'r. One cannot simply be told of and believe in the existence of the Strigoi Morte. Declaring belief upon receiving secondhand information is a very common mortal-minded trait. Be skeptical always and seek validation. Moreover, there are not sufficient concepts within human language or experience to describe a true encounter with the Strigoi Morte. You must *experience* and come to *know* Them for yourself in order to validate Their existence. Such Gnosis comes from making intimate contact with the Strigoi Morte during Communion, where you contact Them and personally verify Their existence. The wisest approach for validating the existence of the Strigoi Morte is to keep an open yet skeptical mind. Observe the results of your investigations objectively and make judgments later. If you are courageous and tenacious, you will thus explore and fulfill your True Nature.

One may ask how to distinguish Strigoi Morte from other disembodied beings. Various lower or parasitic entities exist within the subtle layers of reality. However, as the Strigoi Vii intrinsically recognize others of the Family, so do We recognize the Strigoi Morte. Thus, do not fear that you will be "tricked" by other entities falsely claiming to be Strigoi Morte. If you are True Vampyre, you will simply know their Radiance and experience a deep feeling of love as you would from a fellow Strigoi Vii. The Strigoi Morte have such a focused energy Signature that it is impossible to mistake Them for anything but Family.

In a deep sense akin to love, We build relationships both individually and as a Family with the Ascended. Strigoi Vii can consciously and successfully make Communion with the Strigoi Morte through ritual, meditation, trance, and divination. The True Strigoi Vii creates an intimate bond with the Ancestors. This is one of the things that distinguishes Us from Others such as ethical psychic vampires and other Legacies. The Family's relationship with the Strigoi Morte continues to evolve, as does the Sanguinarium. The Sanguinarium is the Corporeal movement of the Family, inspired by the Strigoi Morte, and the uniting factor that shall gather the Strigoi Vii into an international community for mutual inspiration and agreement.

The Strigoi Morte in Their True form cannot be perceived in a practical mundane sense. Instead, They lend Us a sense of blessing and of being chosen and guided. The True Vampyre allows for more than one possible explanation of the reality of the Strigoi Morte, and each Strigoi Vii may have their own interpretation of contact with Them.

Many amongst the Family theorize that Our Patron Strigoi Morte may also be an aspect of Our higher Self that is free of time and space. In that sense, the Patron is an aspect of Our Immortal soul or Divine Spark. Becoming conscious of all levels and facets of the Self is a grand Awakening of personal awareness. Thus Our experiences with the Strigoi Morte may indeed be simply like looking into a universal mirror and making True and Deep Communion, which is Communion with Our Dragon. The Strigoi Morte, free of time and space, are thus perceived as having personality, shape, form, and image so that Our minds may comprehend the Dragon Itself.

We leave it to you to validate Their existence. The Strigoi Morte are highly discriminating in regard to whom They reveal Themselves. Only the most dedicated and sincere Vampyre will benefit from the vast possibilities of the Current.

The Rovance, or the Patron introduction or acknowledgement, is an exercise in self-meditation during which a Strigoi Vii begins to make contact with their Patron Strigoi Morte. Begin this exercise during a day of solitude, after having tapped Prana to your fill. If possible, try to perform this ritual isolated from the mundane world, such as in a pleasant rural locale. If not, you should at least find a room or residence that can be secured from intrusion. It is important that you not be disturbed or interrupted during this exercise. Be sure to turn off all communication devices so you will truly experience solitude. Tap into the energies of the world and begin establishing a sacred space known as a Sanctum (this process can be found in chapter 25, "Vampyre Ritual"). Once the Sanctum has been established, begin the Rovanne by relaxing yourself from your feet to your head, then center yourself by imagining a serpent from deep within the Earth coming up and wrapping around your spine, slowly sliding through each chakra. As the snake coils up your spine, it moves toward your Throne. Begin the Throning exercise, as described in chapter 12, "Awakening Your Dragon."

Once this has been established, let your Prana flow through your body. Visualize yourself in a long tunnel, on a path in a dark forest, or any other route that manifests in your imagination. Feel yourself walking down this path. Notice what is around you with all your five senses, and listen for direction. Your Dragon will guide you. As you continue the exercise, you will begin to perceive signs on your path. They may take the form of voices, lights, symbols, or even road plinths. These signs have been established by your Patron for you. Heed them, and take note of what they say, following their direction. Do not be discouraged if you do not perceive any signs on your first experience with the Rovanne. It may take several attempts to finally perceive the markers your Patron has set for you on your path of evolution.

The following descriptions represent some of the impressions members of the Family have received upon performing the Rovanne. Use these as examples and inspiration only, as your personal Patron may provide you with a completely different experience.

On this path, you will gradually notice a grand temple far in the distance. You will be magnetically drawn toward a set of immense double doors. The temple looks different to all of Us. Some have seen a large obelisk, while others have seen a cathedral, a pyramid, or ancient Greek temple. Through the cracks in the door, you will notice a beautiful and calming, yet alluring, light. You knock on the door three times, and it swings open with a unique creaking sound. As you enter, you are surrounded by darkness while bathed in the subtle lights you noticed from outside. The light becomes brighter, and before you, in the halls of this temple, one or more figures will be revealed. These will be your Patron Strigoi Morte.

Kneel before Them as a Knight before their sovereign. Look Them directly in the eyes and introduce yourself. They will often not speak. You will experience Their words as whispers or visions inside your mind. Whatever the case, They will find the best way to communicate with you to achieve understanding. Take this opportunity to ask Them Their names, your purpose within the Family, and your personal sigil. This sigil will be your key to calling on Them in meditation and for Communion. At this point, They may choose to reveal a sacred image to you that will be the sigil.

Once you have made contact with your Patron, you can call on Them for guidance, advice, and support. Also, They will often be drawn to you in sacred Communion rites such as the Sanguine Mass.

Chapter 25
VAMPYRE RITUAL

There is a single main definition of the object of all magical Ritual. It is the uniting of the Microcosm with the Macrocosm. The Supreme and Complete Ritual is therefore the Invocation of the Holy Guardian Angel.
—Aleister Crowley, *Magick in Theory and Practice*

Ritual is a strong formula for energetic workings. It creates a "theater of sequences" through the tools of psychodrama by utilizing a system of regimented steps and actions, all for a specific purpose. If the celebrant applies proper will and intent to the ritual formulation, it can be a powerful tool for raising and manipulating energies. The varied tools and symbols of ritual will aid less experienced practitioners, such as the Strigoi Vii Calmae, in entering into nonordinary reality and achieving different states of consciousness. Ritual may also be used to celebrate a specific rite of passage or achievement, such as Initiation.

Below are some of the benefits and purposes of different types of Strigoi Vii ritual:

- Communion with the Strigoi Morte
- Contacting and awakening the higher Self (the Dragon)
- Raising energy
- Entering alternate modes of consciousness

- Creating sacred spaces (Sanctums)
- Focusing will and intent to achieve a specific goal
- Reaffirmation of the Self
- Reaffirmation of collective agreement
- Consecration of tools
- Personal transformation
- Celebration of Initiations and Ascensions
- Celebration of festivals and holidays

A significant benefit of any Strigoi Vii ritual is reaffirmation of the individual Self and the collective Family Pakt. In the past, there have been many different variations of Strigoi Vii rituals presented in various forums. These rituals had their value; however, they were generally tailored to the needs of a particular individual or group and thus did not have widespread applicability. We now present a more generalized formula for ritual with which the Initiate can experiment as they choose. We encourage you to work with this ritual formulation on your own terms, adapting it as best fits your needs. It is a template from which you can make your own system, which will be best suited to you personally.

In "The Vampyre Prospectus" and "Coming Forth by Day," We explored Initiations, psychodrama, and the aesthetics of rituals. Keep these concepts in mind as you now prepare for more advanced rituals. The ritual formulation that follows incorporates the philosophy and the ceremonial aspects of Strigoi Vii ritual. Any modifications you make to this general ritual format should always be in keeping with the spirit of Strigoi Vii ritual, for it is thus that you will gain the most effective results.

However, be aware that anyone attempting Strigoi Vii ritual should be firmly grounded in the Dayside. Mastery of the Dayside is the foundation on which the rituals of the Nightside rest. Without this foundation, the celebrant simply is not prepared to enter ritual, and they will not obtain results. We suggest the celebrant review "Coming Forth by

Day" if they are unclear or uncertain about the foundational principles underlying ritual and the Strigoi Vii Nightside.

The Sanguine Mass

The Sanguine Mass is the most central of all Strigoi Vii rituals of Communion with the Strigoi Morte and is the standard on which many others are based. It is especially empowering for unifying a group ritual into a formulated ceremony to direct and focus energies. There exist many different variations on the Sanguine Mass, but the nine steps below comprise the standard core formulation and are detailed later in this chapter.

1. Prelude (or preparation)
2. Entering the Sanctum
3. Invokation
4. Invitation
5. Offering
6. Recoiling
7. Closing
8. Return
9. Celebration

Although the Sanguine Mass is the cornerstone of all Strigoi Vii ritual, there are other ritual forms. Some forms of Strigoi Vii Communion ritual are akin to a séance, where the celebrant establishes direct communication with the Strigoi Morte. The celebrant may request the Strigoi Morte contact them through various proxies, such as the tools of divination. Some Strigoi Vii use the ritual format as a tool of inspiration, in which they request revelation and insight regarding a specific problem or for a particular personal or Family endeavor. Even if the celebrant does not wish to perform a full ritual, they may apply various elements of Our general ritual format to other workings. Always experiment and discover what best works for you!

Liber Calmae

Solitary Ritual

The vast majority of Strigoi Vii are solitary and independent and often don't even meet their Sorors and Fraters in person. Thus, solitary ritual is the most commonly practiced form of ritual within the Family. The Sanguine Mass is primarily written from the solitary perspective for this reason. However, it is easily adapted to group ritual if necessary.

Group Ritual

Group rituals, most importantly, act as a tool of unity in which all the ritual celebrants are in agreement. Group rituals can be intensely significant psychological markers in situations such as Ascensions and Initiations. The presiding member in group ritual *must* be a MoRoii, Azraelle, or a Magister, as only these individuals are properly trained and experienced enough to channel the flow of energies. The only exception to this rule is if a Strigoi Vii couple wants to perform the ritual together.

Within group ritual, individual celebrants may assume specific roles. The leader of the ritual is known within Strigoi Vii as the *presider,* or *presiding member.* The *Deacons* are individuals who are charged with assisting the presider by taking up specific roles or duties. For example, the presider may request that the Deacon inform the other celebrants that the ritual is about to start and help them prepare their robes and masks. The *celebrants* are those who are directly involved in the ritual, either by contributing energy or being present to celebrate the ritual.

There is no set number of celebrants for group ritual. Traditionally, in witchcraft, the ritual format called for thirteen members. From an Outer Circle perspective, this requirement mainly arose from mortal-minded superstition. Moreover, We Strigoi Vii know that a ritual can be just as effective when held by two people as by twenty! Large numbers do not necessarily make a more powerful ritual. We also suggest that the ritual be limited to the number of celebrants that can comfortably fit in the ritual space and can effectively participate in ritual. A smaller group creates a more intimate and personal experience, often leading to a greater Offering for the Strigoi Morte than does an un-manageably large group.

Performance Ritual

Even though rituals are mostly done in private, there are occasions where some rituals can be done publicly if they are incorporated into performances such as fetish or burlesque shows, dominatrix sessions, DJ sets, or live music or theater performances. One can take example from the "Theater of the Vampires" in Anne Rice's novels. In performance ritual, the audience should be stimulated to produce extra Prana to act as donors to fuel the ritual. For example, as a band performs a live show, the audience will be energized, perhaps singing and dancing along with the music. They will be directing their attention and energy toward the performers in an energetic circuit. This circuit is similar to the Art of Ambient Vampyrism, but in performance ritual the performers are directly involved in raising the energy of the crowd, instead of standing aside and simply tapping it. Such rituals should always employ the Glamour in order to disguise the true intent of the performance and not violate the sacredness of Communion. It is recommended that performance rituals only be performed by Strigoi Vii who are quite experienced in ritual, and who are capable of being discreet in their performance so as not to violate the Black Veil.

A fetish performer might, as an example, wear fangs and traditional "vampire" attire. The audience will merely see the performance as exciting and exotic, while the performer will be utilizing disguised elements of Vampyre ritual. The exception, of course, is during the Endless Night Festival when public rituals can be performed openly, as mortals who are in attendance are more than willing to be the "victims of vampires"!

Timing of Ritual

For those of the Outer Mysteries, this ritual is best done when the Shroud Between Worlds is thinnest, so distractions from the Dayside are at their least intrusive. Strigoi Vii magick and sorcery are two entirely different applications. Magick depends on timing, tools, and psychodrama and can be utilized to create powerful change. Sorcery comes from within the practitioner and needs no tool except the will to master the universe itself. To generalize, Vampyre Magick as performed by those of the Outer Circle is a *thaumaturgic* system, based on ritual actions and tools. Nomaj Sorcery, the province of the Inner Circle, may be likened to *theurgy,* is internally and instinctually based, and often uses no props at all. The abyss between magick and sorcery is both as profound and as simple as the distinction between the Dayside and Nightside.

Adept Strigoi Vii can directly apply Nomaj Sorcery whenever they choose to gain results. However, even the Master does not disdain a useful tool! The main difference is that the apprentice *requires* the tool, while the Master *chooses* it. Specific times of day and dates on the Wheel of the Year have power within the collective human consciousness. The Strigoi Vii Adept and novice alike can tap this power in order to fuel many of their rituals. For example, there still exist numerous legends of sorcerers calling forth demons and ancient gods during their midnight Sabbats for dark orgiastic rites. Playing on such psychological tropes can aid the psychodrama of Strigoi Vii ritual and thus energize it, especially for those of the Family Initiated into the Outer Mysteries.

> *The Witching Hour,* according to a twenty-four-hour daily chronology, begins at the stroke of midnight and continues for the first three hours of the new day. Various writers have called this time the "dark night of the soul." From the Outer Circle perspective, during the Witching Hour, a "door" or "passage" opens between the Corporeal and subtle realities, and Astral beings such as the Strigoi Morte can more easily make contact with the Corporeal world. Mortal legends claim that this time is when predatory spirits such as the Incubus, Succubus, and old hag come to steal the life force of mortals. The Witching Hour is also an efficient time for practicing higher forms of the Art of Vampyrism, since

mortals are asleep and naturally projecting into the Astral by dreaming. We use the belief stamped on the mortal-minded collective unconsciousness through superstitions and legends as a tool to empower Our ritual.

The Dark Moon (also called the *New Moon*) is an appealing time for ritual since this is the darkest time of the month. As viewed from Earth, no moon appears in the sky since no sunlight reflects from it in a manner that is visible from our planet. Psychologically, the Dark Moon aids in a deep Nightside experience where the Outer Circle Strigoi Vii is more easily able to enter the supernatural Nightside.

The Wheel of the Year provides an annual framework of holidays and festivals that may be applied to Strigoi Vii ritual and magick. The holidays on the Wheel of the Year either fall on cross-quarter days, such as equinoxes or solstices, or on other chronologically significant days. They are of ancient origin and have been celebrated by humanity for thousands of years under different names and in slightly different forms. For example, the winter solstice (which falls on December 21 or 22 in the Western Hemisphere and marks the longest night of the year) was celebrated by the Druids thousands of years ago. Now, a huge amount of mortal-minded individuals celebrate this holiday on December 25 as Christmas. We call it the *Long Day Festival,* or the *Night of Immortal Stars.* On this day we tap the huge amount of excess Prana collectively released by the common focus of all the mortal-minded Christmas shoppers! We make use of this and similar days of power to fuel Our ritual intent.

For the purposes of the Strigoi Vii, there are two significant holidays on the Wheel of the Year, as discussed in "The Vampyre Prospectus." The first is All Hallows Eve on October 31, or the *Twilight* or *Endless Night Festival.* On this festival day, secular humans and occultists alike turn their collective thoughts and energies to supernatural creatures and denizens of the night. The second is May Eve on the night of April 30, known in Germany as Walpurgisnacht or Hexennacht. German legends say that on this night, witches would meet on Brocken Mountain to commune with their gods and hold unholy ritual. These and many other dates throughout the year are ideal focus points for aiding ritual due to their prevalence in the human consciousness. Refer to "The Vampyre Prospectus" for more information on each of the festivals.

Again, ritual timing is mainly an aid for tapping the human collective consciousness and helping the celebrant focus. Nomaj Sorcery is not reliant on these concepts of Strigoi Vii magick and ceremony.

Location of Ritual

Strigoi Vii rituals are best done in secure and private Sanctums that are free of distractions from the mundane world. For group ritual, it is best to choose a neutral location. For this reason, as well as issues of personal privacy and confidentiality, it is best not to hold group ritual in a private domicile. Public rituals, both group and solitary, are discouraged in most situations because of the associated distractions and lack of privacy.

The majority of Strigoi Vii who participate in group ritual reside in urban settings, so indoor Sanctums are preferred for two reasons. Firstly, it is very difficult to find a private, isolated space outdoors in a large city. Secondly, an indoor Sanctum screens the rite from mortal-minded eyes while still allowing the celebrants to tap the large repository of excess Prana that surges all about them. If a group of Strigoi Vii wishes to perform an exclusively outdoor ritual, such as the *Rite of Bast,* they should consider renting a private campsite outside the city or making a trip to a secluded wilderness area. It is also possible to rent cabins or houses in rural areas on a short-term basis.

Some solitary Strigoi Vii have the luxury of setting up their own permanent private temple in their home. If possible, this is ideal. If this is not possible due to cohabitation, or simply because of lack of space, We suggest at least choosing a particular area of your residence for ritual use, even if it takes some preparation to ready that area. For example, a living room can be easily adapted to a ritual space once chairs are moved out of the way, the floor cleared, and the coffee table cleaned off for use as an altar. Strigoi Vii tools can be discreetly stored in a chest or drawer when not in use. A space in which rituals are repeatedly performed will build up energy over a time, thus aiding future ritual workings.

For group rituals, We suggest choosing a neutral location. In the old stories, vampires had to be invited across the threshold before they could enter a private home. While this is only a legend, it contains a grain of common sense. Most obviously, it is simply wise to be discriminating in regard as to whom you invite to your home! However, on a subtle level, your personal ritual space is also a place of power. When you invite others to join you in that space, you are allowing them to tap into the energies you have invested in it, and they, in turn, will be investing some of their own energies. Instead, We suggest renting a space that is convenient and affordable for all the participants. Such spaces may include hotel rooms, rehearsal rooms in a dance or music studio, or even a short-term apartment or house rental. Online websites and the classified section of newspapers will list such rentals.

Many Strigoi Vii wish to do rituals in public places such as the Ancient Egyptian wing of a museum or in sacred sites such as the Pyramids of Giza, Stonehenge, or the Mayan pyramids in Mexico. While such locations may yield powerful results, they are also highly public. In such places, the Strigoi Vii must be extraordinarily discreet and careful to blend in with the crowds. Otherwise, they are likely to face unwanted mortal-minded intrusions such as suspicious security guards or curious tourists. Controlled environments are best for ritual. It is difficult to achieve and validate results with constant interruptions.

It is possible for the Strigoi Vii to perform ritual within their own mind by utilizing visualization only. Silent Communion, detailed in the next book, is an example of one such ritual. A Strigoi Vii may choose to perform this type of ritual in very energetically charged locations, such as in churches or tourist destinations like the Eiffel Tower. In this case, the Strigoi Vii taps the vast amount of Prana swirling about them and immediately offers it to the Strigoi Morte before any of it has had an opportunity to dissipate. This sort of ritual is one possible solution to the problems of performing ritual in a public place. However, it is still possible for the Strigoi Vii to inadvertently call attention to themselves during this type of ritual, especially if they begin to "lose themselves" in the Offering or Recoiling. Public ritual should always be veiled from the eyes of the mortal-minded and attempted only if it can be "hidden in plain sight."

Regalia: The Tools of Ritual

Regalia are items and tools used within ritual to focus the will and direct energies. The term was originally used to refer to the insignia and privileges of a sovereign. The word *regalia* itself derives from the Latin *regalis,* which is in turn derived from *rex,* or "king."

Here are some common tools used within Strigoi Vii ritual. Not every Strigoi Vii will use each of these tools in every ritual, but all the tools listed below (save candles) are used in the Sanguine Mass.

The Altar is the center point of the ritual, and on it the tools are placed. Traditionally, the altar faces west and is covered with a black cloth. An altar is usually a sturdy table about four feet high, six feet long, and three feet wide. However, any suitable and available table may be used.

The Ar'thana is a black-hilted, double-edged knife or sword that *symbolically* represents the drawing of blood. It is used for controlling the movement of Prana in the Ethereal realm. It is important to note that the ar'thana is *never* used to draw physical blood. Its function is metaphoric only.

The Bell sets the Corporeal patterns and mood of the ritual. Any material save gold is acceptable. Crystal bells often produce a most delicate chime. Some Strigoi Vii like to use temple bells or other similar instruments, such as gongs or Tibetan singing bowls. When a bell is not available, the celebrant may briskly and loudly clap their hands as an alternative.

Candles are used for lighting and mood in many rituals. However, note that if a Communion with the Strigoi Morte is to take place, candlelight should be avoided. The preferred lighting for rituals incorporating Communion is explained below. Symbolically, red candles represent life force and blood, white candles represent the Dayside, black represents the Nightside, purple the Twilight, and silver the moon.

Chalices or goblets are symbolic in that they represent the Offering of Prana and the Blood of the Family. Silver or pewter are the preferred materials, although glass, pottery, or china are also acceptable. Ornamental designs that include Dragons or Strigoi Vii glyphs are best for decoration. Gold or brass goblets represent mortal greed and should not be used. Red wine is the traditional drink contained by the chalice in ritual, but any natural liquid such as fruit or vegetable juice, milk, or even water may be used, according to personal taste.

The Speculum is a black mirror. It is the gateway to the subtle reality; hence, the Strigoi Vii phrase "beyond the mirror." It is traditionally set at eye level on the western wall, on the altar, or on the floor so that the celebrants can peer into the subtle realities as if they are sailing in a glass-bottomed boat. The speculum may be set in an ornate frame or simply rendered, according to the tastes of the Strigoi Vii. Many Strigoi Vii prefer to obtain a speculum in which the glass is convex, or curved outward, which may create interesting visual impressions. If a black mirror is not available, then any readily available mirror may be used.

The Wand represents the direction of the will. It can be made of any type of wood, metal (except gold), or other substances, such as crystal. The wand will often have the Strigoi Vii glyphs engraved on it to focus will.

The Mood

The Outer Sanctum is a preparation room and is not used for the actual ritual. This room should be open to light. Here, members change into their ritual attire, discuss the elements of the ritual, and meditate in preparation. If Black Swans are present, they should be welcomed in the Outer Sanctum. The Outer Sanctum represents the Dayside world.

The Decompression Chamber is a gate or portal. It should be a doorway or a hallway between the Outer Sanctum and the Inner Sanctum. The Decompression Chamber is where the participants psychologically journey from the Dayside into the Nightside toward the Inner Sanctum.

The Inner Sanctum is the actual chamber where the ritual takes place. The Inner Sanctum should be established in a private chamber, secured from any mundane intrusion. Additionally, it should be completely blocked from outside light. If the Inner Sanctum is an outdoor location, it should be as private and isolated as possible. Either way, it should be separate and secure from the mundane world, so that the Shroud Between Worlds can be safely broken down and crossed.

Lighting is extremely important for ritual in which Communion with the Strigoi Morte is to take place. In this case, any light present in the Inner Sanctum should be that which does not disrupt Ethereal patterns, such as the light from a red bulb as used in a photo lab, the blue light used for night activities in the military, or a Sterno candle. Other light sources, such as sunlight, white light bulbs, or normal candles may disrupt the crossing between worlds. If candlelight is absolutely necessary, it should be kept to a minimum.

Music is a powerful tool in setting the mood of ritual. Drums, rattles, bells, and gongs are common tools in large group rituals incorporating live music. If live music is not available, prerecorded music such as the chanting of cloister monks, tribal rhythms, or ambient or gothic music also will work well. Any music chosen should be appropriate and in accordance with the tastes of the members performing the ritual. Make sure that the music does not drown out the voices of the presiding member and the celebrants.

Incense is an important tool, as scent is sometimes considered the most powerful of the five senses. Any incense scent chosen should be pleasing and should aid in the ritual atmosphere. Suggestions include frankincense or myrrh. Many different varieties of commercially prepared incense are readily available.

Ritual Garb

Clothing within Strigoi Vii ritual can be just as important an aspect as meditation or ritual tools. It is often said that the "clothes make the man," and certainly changing one's clothing changes one's mindset. Consider the mortal-minded leaving behind their ordinary identities and inhibitions upon donning a costume on Halloween. When an actor applies their makeup and puts on their character's costume, they have "become" that character. Think of the office worker who changes her clothing before heading out for a night on the town! Garments, to a great extent, determine one's mood and way of thinking. Therefore, the Strigoi Vii can utilize this tool of the Glamour to their advantage in ritual.

Here are some forms of ritual garb to inspire you.

Nightklad is best used for solitary ritual and groups of individuals who are well-acquainted with each other and comfortable with nudity. Wearing nothing other than darkness is an excellent tool for experiencing and stimulating the free flow of energies. Being Nightklad helps create a psychological and sensual freedom seldom experienced elsewhere. However, always make sure that nudity is used for ritual intent and not abused by those who might try to manipulate others or induce unwanted sexual situations.

Masks often add an element of anonymity to those wearing them, in both solitary or group rituals. They are thus a popular tool for increasing the drama of ritual and separating the celebrants from their Dayside. Masks come in a variety of styles, ranging from theatrical characters to predatory animals to fantasy creatures such as dragons and griffons. One example of inspiration popular amongst many Strigoi Vii is the masked sex ritual performed in the film *Eyes Wide Shut*.

Robes are an alternative when a Nightklad ritual is not possible or desired. Long, hooded robes effectively mask the identity of the wearer when anonymity is a focus of the ritual. Generally speaking, a simple black robe is most popular ritual attire among Strigoi Vii. The robe should have a large hood and be loose and comfortable. Often, individuals will choose to customize their robes with glyphs significant to the Strigoi Vii. While no material is preferred, be aware that synthetic fabrics are often quite flammable, which may be a concern if an open flame is present in the ritual chamber.

Costumes can range from the theatrical to the erotic and may include an ensemble "transforming" the wearer into a deity, stimulating garments of latex or leather, or the attire of an ancient Roman or a Druid priestess. As detailed in chapter 5, in group ritual celebrants who identify with the Currents of Ramkht, Mradu, and Kitra may choose to wear costumes that reflect a particular aspect of their Current. Costumes can aid in the psychodrama of ritual and stimulate the subconscious. Often a costume can be used to "tap into" a particular archetype or godform Egregore, thus enhancing the experience of ritual.

Jewelry and Artifacts can assist in communicating the role or duty of each celebrant or help in enhancing the persona of each individual.

All participants should proudly wear their Legacy Ankhs in ritual, as this communicates dedication to the Family and to life and is a symbol of respect and kinship with the Ancestors. Iron and gold jewelry should be avoided; silver is the preferred material.

Phases of the Sanguine Mass

Depending on the individual, group, resources available, and type of ritual, there are many phases of ritual. The following are the general steps taken in a wide variety of Strigoi Vii rituals, including the Sanguine Mass.

I. The Prelude

This involves the preparation of the Inner Sanctum and the ritual celebrant(s). The celebrant(s) should have tapped their fill of Prana in the days preceding the ritual in order to prepare themselves for the Offering or fueling the ritual. It is best advised that the celebrant(s) not drink or ingest any form of mind-altering substances for at least twenty-four hours before the ritual.

Before the ritual can begin, the celebrant (or presiding member or appropriate Deacon in group ritual) must prepare the Inner Sanctum and tools of ritual. The Inner Sanctum, as explained above, must be an isolated environment free of distractions. Only those who are Initiated or attuned to the Mysteries of Strigoi Vii should enter the Inner Sanctum from the time of its preparation to the end of the ritual. The presence of the un-Initiated will cause unwanted distractions and lead the Strigoi Morte to ignore the ritual and refuse the Offering. However, this obviously does not apply in the case of performance rituals.

The ritual is best performed in darkness and with as little electromagnetic interference as possible. If indoors, electronic devices such as cell phones should be turned off in the chamber where the Inner Sanctum is to be constructed. The lights should be turned off, and all sources of outside light, such as windows, should be covered as completely as possible.

Tools and regalia should be prepared and laid out for ease of use. Getting dressed (or Nightklad) helps induce the mindset of the ritual and serves as a meditative preparation for the celebrant(s). In the case of group ritual, the presiding member should assign ritual roles and make sure everyone knows their place and duties. Assigning duties is essential if the ritual is led by more than one person.

Meditation, yoga, or minor energy work before the ritual can also raise energies and help bring the celebrant(s) into the mindset of the ritual. In the case of group ritual, a communal meditation will also aid in the group agreement and focus. The celebrant(s) should also tend to any Corporeal needs that may interfere with the ritual. Remember that proper planning and preparation can be just as important in achieving results as the ritual itself.

The Sealing and Banishing is very important and should be done within the Inner Sanctum before any celebrants enter. In group ritual, the sealing and banishing is usually conducted by a celebrant associated with the Mradu Current. The celebrant points their ar'thana toward each wall, tracing its borders and thus erecting a subtle barrier. They then state, *"By my will I seal this wall."* The process should be repeated for each wall, including the floor and ceiling. The celebrant should then repeat the process for any reflective surface in the room, including mirrors, television sets, computer screens, and so on. While pointing the ar'thana toward the reflective surface, the celebrant should state, *"By my will I seal this portal."* At this point, the Gate from the Outer to Inner Sanctum should be left open. Once the celebrant has sealed all walls and portals, they should then, using the flow of their breath and the energies of their subtle body, banish all negative energies toward the Gate, pushing them out with their own will. Once this is done, the Inner Sanctum is prepared and the Cleansings can begin.

Cleansings are powerful tools to prepare the mind, body, and spiritual centers before ritual. In solitary ritual, the celebrant should Corporeally cleanse themself by taking a bath or shower before ritual (if possible), or at least washing their hands and face. They should also meditate, focusing on directing stagnant energies away from their subtle bodies, thus allowing an improved energy flow. The solitary celebrant may also choose to utilize a cleansing solution, such as Florida water (a cologne used as a cleansing agent in many South American and Caribbean spiritual paths such as Santeria and Voudoun), as a Corporeal sign and trigger. In group ritual, the celebrants should be cleansed at the Gate to the Inner Sanctum. Again, this is traditionally done by those who associate with the Mradu Current. The individual doing the cleansing may focus their intent and "push" away stagnant energies from each celebrant, or "anoint" them with Florida water.

II. Entering the Sanctum

This should take place only once everything has been properly prepared. Only then is it time to enter the space where the Inner Sanctum has been established. Within the Inner Sanctum, the participant passes from the Dayside of rationality, materialism, and logic into the Nightside, where everything is permitted.

As the Gate is the entry from the Outer Sanctum to the Inner Sanctum, the Portal between the Corporeal and the subtle worlds is the speculum, or black mirror. Thus, the Inner Sanctum is a place between worlds, where the subtle and physical realities touch and merge. For best results in ritual, the celebrant(s) should fully accept that they are at the crossroads of worlds once they enter the Inner Sanctum. Anything that is possible in any world is possible in the Inner Sanctum. These potentialities include extraordinary experiences, the revelation of magickal realities, and, of course, tangible manifestation of the Strigoi Morte.

Once the celebrant(s) is inside the Inner Sanctum, it must be sealed. The celebrant should, with the ar'thana or wand, touch each wall, finishing by reaching toward the gate, and state, *"By my will I seal this Sanctum."*

III. The Invokation

This serves dually as the Invokation of the Current within the celebrant(s) and the declaration of intent and purpose for the ritual and the focus point of will by which the Sanctum will be consecrated. Due to the lack of light in the Inner Sanctum, for best results this and all future spoken parts of the ritual should be memorized or done spontaneously. The presider should face toward the west. Clapping hands loudly twice or ringing the bell a few times is a good way to focus the mood and cleanse the air. Then the words of the Invokation should be spoken slowly and with deep passion. As a sample, the Invokation of Elorath is as follows:

Hear me! *I stand within this Sanctum. Tonight I celebrate with my True Family. Blood calls out unto Blood, and the Blood of Elorath within me cries out to be heard. Let nothing keep me from my purpose, for I am Strigoi Vii! I turn my gaze to You, the Fraters and Sorors of Our Family. You, who share Our Immortal inheritance, are welcome here with me in this sacred space. I have gathered the life of mortals. I offer this greatest of gifts to You, the true Elders of Our Family! I call You forth so I may receive Your Ancient energies and thus join You in the glory of Immortality! I am here to escape death and seize eternal life! Drink from me, and We shall live forever! Ancestors, come forth into this chamber!* Elorath, I invoke Thee! Hail Elorath!

IV. The Invitation

This is mainly used for Communion rites such as the Sanguine Mass or rituals where the Strigoi Morte are invited to aid or protect a ritual. This should be done after the preparation and Invokation. The Invitation is similar to processes such as "calling the quarters" in occult and neopagan paradigms. In Strigoi Vii ritual, the Invitation takes place in three dimensions, with the Calling issued to the four compass points (south, east, north, and west) as well as the zenith (above) and nadir (below). For each of these directions, the celebrant calls the associated

Strigoi Morte. In group ritual, the Invitation is often sent by those individuals associated with the Current of Ramkht.

Once the Inner Sanctum has been sealed and the Invokation declared, the Invitation to the Strigoi Morte is sent forth. The celebrant performs the Invitation by holding the wand upright whilst standing at each compass point and then ringing the bell thrice or clapping their hands after each. The Invitations are first set forth to the nadir and the zenith, then proceed to the invitation to the south, concluding in the west. A sample template for the Invitations to the Strigoi Morte follows:

Nadir—By my will, let the gate in the Earth Below be opened! Kalistree Mothers, Daughters, and Sorors, come to this chamber. I humbly request your presence. Hail Kalistree!

Zenith—Hear my voice! Gates of the sky Above, open before me! Mithu Fathers, Sons, and Brothers, I summon you. Join us in celebration and Communion. Hail Mithu!

South—I turn south and face the gate of fire in passion and love. Kitra, weavers of the Current, I turn my gaze to you. Come now with beauty and delight. Hail Kitra!

East—I face east and gaze upon the gate of the Zhep'rs, the breath of life. Ramkht, I call on your wisdom. Come to this sacred chamber and lend me your insight. Hail Ramkht!

North—To the north I see the gate of stone. Let my own inner power open that gate! Mradu, guardians of the Current, I humbly request your presence. Protect and strengthen me. Hail Mradu!

West—*Elorath,* come to me! Let the Mirror Gates of endless waters swing open between the worlds! It is my True Nature that wills it to be so! I look upon you, and I see no beginning and no end; I look upon the Greatest of all Dragons, and I see my Self. Ancestors, True Lords,

I humbly invite You to this Sanctum, where You are welcome. I have prepared an Offering! Come forth and *feast!* Hail Elorath!

V. The Offering

This takes place after the Invitations to the Strigoi Morte have been sent. This can also be used to offer the Strigoi Morte energy in exchange for support in any specific ritual. The celebrant(s) should subsequently focus all their energies into the speculum, recognizing it as a portal to the subtle world. This is the most sacred of actions; the time when We offer Our most precious gift to Our Ancestors for Their use as well as Ours.

In order to release the stored Prana for the Offering, it is often helpful to control the breath on which it is carried toward the black mirror. The celebrant should inhale deeply through the nose, then release the Offering in an outward, extended breath, exclusively through the mouth. Vocalizing a long vowel sound, such as *hoooo,* with each outward breath may aid in the process.

Placing the speculum on the floor can give the effect of a glass-bottomed boat, whilst putting it eye level on the western wall presents the horizontal view into the subtle world. Some Strigoi Vii prefer to hold the speculum in their hands, so as to bring it close to their face. Various positions should be tried, as some may be more effective than others.

The greater the Offering, the more likely is it that the Strigoi Morte will manifest and return pure and refined energies to the celebrant(s). Smaller Offerings are not as effective, since the entire process of Communion takes a certain amount of energy to perform.

The process of releasing the Prana should be continued as long as possible, even if it means working to the point of exhaustion or experiencing discomfort. The release of Prana should continue until the Strigoi Morte manifest and accept the Offering. Be careful about your own health, as this process is strenuous and those with serious health problems may experience negative results. If you have any doubt as to your own physical ability to participate in ritual, you should refrain from taking part. Similarly, those who are ill, physically hurt, or who are taking prescription medication should abstain from ritual, as these factors will interfere with energy flow and can cause detrimental results to the individual.

In group ritual, the presiding member should be careful to monitor the other celebrants and ensure no one is in danger of being overcome by the Offering process. If a celebrant is overcome to the point of distress or collapse during the Offering, whether in solitary or group ritual, they should immediately stop the Offering and sit quietly or lie on the floor until they have recovered. If the celebrant is drained to a point where they are physically unable to continue with ritual, they should bring a halt to the ritual (if in solitary ritual) or disengage and wait until the other celebrants have finished (in group ritual). In either case, afterward the celebrant should take special care to restore their energies and maintain their health. They should drink water and eat food high in energy, such as carbohydrates or sugars, and of course absorb energy as soon as possible to replace that which was depleted. Often, when a celebrant is overcome during ritual, it means they did not build up a large enough fund of Prana before the ritual. That individual should be careful to absorb a larger amount of Prana when preparing for future rituals.

VI. The Recoiling

In Communion rituals, this is where the real Nightside experiences begin. If the Strigoi Morte have responded to the Invitation and accepted the Offering, They will show signs of Their presence through actual manifestation. In return for the Offering of Prana, They will send a gift of Sorrra to the celebrant(s). Sorrra is highly refined energy that is essential in building Zhep'r and achieving Immortality. Achieving a successful Recoiling is an honor and a sign that one is truly of the Family. Only those worthy will be privileged to experience a Recoiling, during which there is an immense reverse flow of energy through the mirror and into the celebrant's subtle body. The Recoiling of energy can be great or small, if it occurs at all. If the Strigoi Morte have not been satisfied, little or no Recoiling will take place. However, this does not mean the ritual has been a failure, as the simple experience of being in the presence of the Strigoi Morte is enough to potentially increase the Zhep'r of any Strigoi Vii.

The Recoiling of energies will be a fresh infusion of pure Sorrra and Zhep'r from the veins of the Ancients into the celebrant's depleted subtle body. There are many signals of a successful Recoiling, which vary from person to person. Some common signals include a tugging sensation on the solar plexus, the sensation of being touched, the impression of tingling in the fingertips, ringing in the ears, hearing whispers of one's name or other words, or a plethora of heightened emotions such as love, joy, or fear. Some celebrants experience a change in environmental temperature, see sparks of light or afterimages (as if they looked at a bright light and then went into a dark location), or perceive images of shadowy phantasm-like figures in the mirror. It is not uncommon, especially in solitary ritual, for the celebrant to experience a spontaneous and prolonged orgasm during the Recoiling. The more powerful the experiences, the greater the degree to which the Offering has been accepted.

The Communion ritual is the most basic form of interaction with the Strigoi Morte and is an experience that will result in Zhep'r for the Strigoi Vii. It is necessary to achieve a successful Communion, including Recoiling, in order to complete the Mystery of Calmae.

VII. Closing

This marks the formal end of the ritual. Upon the completion of the ritual, the Ancients should be honored as They depart. During the closing, the celebrant(s) bid the Ancestors farewell and thank Them for Their presence. The celebrant or presiding member should raise the chalice toward the portal and state in a firm and empowered voice these or similar words:

> *I raise this chalice to You, oh Ancients. Let it symbolize the Blood that is Our life and Current! I drink in remembrance of the eternal Pakt of my True Family, and my True Nature! I drink in love and loyalty, for I am Strigoi Vii, the Living Vampire, and I am Immortal! Hail Elorath!*

The presider should look into the mirror and into their own eyes, then drink deeply from the chalice. Then the presider should clap their hands twice or ring a bell three times to signify thanks. In group ritual, the chalice should then be passed to the next celebrant counter-clockwise, until each celebrant has drunk, each speaking words of thanks, if they so desire.

The presider should point the tip of the ar'thana or wand into the mirror, then to the west, then toward the north, east, south, zenith, and nadir. They should then extinguish all light and, in the absolute darkness, sincerely pronounce: *"So now it is done!"* followed by clapping the hands or ringing a bell twice to mark the conclusion of ritual.

VIII. The Return

Once the ritual has been finished, it's time to return to the Dayside. The lights should be reignited, the ritual tools removed, and the altars covered. Everyone moves on to the celebration.

IX. The Celebration

After the ritual is completed and the celebrant(s) have returned to the Dayside, they need to acknowledge the need for restoration and balance. Drinking or eating is a good way to restore one's equilibrium after an especially intense ritual. Foods containing carbohydrates, such as bread, cakes, or rice provide high levels of Corporeal energy and are especially grounding. Chocolate is preferred by many Strigoi Vii, as it has been long considered a delicacy and associated with magic and ritual.

Summation

In the preceding pages, We have presented the core elements and traditions of Strigoi Vii ritual, including the format for Communion ritual within the Sanguine Mass. The aspiring Calmae should assiduously experiment with these ritual formulations and elements. Each individual and group is different, as We of the Family are all individuals; therefore, no one form of ritual will be most effective for all celebrants or ritual groups.

The guidelines We offer here are tested and proven to yield results for those of the Family with dedicated practice. However, you should always feel free to adjust them as suits your needs. Discuss your ritual experiences with others of the Family and contribute your own. The Family evolves both individually and collectively. However, the aspiring Calmae should first experiment alone and achieve results before progressing to communal ritual work. Remember that you cannot solve the Mystery of Calmae until you have achieved a successful Communion with the Strigoi Morte.

For in the end, only results matter.

Chapter 26
TECHNIQUES AND ENERGY MANIPULATION

Change your thoughts, and you change your world.
—Norman Vincent Peale

The True Vampyre is more attuned to the subtle layers of reality than the average mortal, due to the higher vibration of their subtle bodies. This is spiritual alchemy; even before an awakening, the potential Vampyre may have experiences that are undisciplined uses of energy manipulations. With training and discipline, "techniques" can be used to focus and amplify these abilities. Those who are of the Current, awakened or un-Awakened, are sensitive to fluxes in subtle energies and have what would seem like latent psychic abilities. Some potential Living Vampires un-Awakened to their nature have become professional psychics, healers, and mediums. Many turn away from their nature, attributing these experiences to delusion, and never taste the fullness of Zhep'r. They deny themselves this freedom out of social conditioning or a sense of displacement. To them, the apprehension of the subtle nature of reality keeps them from "fitting in" to mortal society. They will create excuse after excuse as to why they do not rise into their own opportunity of accepting their potential for Immortal-mindedness. These individuals are the iconoclasts of Strigoi Vii society—they reject their own potential and continue to identify with the mortal mindset.

Knowledge of the difference between Invokation and Evokation is an essential step toward mastering techniques. Evokations are outside the subtle body, whilst Invokations are internal. Grounding, for example, is an evocation because is deals with pushing energies and manifesting external workings, whilst centering is an invocation and works inward.

For many of the un-Awakened, potential Vampyres or not, the process of seeing beyond the five senses can be a terrifying prospect. The perceptions of children are usually not considered "normal," as the child does not hold the agreed-on adult perceptions of what is "real" and what is not. Instead, the child simply perceives and experiences without measuring their experience against a standard of what is deemed possible, normal, and rational. It is not uncommon for children to see spirits or "invisible friends," engage in psychic activity, or have premonitions and lucid dreams. Some other markers of the potential to sense the subtle realities include an intrinsic sense of geography, a unique sense of humor, love of life, strong sense of empathy, love of ancient cultures, interest in the mysterious or supernatural, and an abiding sense of personal strength. However, one must realize there is no one set of these markers. Strigoi Vii are often well-rounded individuals who have many varied interests, many of which are strongly rooted in the Corporeal, such as sports or other physical activities. This reflects Our need for a powerful connection to the Corporeal, which is the foundation for the flow of energies.

While the Vampyre is wise to solve the Outer Mysteries, it serves to bring their understanding toward the first steps of Mastery. This intimate connection to the subtle realms offers the Strigoi Vii the experience to interact with energies most mortals will never experience. There are many mortals, other species of Awakened beings and, of course, other tribes of vampires/Vampyres, who also interact with these energies. Most Strigoi Vii have a strong and unique connection to these subtle realms.

Here are a few of the "techniques" that are essential for the Nightside perspective to be fully embraced and for Zhep'r to flourish.

Meditation techniques are at the center of all successful energy work and manipulation techniques. We have already explored a standard regimen of meditations such as Throning and the Surjaah. A meditation is a shift in consciousness and focus from the normal reality to one of relaxation and alternative states of consciousness, usually achieved without the influence of drugs. It brings our energy into focus and creates equilibrium between the layers of the Self. One does not have to be in a lotus position or use charms or chants to "properly" meditate. There are many forms of meditation, which the average mortal-minded person does not consider. For example, intense and focused activities such as dance, performance, yoga, running, sex, creating art, and even driving can allow your mind to move into these alternative states. What is most effective for each individual depends on their nature and the state they wish to enter.

Once the shift has come, meditation is essential not only for higher levels of energy work, but the most basic steps of filtering, grounding, and centering energy. Breath and breathing are the most basic elements of meditation. Breath controls your flow of Prana in and out of your body, and breath control naturally centers and grounds you.

Deep breathing should begin any meditation. Many breath techniques advise you to begin breathing in through your nose and out through your mouth, expanding your diaphragm and using it as your focal point of control. This simple technique, if practiced correctly and continuously, will result in relaxation of the mind and body as the two come into balance.

Once breathing has been mastered, bring the mind into the equation. Begin Throning or simply sit still in a relaxed position for as long as you can. Let your mind wander for a while, then try and bring it into focus. Cleanse your mind of all random thoughts and visuals. Focus on the pleasure and calmness of just existing. If you have a specific focus for meditation, which you often have prepared beforehand, bring it forth when you feel it is the best time to focus on it.

Rituals are meditations and can be truly empowering. Many paradigms and groups employ ritual, from African tribes to Voudoun practitioners. Meditative states can be created through dance, scent, melodrama, and music. These are done to achieve a trancelike state that can be used for Astral projection, dreaming, celebration, or Ascension, among many others. Chanting is a powerful way to evoke trance, but is best done in a group as it depends on harmonizing with others' voices.

There are many levels on which we can achieve meditation. Most effective meditation comes from sensory modification, stimulation, or deprivation. One can simply meditate, such as in the Surjaah, in order to plan their day and harmonize themselves. A deep level of meditation and trance can be achieved by body suspension and similar procedures practiced by modern primitives. Tattooing and permanent body modifications are also a powerful experience. However, deep meditations should be prepared in advance in order to be truly meaningful. The Strigoi Vii should also use good judgment when embarking on any process, such as tattooing or piercing, which is not easily reversible.

In closing, explore and test, experiment and validate. Each of us is a unique being and what works for one person will not be of benefit to the next.

Perceiving is the ability to discern subtle energies to which We are Awakened, such as auras of the Ethereal body and the flow of Prana. Perception of deeper forms of energy are most often done through Astral projection and dreamwalking, as they are less tangible. Use of psychic abilities is actually perception on this level, and many use the Astral as their gateway, especially when working over long distances, as time and space are perceived differently in the subtle layers of reality.

Energy can be also perceived in ways analogous to the Corporeal senses, such as a scent or sound. This is most often the case with Ambient energy. One can simply "smell" or "listen," and even those who are only slightly Awakened can sense such energies if they pay attention.

The aura is the most basic form of energy sensing beyond Ambient energy. Auras are the excess energy radiated from the outermost Ethereal layer of the subtle body. Astral energies such as emotion appear as colors and can be used to determine the nature of the being emitting the aura, their emotional state, and their state of health and spirit. There are countless books on this, so we will only go into basic details on aura perception.

The first and foremost technique is manifesting energy into the hands and holding them up toward a dim light in order to perceive the energy. Of course, first try this on the most convenient subject: yourself! Push the energy into your hands and begin to focus on them. Once you have begun to feel heat and vibration, you will begin to see a dim and blurry halo a few inches off the skin. Like a mime, hold your hands upward toward an invisible wall, and the halo will become visible. You will also be able to feel the energies between the hands as a subtle pressure and resistance. This is the thickness of the focused and dense Prana in the Ethereal body.

One experiment involves manifesting tendrils of energy. What differentiates a human aura from that of a vampiric spirit is these tendrils, which are in effect the "subtle fangs." Once you have learned to perceive auras, this will allow you to differentiate between mortal and Vampyre. More advanced techniques will allow you to actually read auras and determine the nature of a being. Strigoi Vii have radiant and powerful auras of swirling colors with a high rate of vibration, almost alight with what could be perceived as a divine fire. The auras of psychic vampires are dark and often contain small streaks of purple and very disparate tendrils. More advanced ethical psychic vampires have been able to manage their auras and heal them temporarily as they feed properly. This is their curse and shows their true nature. Human auras vary in comparison to the consistent nature of the auras of Awakened beings.

Auras also vary in size and health according to the individual. Divinely empowered individuals can be as radiant as Strigoi Vii; this is how they channel their abilities either consciously or unconsciously. Auras vary in distance from a few millimeters to about a meter away from an individual, again depending on the health and strength of the individual's subtle body. The auras are also layered, with the core being the actual double of the individual, their "second skin." Layers of aura move out and become imperceptible to all but the most sensitive. When we perform the Art of Vampyrism on a surface level, We are making contact with the outer layers of the aura. Deeper forms of Vampyrism must pierce these layers to tap directly from the source, or "soul" of the human.

Perceiving the aura with your hands is entirely possible. A good example is "energetic play" between two individuals. You can use the force of the aura to "disarm" the other individual, or to experiment with pressure. You can touch the outer layers of the aura or mix them. This is one of the ways in which We penetrate the aura. Remember, aura contact between two individuals is Ethereal contact.

There are many tools which the un-Awakened use to scientifically attempt to perceive the aura. Approach such tools with a skeptical mindset, as they are not fully scientifically validated. Some examples include Kirlian photography, which was accidently discovered and pioneered by Semyon Kirlian in the 1930s. It is often used to photograph the subtle body, most particularly the aura. Scientists working with Kirlian photography were able to photograph a portion of a leaf, working under the assumption that all parts of a living thing possess a residual energetic aura of the whole. The "phantom limb" showed up as a complete leaf. There was even an experiment involving Kirlian photography in 2006 for a History Channel special called "Vampire Secrets." In this experiment, a Kheprian priest showed a darker aura than a Strigoi Vii Kitra, who had a radiant, fiery aura. Brighter and more vibrant auras are the signatures of Living Vampires, whilst the darker ones are often the signatures of psychic vampires. The touch of the psychic vampire left a black mark on the subtle body of the Kitra, which of course healed quickly.

Utilize the applications and techniques listed here, and experiment to discover your own methods. Each of Us has Our own talents and abilities. We should focus on and hone those manipulations.

Filtering is a defensive technique for Vampyres selecting which energies to procure. The adept Living Vampire never shields, because shielding partially blocks and cuts off the Strigoi Vii from the flow of energy, which they must interact with at all times, as every being must interact with energy at all times. However, sometimes there are energetic attachments that we do not wish to bring into ourselves, and we must be selective with them. The foundations of filtering are important at the Nightside level and for more advanced forms of the Art of Vampyrism.

In order to properly filter, one must have an understanding of the difference between Ethereal and Astral energies, as we are filtering out Astral energies and keeping the Prana of the Ethereal. Astral "baggage" such as negative emotion can be absorbed into our subtle bodies and affect us if we do not filter properly. Filtering is often unconscious and varies with the stability of mind; however, as with the Art of Vampyrism, We benefit from directing this consciously with the will as a manipulation. We can choose which energies benefit us the most, and the others are simply converted. Of course, not all filters will be perfect, and this technique takes time to master and develop. Filters can also be reversed to project "negatively charged" to ward off psychic attacks and subtle beings.

To consciously filter, one must ground and center, then envision a bubble or focused layer of the aura, which is like porous parts in the Corporeal skin. Fuel the filter with Prana and shape your Ethereal body into a bubble-like shape, often visualized in a violet color. This technique is facilitated by Ambient Vampyrism, as the absorbed Prana will give your Ethereal body strength and form. One advantage of filtering is that it keeps out harmful energy such as that of diseases and drugs. Filtering is the first technique used to protect the Vampyre and their spiritual health. There are more advanced techniques, such as converting energy, which eliminates the need for filtering in most cases.

Once the Ethereal bubble has been created, apply will, visualize, breathe, and pull inward to the contours of the Ethereal subtle body. This will become like a suit of armor through which you can choose to allow specific energies in and out. Let the filter function like a wetsuit, keeping "warmer" energies in and keeping out the "colder" energies. More advanced filters can act as environmental suits that can open and close according to your preferences and how much energy you wish to absorb.

Filtering can also be used to cleanse yourself of specific energies already in your system. Simply visualize the filter going through your subtle body like an X-ray scanner. It will push out the negative energies.

Grounding is the process in which one brings energy under control and releases the stagnant or unwanted energies. We use a system similar to grounding in the Throning exercise. Strigoi Vii grounding is more about direct energy than focus, and is metaphorically equivalent to grounding an electrical wire. Grounding is very important, especially for the more advanced Vampyre working with large amounts of energy. Most people use the Corporeal Earth as a grounding tool; however, this is only one example, as the zenith and the heavens can also be used in what can be seen as reverse lightning. There are many people who are naturally grounded and do it instinctively, whilst others have difficulty grounding themselves. Of the Strigoi Vii Currents, the Ramkht are the least grounded; Mradu are commonly exceptionally grounded individuals. Due to the intense interactions with and cycling of energy, the Kitra are often most in need of grounding. The Vampyre Middle Pillar exercise found in Liber MoRoii "Coming forth by Twilight" not only stimulates energy flow, but it is a powerful grounding tool.

Even with filtering, the emotional and negative energies will sometimes seep through. Grounding helps get rid of these and is almost a personal cleansing. It is possible to ground others and to ground in group ritual. This is exactly where the Mradu are most proficient. The Mradu can ground others through a laying-on of hands and then grounding themselves. This is why they are most powerful at filtering and are naturally larger.

Grounding is essential for preparing for ritual, for practicing healing, and for after practicing the Arts of Vampyrism. One of the most effective techniques for grounding amongst the Strigoi Vii is known as the Serpent Spear. Visualize at the base of your spine a coiled snake.

Then imagine it's eyes opening as it begins to uncoil up your spine and through your chakras until it becomes a long lightning rod which extends deep into the earth. The top of the rod ("zenith" or "up") can release energy like lightning into the heavens, and the lower portion of the rod can release energy into the earth. However, be aware that being too focused on the ground does not create buoyancy. This is done by also releasing these energies into the heavens, where they will offer a balance as a reverse lightning leaving the tree. Of course, these techniques work from both a Dayside and Nightside perspective; however, they contribute to a balanced energy of the Twilight.

Grounding is most effective when you are around traditional psychic vampires and you are overloaded with excess energies. It allows you to more firmly defend against their energies and more efficiently absorb the Prana they offer to you through normal interactions. One can use metals as symbolic tools for grounding. This technique is like using a rod, blade, or wand for directing energy.

Centering, as it is called in most esoteric paradigms, is a different form of controlling energy and is the next step beyond grounding. At its core, centering is a meditative application of energy manipulation. With focusing, you bring your energy into a specific state of relaxation. This can be done in conjunction with grounding or separately, depending on the situation and goals. The best formal use of centering is meditation and breath work, including forms of yoga. In coming forth by Twilight we will explore the Vampyre Middle Pillar, which is in itself a grounding, focusing, sealing, and centering exercise that can be broken down or used efficiently to inspire other forms of energy manipulation. Centering is different than focusing, as it is used for bringing energies together, whilst focusing is for directing energy toward a specific goal.

To begin centering, focus on your Center Chakra, the solar plexus, and then bring your energy into a vibrational swirl around this chakra. Do not let it be static, but alive and fluid, moving and rotating like the sun. It is best to begin Throning partially at this time, but if this is not possible, focus on a specific point, such as a point on the wall, for as long as you can. Focus on the Self and do not get lost in selflessness in the eternity of Throning. Create a balance between eternity and the focus on the Self.

Once you have achieved this, center your hands around your solar plexus as if you were holding an energy ball. Then, like a puppeteer using a marionette, pull the energy outward until it fills the inside of your body. This should be molded inside your Ethereal double and line the inside of your aura.

Maintain this for as long as you can and ground out any distracting energies. This may be done sitting, standing, or reclining, and can be used to begin to apply the technique of focusing energy and even sealing.

Cycling is the use of exchanging energy between two Vampyres and can be used for energy play or exercise, sexual and erotic encounters, and many other things. Such practices essentially involve the conscious exchange of energies between two consenting Strigoi Vii. This does not always or even often involve intercourse, but does require physical contact. Since the Art of Vampyrism requires intent, cycling involves two individuals applying the Art to each other with specific and mutu-ally informed consent. The process is called "cycling" because the flow of energy will cycle back and forth between the two Strigoi Vii, like a pendulum swinging between two points in an arc. Each Strigoi Vii, as they absorb the energy at their point in the cycle, will enhance and augment it. Chakra Kissing, as explained in "Coming Forth by Day," is a Dayside example of this technique.

Sealing is the technique of preserving Prana so as to stop any leakage. Many Vampyres know how to draw in energy, yet they do not really know how to keep it. There are many things that may cause a practitio-ner of the Art of Vampyrism to lose Prana.

Just consider water poured into an uncovered bowl. Over time, unless the bowl is covered and sealed from contact with the air, the water will evaporate. Any liquid poured into a container with small holes will eventually drip through those holes. Numerous factors, such as personal worry, stress, anger, and ill health of the Corporeal body can cause a leakage of Prana, just as a crack in a vase will cause the water inside to leak away. The Strigoi Vii focuses on metaphorically "covering the bowl" or "repairing the holes or cracks in the vessel" in order to preserve the precious life force within.

Meditation is a powerful tool to reduce Pranic leakage, as a calm and centered mind does not waste energy on unneeded worry and destructive thought patterns. When the mind is functioning in a healthy and productive manner, the Ethereal body often follows suit. Since the Corporeal body is connected to the Ethereal body, maintaining the health of your physical body will help ensure your Ethereal health. Energy practices such as chakra work or Reiki may also help you sense any "holes" in your Ethereal body, so you can turn your attention to "repairing" your Ethereal Self.

Sealing is important for the digestion of energies. It allows the digestion of Prana so the physical body can rest and recharge. Such a process can be seen on Thanksgiving, when humans eat large gluttonous meals and become sleepy. During sleep, the body is free to concentrate on digesting and processing the large amount of food consumed. After eating, one must digest, and sealing is that technique. Sealing slows leakage and creates a contained energy pool. Once an individual is sealed, they can then proceed to more efficiently focus their energies.

Summation

The techniques listed here are the most elementary of energy manipulations and should be practiced and developed as skills. Not every Vampyre will be able to master these immediately, whilst others will find they come naturally and can be improved on. They are the foundations of full Initiation, and more advanced versions of these techniques are explored in the Higher Mysteries.

Chapter 27

EMBRACING THE CURRENTS

But when Zarathustra was alone he spoke thus to his heart: "Could it be possible? The old saint in the forest has not yet heard anything of this, that God is dead!"
—Friedrich Nietzsche, *Thus Spake Zarathustra*

Elorath is Our spiritual Blood, collective consciousness, group mind and will, mutual "high guardian angel or spirit," and the united karma and dharma of the Family. Those who Initiate into the Mysteries, pursue Zhep'r, and gain results are activating and attuning to this Current, consciously and willingly. We as a Family are aware of the nature of Elorath and know It is not like any previous or future concept of "blood ties" or divine being. Our Current is unique, and thus We do not worship Elorath as the mortal-minded would a deity. The totality of Our Current is far more unique, and at its foundation is the Trinity Choir.

The Calmae need not concern themselves with the precise source or origin of Elorath. This is indeed a very deep and sacred Mystery, which only generates more questions with every answer. We know that Elorath is of immense antiquity. Today, It is alive and flourishing, growing and self-aware, sentient yet not in the manner in which sentience is commonly understood. The Current of Elorath flows around and through Us, ever speaking to Us in Our dreams and Calling the members of the Family together for the purpose of a conclave of Awakening. Elorath is truly the Greatest of all Vampyre Dragons.

The Nature of an Egregore

The word *Egregore* derives from a Greek word meaning "watchers," which is also sometimes translated as *grigori*. Egregores are elemental beings created by a collective spiritual consciousness and group mind, and thus they manifest specific characteristics. Each Egregore has its own individual personality traits, karma, dharma, function, and will. The precise nature of an Egregore depends on who created it and for what purpose. Elorath is the most ancient and revered Egregore of the Strigoi Vii Family. Its function is unique and sustained. Younger Egregores are dependent on the energies of sacrifices and Offerings provided for them by their creators or worshippers. Once an Egregore is established and reaches a specific level of momentum, those who helped create it commonly make Offerings to it in exchange for resources and favors. The Egregore can also be tapped as a source of guidance and power for the members of the creating group, with the appropriate Offering of collected Prana.

Many Egregores die or lie dormant when they are no longer fed by belief and thus receive no Offerings. Many "dead gods" from ancient religions are simply Egregores who weakened when they lost their worshippers. These are a specific type of Egregore known as a *godform*. For example, for many years the ancient Greek gods and goddesses had no worshippers as Christianity overtook Europe. However, the memories of these gods were kept alive through art, poetry, and literature. Even if the poet did not believe in Pan, she still composed an ode in his honor. Therefore, these Egregores did not "die" but no longer maintained the level and frequency of power and manifestation they once had. Yet these dormant Egregores can be revived, as has recently happened with the contemporary occult and neopagan interest in ancient godforms. Now thousands of people hold rites to invoke and honor Pan and other such deities! For example, when performing ritual, many pagan groups "feed" these deities by projecting their collective energy and intent. The more people who do so, the greater the strength of the Egregore.

Elorath, in Its current form, is effectively a modern incarnation of the same Egregore established by the members of Our Family in a time so ancient it retains no record, and which is only truly known to the eldest and wisest of the Strigoi Morte. Elorath, like Our own higher Dragon Self, has no shape, no gender, and no graven image. We would not disrespect Elorath and worship It as what It is not: a god! Rather, We respect and honor It as the collective soul of the Strigoi Vii. As a member of the Santeria religion would esteem their Orishas, so do We esteem Elorath, as It is the deepest connection and the most spiritual Blood bond between the members of Our Family!

Dealing with the Egregore of Elorath is something that always should be done with respect, and only by those who are Initiated. Those inexperienced in the Mysteries of Strigoi Vii should not attempt to work with Elorath directly, and even experienced Strigoi Vii should always exercise utmost caution. Elorath solely exists on the subtle layers of reality, and can be invoked and tapped as a source of power. Advanced summoning and direct manipulation of the Current of Elorath is magick too advanced for the Calmae level of Initiation and is one of the Higher Mysteries. At this stage of Zhep'r, the Calmae should attempt to merely familiarize themselves with the idea of Egregores and the nature of Elorath at the most introductory and elementary level—through the Trinity Choir.

There are three base Currents of Elorath, or *Choirs.* Each is a balanced and actualized Current within the whole of Elorath. As an analogy, you might consider a research team working on a scientific project—each member of the team has their own unique scientific specialty, but they all strive toward the successful completion of the overarching project. Within Elorath, the first Choir is the *Singularity Choir,* which represents Elorath as a unified representation of the soul and Blood of the Strigoi Vii. The second is the *Duality Choir* of the *Kalistree* (feminine) and *Mithu* (masculine) aspects of the Currents of Elorath. It should be noted that the Duality Choir is not an absolute division by gender, for masculine and feminine are complex concepts. Nor does the Duality Choir necessarily correspond to physical gender.

Many Strigoi Vii possess aspects of both the Kalistree and Mithu, and there are Vampyres who are even "spiritually transgendered." In other words, a Strigoi Vii need not be a female to strongly identify with the Kalistree Current! Additionally, many Strigoi Morte have blended aspects of the Duality within Themselves. Understanding and working within the Duality Choir is part of the evolution of Zhep'r for the Strigoi Vii. Finally, there is the Trinity Choir, comprised of the Currents of Elorath, entitled Kitra, the weaver; Mradu, the guardian; and Ramkht, the inspirator. Some Strigoi Vii view the Trinity by how the specific Strigoi Vii interacts with or is attuned to energy.

As stated in "The Vampyre Prospectus," all Strigoi Vii have these three Currents running within their soul; however, only about one in five members of the Family truly and strongly resonate with one of these three basic Currents. Such Family members attuned to or resonating with a specific Current are collectively called Kharrus. Once they have graduated as an Azraelle, they may choose to be subsequently Initiated into a specific Current. Most Kharrus can function outside their Road and perform the duties of another Road, yet without quite the same level of expertise. Kharrus tend to be much more social and drawn to interaction with other members of the Family. The Strigoi Vii can view the Trinity Choir as a fluid framework of initiatory optional roles that may be adopted and developed by an individual Strigoi Vii.

Within ritual, individual Kharrus of specific Currents are often assigned particular ritual tasks. However, the importance of the Trinity Choir reaches far beyond ritual roles. The Trinity Choir describes the spiritual predilections of the individual Strigoi Vii, which in turn may be useful in a ritual format. During ritual the celebrant calls on the Choirs during the Invitation to the Strigoi Morte. This is no coincidence. Remember, the aspects of Elorath are not gods and do not represent the totality of the Strigoi Morte. They are instead aspects of the Current's archetypes inherent in each of Us, as well as *within* the Strigoi Morte. This may be confusing and hard to understand, but it is an essential aspect of Our Mysteries. However, these are teachings that must be left for higher levels of Ascension. The Calmae is most rewarded when they first experience Communion with the Strigoi Morte, before beginning to perceive the multiple facets of Their Blood through the aspects and Choirs of Elorath. The Calmae is thus taking the first step on the path to a deeper and more profound apprehension of the great Secrets of Our Blood.

Together, three Strigoi Vii who each identify with one of the Currents of the Trinity Choir can perform a special form of Communion known as the *Vinniculum.*

In the early days of Strigoi Vii, the Family used rudimentary applications of the Kitra, Mradu, and Ramkht Currents. When We encountered the Kheprians, they inspired the evolution and re-envisioning of Our Trinity Choir. Therefore, Our Trinity Choir is similar in some ways to the Kheprian castes. However, the significant difference is that the Kheprians view their castes as direct modifications of the actual subtle body, while the Currents of Our Trinity Choir are expressions of a natural energetic attunement on the part of the individual Strigoi Vii.

The Current of Kitra is that of the weaver, councilor, healer, and lover. The Kitra cycles energy easily and frequently acts as the "conscience" of the Family. They often are highly drawn to sensual acts and are catalysts of Pranic energies. In Hebrew, *Kitra* also means "crowned one." Kitra are drawn to the Ethereal plane and thus their Ethereal bodies are the most developed, adaptable, and active of the three Currents. This is why they are the most attuned to healing, cycling, and sensual techniques within the Arts of Vampyrism. Kitra are often called weavers because they are constantly cycling Pranic energy at an extremely high rate, always pulling in and releasing Prana. Therefore, they are often the best suited of all Currents to act as donors, if necessary, and contributors of energy in ritual. With such a deep connection to the Ethereal and a high flow of energy coming in and out of their subtle bodies, Kitra can also recover energy more quickly than individuals of other Currents.

The Corporeal form of a Kitra is often attractive and fey, as this image best suits their duties. However, as with the other Currents, each

Kitra is a unique individual and thus they cannot be said to absolutely conform to any guidelines of appearance, profession, or predilection. Many Kitra may seem initially to possess a passive and agreeable personality. However, most Kitra are ultimately very forceful and emotionally intense. When they disagree with others, they can be very assertive about their own preferences. They are naturally resourceful and play a creative role within the Current of Elorath.

Due to their extremely active subtle bodies, Kitra must learn to filter out Astral energies and may succumb to emotional overloads if they are not skilled in such techniques. This is why so many Kitra seem to have emotional outbursts and forge emotional links with others so easily. Yet, in reality, such sensitivity makes the Kitra extremely adaptable to different situations. A Kitra may seem giving and altruistic at one moment, self-centered the next. Such seeming contradiction is due to the constant flow of energy through their subtle bodies, which in turn may be reflected in their emotions and associated behavior. The Kitra functions very well when balanced by the other Currents, as that balance prevents them from neglecting their Self.

Since they form links so strongly and rapidly, Kitra may become extremely attached to those with whom they connect. The Kitra must be wary of jealousy, as they have the potential to become very obsessive when links reach too deeply. However, once lasting and profound links are formed over a prolonged period of time, they will be loyal and passionate in their relations. This is why they have an intense need to be loved and can be very talented in regard to lovemaking and sensuality. Kitra are known throughout the Sanguinarium for being intense lovers.

Out of all the Currents, the weavers are the most social, due to their deep need for affection. They are also the most common of all the Kharrus. This ratio may seem unbalanced, but in actuality it is not, since the Kitra provide the most important of all functions: the weaving, cycling, and flow of energy throughout the Current of Elorath. They are the "Blood of the Family."

The energy signature of the Kitra is very much charged from the Kalistree Current, yet there is a definite streak of Mithu within their souls. As a consequence, many male Kitra are "dandies" or manifest typically feminine characteristics, while female Kitra are often extremely feminine in their behavior and personal predilections.

In group Communion rituals such as the Vinniculum, the Kitra usually are charged with stimulating the flow of moving energies, as they are more skilled in processing energy than Strigoi Vii belonging to the other Currents. During group ritual, the Kitra enter the Inner Sanctum immediately after the Mradu (who enter first), as they must begin the flow of energy. Within the Family, Kitra often find themselves in the role of advisor and confidant, as they are known to possess a quick wit and a poetic way of stating their opinion. Those who attune to the Current of Kitra often will find cycling energy from the Mradu to be quite beneficial, as individuals of these two Currents often complement each other.

Throughout history, many members of the Current of Kitra acted as sacred priestesses or temple concubines, serving the gods and goddesses of various religions. They could be seen amongst the temple maidens of the Second Temple in Jerusalem, the Maenads or the female worshippers of Dionysus in ancient Greece, or as priestesses of Isis in Ancient Egypt or Greece.

The Current of Mradu is that of the warriors and Guardians. Of all the Currents, the Mradu are most intimately connected to the Corporeal plane. Mradu are not as common as Kitra, yet are much more common than Ramkht.

The Mradu are renowned for their honesty, loyalty, and dedication to the Family. However, for most Mradu, a strong streak of stubbornness manifests alongside these traits. The core purpose and instinct of the Mradu is to protect and defend the Family against all threats, external and internal. Somewhat contradictory in their nature, the Mradu may be seen as a "two-sided coin," as their strong protective instinct may lead to personal inflexibility and obstinacy. Partially for this reason, some Mradu are antisocial and withdrawn. However, they may also be extremely charming and gregarious when they so choose.

The Mradu are primarily grounded in the Corporeal plane and are very much creatures of the world of the five senses. Nevertheless, they are still connected to and skilled at manipulating the Ethereal and Astral layers of reality. Their groundedness and the way in which they channel energy is often reflected in their physical form. Physically, the typical Mradu is broad-shouldered and muscular, and many Mradu are larger than average. Due to their subtle metabolism, the Mradu generally are of excellent physical health and may even possess overdeveloped immune systems.

Their Ethereal bodies are composed of very dense Prana, which flows slowly and almost thickly. Some members of the Family have jokingly dubbed the Mradu "Strigoi Vii Camels," because they have the lowest thirst for Prana to fuel Zhep'r and the most efficient subtle bodies within the three Currents. They are able to go for long periods without employing Vampyrism consciously and can even combine Prana with elemental energies in connection to the Earth to fuel their needs.

Mradu naturally filter, ground, and shield energy, which makes them the best-equipped defenders and protections of the Family. Quite often, they are skilled in martial arts or other forms of combat and gifted in military strategy. Mradu are well known for their tempers and, due to their intense loyalty, hold powerful grudges against those they see as betrayers. They will present a very hostile face to anyone who has betrayed or angered not only them, but their Family or close associates as well.

Some of the Mradu find themselves facing a conundrum, for while they have an intense need to give love, it is often difficult for them to forge links and cycle energies deeply. In response, the Mradu may adopt an "old-world" romantic or chivalrous personality. Once they bond with someone, they are completely dedicated and loyal to that individual. Knowing this side of a Mradu is truly an honor, as they are often very slow to open themselves to others and very selective about whom they choose as friends and associates. The loving, outgoing nature of the Kitra thus often complements the steadfast, reserved Mradu. Mradu are often also drawn to those of the Ramkht Current, as "opposites attract," and the Mradu and Ramkht are the most separated of the three Currents.

The Mradu often have difficulty with out-of-body experiences and Astral projection, but have great success in limited shape-shifting on an Ethereal level. This is why so many Mradu are often drawn to the totem of the wolf, predator bird, great cats, or bear. Even though they may have difficulties with Astral projection, they are still able to be highly effective in the Astral realm. Mradu are renowned for banishing and combating hostile subtle entities.

A Mradu with a fully manifested Zhep'r will project a very strong presence. They excel in tasks of guardianship, as these roles are fulfilling to them. It is dishonorable and even unthinkable for a Mradu to turn down such a duty when they are needed. No task that requires protection, grounding, or active defense is foreign to the most dedicated and sincere Mradu, as they take the initiative to find all the potential threats to the individual, group, or Family, and respond quickly and effectively.

Within ritual, Mradu are called on to ground energies and are always the first to enter and begin establishing the Inner Sanctum. Throughout history, examples of Mradu-like groups have served as templars, holy warriors, and temple guardians. The Knights of the Round Table in Arthurian mythology is a well-known illustration of legendary Mradu.

The Current of Ramkht is known to Us as the priests and inspirators. The Ramkht are the rarest of all the Kharrus, yet are the most influential in regard to their impact and role within the Family as a whole. Ramkht are known for their talents in energy manipulation, spiritual guidance, and the ability to fuel intent and inspiration into manifestation. Since the members of this Current prefer the role of ritual leader, they often preside over rituals, group Communions, and other Family functions, such as Ascensions or weddings. Ramkht focus their talents on providing intent and direction in ritual. Foresight and intuition are common characteristics of the Ramkht Current.

Ramkht are most deeply tied to the Astral plane and least connected to the Corporeal. This is why they are often called the "Dreamers." The Ramkht can easily fall into the trap of neglecting their Corporeal development or physical body and will thus have to consciously remember to ground themselves. The Ramkht will sometimes choose to spend as much time as possible dreaming, creating visions, and dancing within the Astral realm. However, this does not mean that Ramkht are dissociated from everyday concerns or seek to "escape" the physical world! They often choose to work within the Astral realm so as to manifest their goals and desires into reality. Many Ramkht are as at home in the Astral as a bird is in the sky, and thus, of all Currents, they have the best potential for mastering Astral Flight.

As their Zhep'r advances, Ramkht develop a very strong "thirst" for Prana due to a specifically developed subtle metabolism. Unlike Kitra, who cycle energy constantly, Ramkht draw energy in and expend it, due to their specific frequencies and energy attunements. They also have the greatest potential for Inviting the Strigoi Morte during group ritual and are often skilled in communication with subtle entities. When employing the Arts of Vampyrism, Ambient Vampyrism rarely sustains them for long periods of time, and they require larger doses of energy from deep tapping or other forms of the Art.

Physically, many Ramkht tend to be somewhat hermaphroditic in their appearance and demeanor. Many see the Ramkht as "bi-gendered" or "androgynous," a perception that is in many ways due to the Ramkht being equally balanced between the Mithu and Kalistree Currents of Elorath. Even if they first appear solidly grounded in one gender, many Ramkht assume traits or behaviors commonly associated with the other gender. Male Ramkht, for example, may be drawn to appearances or pastimes normally considered feminine, while the female Ramkht may be correspondingly drawn to seemingly masculine behaviors.

When in ritual, Ramkht are most drawn to the energy of the Kitra, while the Mradu is strongly drawn to the Ramkht. You can see examples of the Ramkht Current throughout history in the high priests and priestesses of many religions, from Catholicism to the ancient pagan temples of Egypt and Mexico. Several legendary philosophers and sages have also borne traces of Our Ramkht Current, from St. Augustine to Jeanne d'Arc (Joan of Arc).

Summation of the Currents is one which must be taken seriously. Recall that not all Strigoi Vii are Kharrus, and only a minority of Us resonate with one of the Trinity Currents. Those who are not Kharrus can, of course, practice and become skilled in these roles if they so choose. The path of Kharrus requires focus and dedication in order to successfully reach Mastery.

Conclusion

Within the Nightside, one revels in darkness and the unknown. In the Nightside, the Strigoi Vii will experience that which the mundane world considers magic, legend, and superstition. The aspiring Calmae should stride firmly and confidently into the darkness of the Nightside, personally testing and validating the wonders that lie within. There are no "rules" or "musts" for this journey of exploration—it is a journey of the Self, a process during which the Initiate comes into agreement within their Self and with others of like mind.

Coming forth by Night is a journey that can only be made with personal dedication and a firm foundation in the perspective of the Dayside. All beliefs must be cast away and dangers accepted. Truly, then, in the Nightside "there be Dragons," for agreement with the Dragon is the only truth.

With this foundation, the Initiate is then prepared to take the next step and investigate the deeper challenges beyond mere mortal survival. You are on a glorious Quest for genuine Immortality of the Self and personal divinity!

Embrace the duality of your nature—civilized, spiritual, and noble as well as primal like the predators in nature!

Zhep'r! Hail Elorath!

Appendix I
THE VAMPYRE LEXICON

Here we present the simplified Vampyre Lexicon. There are notes next to many of the terms. A superscript 1 denotes words specific to the Strigoi Vii "Elorathian" language. A superscript 2 denotes words that originate from other historic or esoteric sources, but which have been modified for SV use. A superscript 3 marks a word that is used by other groups and systems, such as Legacies or occult traditions, but with a different meaning from how it is used by Strigoi Vii.

The terms here are specifically related to the Outer Mysteries, particularly those teachings found within the *Sanguinomicon*.

There are two levels of terminology in this Lexicon: informal and formal. For example, *Mradu* is the formal of "warrior": *Jahira* is formal for an Initiate who has Come forth by Day. The Outer Mysteries present the informal terms first, whilst in the Inner Mysteries the formal is primarily used.

Please note that all words specific to the formal Strigoi Vii "Elorathian language" are gender neutral, so their English equivalents are sometimes defaulted to male or female at random. For example, a Jahira is just a Jahira; there is no gender. However, sometimes they may be referred to as a Magistra, and sometimes as a priestess, unless they are used to refer to a specific individual.

Special thanks go out to Lord A., Lilith Madleh, Lucius, Irhandi, and Mael for their assistance with this Lexicon.

Abani[1] /aban'nie/—the formal term for being of a certain Halo or legacy. Ex: Gryphyn abani Gotham Halo.

Abbon[1] /ab'bon/—The formal term for an ally and friend of the Strigoi Vii Family from another Legacy.

Acolyte[2]—informal term for Azraelle.

Adept[2]—the informal term for MoRoii.

Adra[1] /od'dra/—the formal term for a mentor or teacher of the Strigoi Vii Mysteries. Adra usually are Magisters or MoRoii, but never teach above their level of initiation; for example a Calmae should never teach MoRoii teachings.

Aeons—Spiritual ages of approximately 2,300 years.

Albion Halo[3]—The first Halo of the United Kingdom, centered in London.

Altar—A physical table in a Sanctum that is used as the center point in ritual.

Ambient—Excess energy "evaporated" from the subtle body that "radiates" into the surrounding area. This can be tapped as a basic form of Vampyrism.

Ancestors[2]—an informal term for the Strigoi Morte.

Ancients[2]—an informal term for the Elder gods; these are not Strigoi Morte.

Angael Halo[3]—Los Angeles metro area Halo. Includes most of Southern California.

Antares Halo[1]—The Halo of São Paolo, Brazil. The term was coined by Lord A:.

Art of Vampyrism[3]—The process of tapping Prana (life force) radiated by the human subtle body.

Ardetha[1]—the formal term for Made Vampyres.

Ar'thana[1] /ar'tana/—The Vampyre term for an athame, a double-bladed, black-handled ritual knife.

Asarai[1] /ass'r'aye/—The formal term for traditional psychic vampires; parasitic mortal-minded or mundanes who have an energy deficiency and must feed from Pranic energy. This can also include mundanes who "fake" an energy deficiency and think they must feed from Pranic energy.

Ascension[3]—The informal term for an Initiation and recognition of completing one Ordeal and moving to the next.

Ascension Festival[3]—The "Vampyre birthday" of a Strigoi Vii Initiate, marking when they took their first steps to Zhep'r. Celebration of this festival is of the individual Initiate's choosing.

Astral Body—The aspect of the Self that exists on the Astral plane.

Astral Plane—The deepest of the outer layers of the subtle planes, where dreams, emotions, and spirits exist.

Astral Projection—Pushing the consciousness into the Astral plane, out of and away from the Corporeal body. Also known as out-of-body experiences or OBE.

Awakening—To come into awareness of one's Vampyre nature and abilities. This is the beginning of the process Strigoi Vii call Zhep'r.

Azraelle[1] /azz'rae'elle/—The formal term for a Vampyre Acolyte, they have made the Oath of Loyalty, but have not completed full Initiation as a Magister.

Azralim[1] /azz'rael'im/—The Strigoi Vii formal term "old-school vamps" of Gotham Halo before 1996.

Bast Festival[3]—Lammas, in August, celebrates the primal nature of Our Selves. The Hunt of Bast is enacted during this festival.

Beacon—The Kheprian and psychic vampire term for the equivalent of Radiance.

Becoming—To experience Zhep'r and achieve your potential as a Strigoi Vii.

Bellah[1] /bell'laah/—An old-school formal term for a Prospectii.

Black Flame[2]—The potential within an individual to achieve Zhep'r.

Black Swan[3]—A lover, friend, ally, or donor of a Strigoi Vii who is mortal-minded but supportive and accepting of Strigoi Vii. This term was originally coined by Father Sebastiaan at Long Black Veil in spring 1997.

Black Veil[3]—The five core principles of the Strigoi Vii and the

Sanguinarium. The Strigoi Vii Black Veil is taken from the original code of conduct for the Vampyre gathering Long Black Veil in New York City.

Blood, The²—(capital B). The metaphorical term for Prana and the Current of Elorath. *See also* Sanguine.

Blood and Roses³—A Strigoi Vii term for a handfasting or wedding ceremony.

Born Vampyres—Individuals who were born awakened to the Current. The formal term for this is *Quissain*.

Calling, The²—An un-Initiated potential's drive to explore the Mysteries.

Calling—Use of techniques and energy manipulations to pull on links to summon an individual.

Calmae¹ /kal'may/—A Strigoi Vii Initiate who has Come forth by Night; a Strigoi Vii Soror or Frater.

Carroll, Peter J.—The founder of Chaos Magick and cofounder of the Illuminates of Thanateros (IOT).

Caste—The Kheprian equivalent of Strigoi Vii Currents, composed of priest (Ramkht), councilor (Kitra), and warrior (Mradu). This term was once used amongst the Strigoi Vii; however, it is now simply called Currents within the Strigoi Vii paradigm.

Centering—An energy work technique in which one moves to the core of the Self and pulls energy into their core; similar but different from grounding.

Chakras—Seven recognized energy centers within the subtle body. Each has a different function.

Chaos—Change, breaking of old ways and energies, and rebirth to new. The Strigoi Vii embraces chaos, an essential aspect of Zhep'r.

Chaos Magick—Originated in the 1970s by Peter J. Carroll, mixing Discordianism, Thelema, Tantra, Taoism, and Sex Magick. The Chaos Magician is without a fixed paradigm, as they can shift spiritual/religious traditions and systems of magick as one would change clothes.

Claude/Claudia[3]—A Vampyre Lolita, usually an individual who looks under the age of majority and plays on this childlike aura for use in Glamour.

Coming Forth by Day[2]—the Jahira Ordeal, which is a process of understanding the Corporeal and material world.

Coming Forth by Night[3]—The Calmae Ordeal leading to an elementary understanding and Gnosis of the Nightside of Strigoi Vii theology and the Ethereal plane of existence.

Coming Forth by Twilight[3]—The MoRoii Ordeal leading to an elementary understanding and Gnosis of the Twilight of Strigoi Vii theology and the Astral plane of existence.

Coming out of the Coffin—Openly admitting to friends and family that you are a Vampyre. This humorous term originated at Long Black Veil in fall 1997, because MOTHER, the club hosting the event, was a gay club.

Communion[2]—The circuit and exchange of energies in ritual between a Strigoi Vii and the Strigoi Morte. This term is inspired by the Tiamantis concept of Communion.

Conclave—A continental meeting of Strigoi Vii.

Corporeal Plane—The physical/tangible world experienced through the five senses.

Councilor—The informal term for an individual ordained into the Kitra Current.

Courtly Garb—Clothing with imbedded Strigoi Vii symbolism for use in formal gatherings, masque balls, and special occasions. Often, courtly garb is historic or theatrical in nature.

Crimson Festival[3]—February 14, Valentine's Day. The Crimson Festival celebrates loves past, present, and future.

Crimson Muses[3]—individual ladies who are consorts of Elorath. Equivilent to Crowley's definition of the Scarlet Women.

Crowley, Aleister—"The Great Beast," occult writer, and magus. He inspired much of the occult literature and practice of the twentieth and twenty-first centuries.

Crown Chakra (AK)[1]—The divine chakra, residence of the Dragon, the seat of the Immortal Self, wisdom, will, and balance.

Cult of One[2]—Refers to the individual being their own leader and adhering to their own validated perceptions through experience.

Current, The[3]—The spiritual "Blood" of the Family.

Current of Elorath[1]—*See* The Current.

Currents[3]—Various aspects of the Blood. *See* Elorath, Kalistree, Kitra, Mithu, Mradu, and Ramkht.

Cycling—A technique of energy work in which the Vampyre flows energy through Their body. This aids in sealing and self-cleansing.

Dark Moon—The time of the month when the moon is not visible from Earth. Also known as the New Moon, it is a time of power for the Strigoi Vii.

Dayside[2]—The physical world of the five senses, the physical Corporeal reality of how a Strigoi Vii interacts within the mundane world.

Deep Tapping—A form of the Art of Vampyrism in which the Vampyre penetrates deeply into the subtle body of their donor. If done forcefully or too often, it can cause wounds or permanent damage to the donor's subtle body.

Dominus—The older reference to a Grande Magister or Iminus.

Dragon[2]—The Strigoi Vii term for the higher Self—a symbol of power, fire, mystery, and magick.

Dragon Festival[3]—May Eve/the pagan Beltane, celebrates the higher Self, the Dragon.

Edorsia[1] /ed'or'see'yah/—Regression in Zhep'r caused by ego inflation.

Egregore—A self-aware created spiritual elemental made up of common will, karma, dreams, and agreement.

Elder—An individual who has been active in the Sanguinarium for five or more years and or has made Ascension to MoRoii.

Elorath[1] /elle'or'ath/—The soul of the Family, the collective will, spirit, and consciousness of the Strigoi Vii and the Sanguinarium. *See* Egregore.

Endless Night—The annual gathering of the Vampyre and vampires tribes in New Orleans on Halloween and during the Twilight Festival.

Ethereal/Etheric Body—The most solid part of the subtle body, where Prana, auras, and chakras reside.

Ethereal/Etheric Plane—The substructure of reality and life force (Prana, *Chi, Ki,* etc.). The Ethereal plan is located above the Corporeal and below the Astral. The Ethereal plane can be considered analogous to liquid water, whilst the Corporeal is akin to ice and the Astral to vapor.

Ethical Psychic Vampire—Individuals with an energy deficiency (such as a damaged subtle body) who are aware of and seek to manage their condition ethically through consuming human Prana.

Evokation—Refers to invitations to spirits and entities that are external to the summoner.

Excommunication—*See* Sin Nomine.

Ezerix[1] **/ezz'are'ix/**—The formal term for a metaphysical tattoo which is not only on the Corporeal body but also imprinted on the subtle body.

Familiars—Animals that carry the Current of Elorath within their Pranic bodies. They are excellent companions for the Strigoi Vii and can be beneficial in magickal workings.

Family Dentist—*See* Fangsmith. This name for a fangsmith was coined by Lady Vi Johnston of the House of Lilith.

Fangsmith[3]—A specialist craftsperson of custom-made theatrical fangs. This term was coined by Mavenlore.

Father[3]—The term for a fangsmith within the Family.

Fifth Principle of the Black Veil—The Principle of Secrets. "What happens within the Sanguinarium, stays within the Sanguinarium."

Filtering—The ability to filter out negative or harmful subtle energies when tapping or doing energy work.

First Death—The death of the physical/Corporeal body.

First Principle of the Black Veil—Law.

Flight—Astral projection.

Fourth Principle of the Black Veil—the Quest.

Gaja[1] **/ga'jah/**—The formal term for "wannabe" vamps who sometimes are immaturely obsessed with and/or contemptuous of the Strigoi Vii.

Garb[2]—Attire worn by a Strigoi Vii to enhance the Glamour or for symbolic reasons. This can include courtly garb for formal gatherings, temple garb for Quorums and ritual, and mundane garb for Dayside life.

Glamour[3]—The use of NLP, body language, aesthetics, scent, etc., to maneuver through the mundane world. The Outer Glamour is the use of the vampire archetype, often by newer Strigoi Vii Initiates and Ronin.

Glueve /gloove/—A large ritual blade (ar'thana) specifically used by Mradu.

Grounding—A technique of energy work in which the individual pushes energy out into the ground and finds a sense of calm and stability.

Gnosis—To accept and validate spiritual knowledge for oneself.

Gotham Halo[3]—The Strigoi Vii term for the Halo of the New York City metropolitan area.

Grimoire[2]—A personal magickal and spiritual journal used by a SV.

Halo[2]—A designation for a geographic area, such as a large city. *Halo* refers to the large amounts of ambient Pranic energy in these areas due to the large numbers of humans.

Heart Chakra (SA[1]**)**—Emotions, balance of ego, self-love, and self-acceptance.

Hermetic Magick—The most influential form of Western magick, which was inspired by the meeting of Greek and Egyptian systems.

Hurin /hur-inn/—The formal term for fundamentalist "vampires" who can be sanguinarians or either type of psychic vampire. Hurin consider all other types of Vampyres/vampires to be illegitimate because they do not have an energy deficiency nor the need to consume physical human blood.

Hyle /high'el/—The Gnostic term for mortal-minded humans, used by the Strigoi Vii to refer to mundanes.

Ingluum /ing'lum/—A wand or rod related to those of the Ramkht Current for ritual and magickal workings.

Initiate—An individual who formally Initiates into the Strigoi Vii system of Ordeals and achieves a degree. This can also refer to an individual who has Come forth by Day as a Vampyre Jahira.

Inner Circle—Those Initiated to the Inner Mysteries, Magisters, and practitioners of Nomaj Sorcery.

Inner Mysteries—The secrets of the Magisters, forbidden for the mortal-minded or Outer Initiates to know.

Invokation/Inkorporation—To summon an entity (spirit, ancient, Ancestor) to possess the subtle body of the summoner.

Ipsissimus—The highest level of Magister Initiation, the Ipsissimus cannot be measured in Ordeals or Initiations. The true journey begins at this level. Rarely involve themselves directly in Family affairs.

Jahira[1] /jah'here'ah/—A Strigoi Vii Initiate who has Come forth by Day, I°.

Kalistree[1] /kal'ist'er'ree/—The feminine aspect of Elorath, the Duality to Mithu.

Keepers[3]—Members of the Synod charged with protecting Sanctums and guiding the Current.

Kharrus[1] /car'rus/—Known as the "Chorus of Elorath," these are individuals who exhibit the traits of one of the three Trinity Currents of Kitra, Mradu, or Ramkht.

Khaskt[1] /kask/—The Strigoi Vii equivalent of negative karma for opposing the Black Veil or the Current.

Klavasi[1]—The formal term for Latent Vampyres.

Khem—"The Black Land," a name for Ancient Egypt due to the black soil deposited around the Nile.

Khemetic—A system of Ancient Egyptian magick and religion.

Kheprian—Another Legacy, a tradition of vampyrism from Ohio.

Kitra[1] /Keet'trah/—The formal term for weavers and councilors of the Trinity Current of Elorath. In Hebrew, this means "crowned one."

Knight—A male Strigoi Vii who has Come forth by Day; a male Calmae.

Krere[1]—A formal term for renegade Vampyres who have tasted Zhep'r yet still identify more as a mortal-minded than Immortal-minded.

Kull[1]—A discussion circle on the Strigoi Vii Mysteries.

Latent—Another term for an un-Awakened Vampyre who has the potential for Zhep'r. *See* Nasarim.

Latent Vampyre—An individual who has the Current within their spirit yet does not Awaken until a trigger occurs, such as being fed on, being exposed to the Quest, or a traumatic event takes place. The formal of Latent Vampyre is *Klavasi*.

Legacy[3]—A non-Strigoi Vii tradition of vampirism/Vampyrism.

Legacy Ankh[3]—The sigil of the Strigoi Vii and the Sanguinarium, a bladed ankh created by Master Metal Manipulator D'Drennan in 1996.

Links—Connections between Ethereal subtle bodies, often reinforced over intimate or prolonged contact between two individuals or objects.

Long Day Festival[3]—Summer solstice, celebrates the Dayside. The Long Day Festival falls on June 20 or 21 in the Northern Hemisphere, December 20 or 21 in the Southern.

Long Night Festival[3]—Winter solstice, celebrates the Nightside. The Long Night Festival falls on December 20 or 21 in the Northern Hemisphere, June 20 or 21 in the Southern.

Lutetia Halo[1]—The Strigoi Vii Halo of Paris, France. The name comes from the most ancient name of the first settlement where Paris currently stands.

Lycanthropy—The ability/skill to shape-shift the subtle body into a wolf.

Made Vampyre—A concept in which an individual who is not a member of the Family is given the potential of Awakening through a ritual only known to select Magisters. This is known as the "Kiss of Elorath."

Mael[3] **or Mael'elle /may'elle/**—The name for the "Voice of the

Synod," a spokesperson for community and noncommunity affairs. This term means "king" or "prince" in Gaelic.

Magick—The application of the will over the layers of reality. This spelling was coined by Aleister Crowley.

Magister[2]—An Initiate of the Strigoi Vii Inner Mysteries who has made an eternal commitment to the Mysteries by personal validation.

Magister Templi[2]—A Magister who takes up duties of a priestly nature such as presiding weddings, initiations, funeral rites, etc. This is more of a duty and a title than a type of Initiation.

Mentor—To teach another; not a title but an action. *See also* Adra.

Meridians—Energy lines in the Ethereal body, the equivalent of subtle veins and arteries.

Mithu[1] /myth'oo/—The formal for the masculine aspect of the Current of Elorath, the Duality to Kalistree.

Moot[2]—An informal gathering of Strigoi Vii for dinner, cocktails, celebration, or socialization.

MoRoii[2] /moor'roy/—The formal term for a Vampyre Adept who has Come forth by Twilight.

Morta—The New Orleans Halo.

Mortal—A mundane, the mundane realm. *See also* Hyle *and* Mortal-Minded.

Mortal-Minded[3]—Individuals who have not Awakened to the potential of eternity. They are sometimes referred to as *mortals*.

Mradu[1] /mrad'oo/—The formal term for the guardian or warrior aspect of the Current of Elorath.

Mundane[2] or "Danes"—Inhabitants of the normal world, generally un-Awakened to the world beyond the five senses and the subtle reality. This term was used in the early days of the Sanguinarium and was used by the Renaissance faire "Rennies" to refer to normal people.

Mundane Garb—Clothing for use within the mundane world. Aesthetically chosen according to the situation to subtly enhance the Glamour.

Nasarim[1] /naz'ar'im/—The formal term for a Seeker who may be aware or unaware of their nature, yet has not formally become a Vampyre dedicant or Prospectii.

Nietzsche, Friedrich—A German philosopher and Social Darwinist who wrote *Thus Spake Zarathustra, Beyond Good and Evil,* and *The Birth of Tragedy.*

Nightside—Focused on the Ethereal plane, this is the subtle, magickal, and spiritual world beyond the Corporeal plane.

Noir Haven[3]—A Strigoi Vii–run event, usually gothic, fetish, or steampunk, with a dress code and back room for members of the Family.

Nomaj[1] **/no'moge/**—The formal term for the vibrational sorcery of the Inner Mysteries only taught to Magisters.

Noviomagus Halo[1]—The Halo that comprises the Netherlands and Flanders. The term originates from the Roman name for one of the first settlements in this area. Coined by Morikell.

Oath of Fealty—An Oath made before the transformation to become a Vampyre Acolyte.

Offering—The offering of Prana to the Strigoi Morte in Communion, a most sacred Strigoi Vii act.

Ordeals[2]—Rites of passage within the Strigoi Vii Mysteries, such as Jahira, Calmae, MoRoii, etc.

Ordo Strigoi Vii (OSV)—The outer court of the Synod, an invitation-only Initiatory order of Strigoi Vii who set forth a prime example for the Family through actions and deeds. Formally only Magisters may be members of the OSV.

Outer Circles—Those Initiated to the levels of Prospectii, Jahira, Calmae, and MoRoii, including Ronin and Black Swans.

Outer Mysteries—The open secrets published in the *Sanguinomicon* and the *Mysteries of Prospectii, Jahira, Calmae and MoRoii.*

Paradigm—A school of mortal thought, most often a spiritual or religious preference of the individual Strigoi Vii. Examples include Dark Pagan, Chaos, Lilith, Discordian, etc.

Paradigm Shift—The ability for an individual to shift perceptions from one set of beliefs to another.

Poser—The informal term for *gaja.*

Posthumanism—*See* Transhumanism.

Prana—The subtle energies, which are vital life force (*Chi, Ki,* etc.), on the Ethereal plane.

Priest/ess—The informal term for an individual ordained into the Ramkht Current.

Primus[3]—The official title of the founder of the Sanguinarium, who is also the first Keeper of Elorath. This is Father Sebastiaan.

Principles—The five core ethics of the Black Veil.

Prospectii[3]—A prospective or Seeker who has formally displayed a serious personal interest in Strigoi Vii. This is also known as a Vampyre dedicant.

Prospectus—The first book of the *Sanguinomicon,* containing the elementary mysteries of Strigoi Vii.

Psychic Vampire—For traditional, *see* Asarai; for converse, *see* Ethical Psychic Vampire.

Quest of Family[3]—The search for others of Our kind to let them know We exist and to provide subtle invitations without force and with respect for free will.

Quissain[1]—the formal term for a Born Vampyre.

Quorum[3]—A private, face-to-face gathering of Strigoi Vii Initiates for ritual, usually held in conjunction with a Moot. This term means "select group" in specific esoteric circles.

Radiance[3]—The signature of those who are of the Current, a beacon.

Ramkht[1] **/rohm'ket/**—The formal term for the inspirational and priestly aspect of the Current of Elorath.

Recoiling[2]—The receiving of Sorrra in Communion from the Strigoi Morte.

Regalia—Tools used within a ritual, such as ar'thana, masks, and rods.

Renegades—The informal term for Krere.

Rite of Transformation[2]—The ritual and Ordeal one must go through to be formally Initiated as a Magister and enter the Inner Mysteries.

Road[3]—An outdated term for following one of the Trinity Currents of Kitra, Mradu, or Ramkht.

Ronin²—An individual who is of the Current yet does not use formal Initiations or Ordeals.

Root (NE)¹—The chakra focused on grounding of the Self, the Elorathian aspect of Mradu.

Sacral (AE)¹—The chakra associated with the Elorathian aspect of Kitra, the weaver of life, self-gratification, sexuality, and instincts.

Sanctum²—A sacred space for the Strigoi Vii to escape the "noise" of the mundane world.

Sanguinarian—A vampire who claims they must drink blood to survive. Not to be confused with a member of the Sanguinarium.

Sanguinarium²—The international movement of the Strigoi Vii, particularly the Outer Mysteries.

Sanguine³—1) Refers to being of the Family, the Current of Elorath; 2) short for a blood-dinking vamp in the online vampire community.

Sanguine Mass—A formalized and ceremonial Communion ritual.

*Sanguinomicon*¹—The core texts of the Strigoi Vii Outer Mysteries.

Sealing—The technique of digesting harvested Prana, often combined with cycling.

Second Death—The death of the subtle body, the Ethereal and Astral elements of the Self.

Second Principle of the Black Veil—Responsibility. Strigoi Vii is for adults only, no minors under the age of majority (eighteen in the United States).

Shielding—The ability to block energy or subtle attacks.

Signature—The subtle fingerprint or sense of an individual. Similar to the Radiance.

Sin Nomine—To be excommunicated, stripped of name and Ascensions amongst the Strigoi Vii and within the Sanguinarium. Only officiated by the Synod and very rarely used.

Sobriquet² /sob'ree'kay/—A specific chosen name to be used within the Sanguinarium, separate from a mundane name and the equivalent of a "magickal motto" in the Hermetic Order of the Golden Dawn.

Solar Plexus (TA)[1]—The chakra that is the center of the Self, the core, the seat of the Dark Flame and Self-empowerment.

Somnisium—Taking a break from the Sanguinarium and/or vamp community, a sabbatical. This term was coined by Daemonox.

Sorrra[1] **/sore'rah/**—The divine and Immortal subtle Blood of the Strigoi Morte, which is exchanged in Communion for Prana. Other similar words in history include *ambrosia, numina,* and *somna.* It is also referred to as the Philosopher's Stone.

Strigoi Morte[2] **/strig'oy mort'a/**—Our Ancestors; often called undead, as they have defeated the Second Death and achieved Immortality.

Strigoi Vii[2]**/strig'oy vee/**—The plural translation from Romanian for "living vampire witch," the namesake of the Strigoi Vii Mysteries, teachings, and tradition.

Strigoi Viu—The singular of Strigoi Vii.

Strix—An undead vampiric shrieking bird in Romanian mythology.

Subtle Body—The Ethereal and Astral aspects of the physical body beyond the Corporeal.

Swan[3]—Short term for a Black Swan. This term originated within the Sanguinarium.

Sympathetic Vampire—A temporary condition of traditional psychic vampyrism in which a mundane has been fed on so deeply that their subtle body instinctively engages in an act of vampyrism to replenish its depleted Prana.

Synod[2] **/sin'odd/**—The spiritual and administrative body of the Ordo Strigoi Vii and the architects of the Sanguinarium and Current of Elorath.

Temple Garb—Clothing such as robes, masks, and paraphernalia used in ritual, Sanctums, and Quorums.

Tactile—The Art of Vampyrism as performed through touch.

Techniques—energy manipulations such as shielding, filtering, sealing, cycling, etc.

Tendrils—Cords of subtle energy that extend from the Ethereal body. These can be used to tap and absorb energy.

Third Principle of the Black Veil—Blood. Strigoi Vii do not consume physical blood for the purposes of the Art of Vampyrism.

Thirst—The "Need" or "hunger" for Prana, which results from Zhep'r and the enhanced frequency of the subtle body.

Throat Chakra (AY)[1]—Power, voice of telepathy, self-expression, voice, and creativity.

Throne Chakra (AH)[1]—The seat of perception and the sixth sense, which sees into the subtle reality. The main chakra of the Ramkht.

Throning[3]—A Calmae exercise of "nothingness," experiencing the Dragon and eternity. This is a Strigoi Vii–specific term.

Thrumanti Halo[2]**/through'mant'ee/**—The Halo comprising the area of Germany around Essen, Cologne, and Dortmund. Term coined by Ventear.

Tiamantis[1] **/tee'a'mont'iss/**—The Strigoi Vii term for the Temple of the Vampire, their philosophies, and traditions.

Traditional Psychic Vampire[3]—*See* Asarai. Specifically used within Strigoi Vii.

Traditionalist Strigoi Vii[3]—An Initiate or Ronin who has validated the Strigoi Vii Mysteries almost identically to the ones described in the *Sanguinomicon*.

Transhumanism—Also called posthumanism; to seek conscious personal evolution through science, technology, philosophy, and medicine.

Tribes[3]—the Strigoi Vii term for those of other interpretations of vampirism or Vampyrism, such as Kheprians, psychic vampires, Tiamantis, etc.

Trinity, The[3]—The term for the three Currents of Mradu, Kitra, and Ramkht.

True Vampyre[3]**/True Vampire**—A Strigoi Vii–specific term for a Strigoi Vii Initiate or Ronin who is True to their nature.

Twilight[3]—A balance and equilibrium of the Nightside and Dayside, which Strigoi Vii strive to achieve.

Unconscious Vampyrism—A type of Vampyrism that happens

when an individual has not yet Awakened and is usually unrefined in the skills of the Art of Vampyrism.

Undead—An informal and little-used term to refer to the Strigoi Morte, as they are between the First and Second Deaths.

Vampire—The newer spelling of *vampyre*, used primarily in the on-line vampire community (OVC). Traditionally within Strigoi Vii, this term usually refers to mythical and Hollywood vamps like Dracula and Lestat.

Vampyre—The older eighteenth- and nineteenth-century spelling of *vampire*, used primarily by the Strigoi Vii.

Visual Vampyrism—The Art of Vampyrism via sight or eye contact.

Warrior—The informal term for an Initiate of the Mradu Current.

Weaver—A primary and informal term for an Initiate of the Kitra Current.

Whisperer[3]—Another term for a Strigoi Morte.

Witch[2]—The informal term for a female Strigoi Vii, not always used.

Xeper—In the terminology of the Temple of Set, this means to "come into being"; it is their equivalent of the Strigoi Vii term *Zhep'r.*

Xion[2]—The old name of Halo Novoimagus.

Zadyrere[1]—The formal term for the Outer Mysteries.

Zhep'r[1] /**zep'fher**/—The SV spelling of *Kheper,* which means to evolve, transform, and become.

Appendix II
MUSICAL INSPIRATION

The following list is inspired by the playlist of Lord A:. from Brazil, with some additions from Father Sebastiaan and others. There is no specific form of "vampire music," nor are vampires limited to the gothic rock genre. The following is just a sample of the music that has been popular amongst the Strigoi Vii over the years.

Bauhaus, "Bela Lugosi's Dead"
Bella Morte, "The Coffin Don't Want Me"
Blutengel, "The Oxidising Angel"
Brotherhood of Pagans, "Resurrection"
Carfax Abbey, "Angels Hesitate"
Cicuta, "Vende-se um estido" (Poesida)
Concrete Blonde, "Bloodletting"
David J, "This Vicious Cabaret"
Dead Roses Garden, "Nosferatu"
Elegia, "Underworld"
Gargula Valzer, "Ignominous Phalazaious"
gODHEAD, "Paint It Black" (Rolling Stones cover)
Ikon, "Psychic Vampire"
In Auroram, "Interludium (Invocation of Fire)"
Inkubus Sukkubus, "Call Out My Name"
Inkubus Sukkubus, "Dark Mother"
Inkubus Sukkubus, "Paint It Black" (Rolling Stones cover)
Inkubus Sukkubus, "Sympathy for the Devil" (Rolling Stones cover)
London After Midnight, "Kiss"
Mediaeval Baebes, "Dringo Bell"
Nick Cave and the Bad Seeds, "Long Black Veil"

Olam ein sof, "Hecate Chant"

Paralysed Age, "Self Control" (Laura Branigan cover)

Porifira, "Images of Memories"

Rasputina, "Transylvanian Concubine" (Marilyn Manson remix)

Scary Bitches, "Lesbian Vampires from Outer Space"

Sunseth Midnight, "The Bat"

The Damned, "The Shadow of Love"

The Downward Path, "Black Tears"

Two Witches, "The Vampire Empire" (Crimson mix)

Appendix III
BLOOD AND ROSES: THE VAMPYRE WEDDING

The Vampyre Wedding Rite is known as Blood and Roses. This is similar to a handfasting in that there are three exchanges of "Rings." Each ring represents a deepening of the marriage. Unlike other forms of marriage, the Vampyre wedding is done by the couple, who determine their own vows. A Magister or Azraelle may preside over the ceremony; however, their focus is solely on observation.

The First Ring is equivalent to an engagement and allows members of the marriage to test out their relationship and compatibility in an official and ceremonial format. The First Ring traditionally lasts for a year and a day. It can either be renewed, allowed to expire, or the members of the agreement can move to the Second Ring.

The Second Ring is a formal marriage, which traditionally lasts seven to ten years. This limited scope acknowledges that individuals evolve and change throughout their own personal evolution. As with the First Ring, the members can allow the Second Ring to expire, renew it, or move to the Third Ring.

The Third Ring is the most intimate commitment and is equivalent to a renewing of vows and bonds between the lovers' souls on an eternal basis, beyond the First Death. This is the highest of all Vampyre commitment rituals.

BIBLIOGRAPHY

Works Cited

The various literary works listed in "Further Reading," following this section, are also all highly recommended reading for Strigoi Vii. You should seek to build a solid foundation in all fields of thought influenced by Our Current, be they poetical, literary, philosophical, psychological, or any other.

Aiken, Conrad. *The Jig of Forslin* in *The Divine Pilgrim*. Athens: The University of Georgia Press, 1916, 1949; 39–102.

—————. "Preludes for Memnon," *Selected Poems.* New York: Oxford University Press, 1961, 2003.

The Bible, King James Version.

Blake, William. "All Religions Are One." In *The Complete Poetry and Prose of William Blake,* David V. Erdman (ed.). Garden City, NY: Anchor Books, 1982; 1–2.

—————. "Augeries of Innocence." In *The Complete Poetry and Prose of William Blake,* David V. Erdman (ed.). Garden City, NY: Anchor Books, 1982; 490–492.

—————. "The Four Zoas." In *The Complete Poetry and Prose of William Blake,* David V. Erdman (ed.). Garden City, NY: Anchor Books, 1982; 300–407.

—————. "The Marriage of Heaven and Hell." In *The Complete Poetry and Prose of William Blake,* David V. Erdman (ed.). Garden City, NY: Anchor Books, 1982; 33–44.

Budge, E. A. Wallace (ed. and trans.). *The Egyptian Book of the Dead (The Papyrus of Ani).* Brooklyn: A&B Book Publishers, 1994.

Chaucer, Geoffrey. "The Franklin's Tale," *The Canterbury Tales*. In *The Riverside Chaucer,* 3rd Edition, Larry D. Benson (ed.). Boston: Houghton Mifflin Company, 1987.

Coleridge, Samuel Taylor. "Christabel." In *The Standard Book of British and American Verse,* Nella Braddy Henney (ed.). Garden City, NY: Garden City Publishing Company, 1932; 301–319.

Crowley, Aleister. *Magick in Theory and Practice*. New York: Dover Publications, 1976.

Fitzgerald, Edward. "The Rubaiyat of Omar Khayyam." In *The Standard Book of British and American Verse,* Nella Braddy Henney (ed.). Garden City, NY: Garden City Publishing Company, 1932; 438–455.

Gaiman, Neil. "Desire," *The Sandman: Endless Nights*. New York: Vertigo/DC Comics, 2003; 37–56.

H. D. "The Walls Do Not Fall," *Trilogy*. New York: New Directions, 1998; 1–60.

Hesse, Hermann. (Michael Roloff and Michael Lebeck, trans.) *Demian*. New York: Bantam Books, 1925, 1969.

———(Hilda Rosner, trans.). *Siddhartha*. New York: Bantam Books, 1951, 1971.

———. (Basil Creighton and Joseph Mileck, trans.) *Steppenwolf*. New York: Bantam Books, 1927, 1963.

King, Dr. Martin Luther. (Marlene Clark, ed.) "Letter from Birmingham City Jail," *Juxtapositions,* 1st Edition. Boston: Pearson Custom Publishing, 2004, 2005; 95–111.

Lee, Stan. *Amazing Fantasy,* no. 15. New York: Marvel Comics, August 1962.

Le Fanu, Joseph Sheridan. *Carmilla*. In *Vamps,* Martin H. Greenberg and Charles G. Waugh (eds.). New York: BP Books, 1987; 322–420.

Longfellow, Henry Wadsworth. "Hymn to the Night." In *The Standard Book of British and American Verse,* Nella Braddy Henney (ed.). Garden City, NY: Garden City Publishing Company, 1932; 432–433.

Lovecraft, H. P. "The Descendent," *The Dream Cycle of H. P. Lovecraft: Dreams of Terror and Death*. New York: Ballantine Books, 1943, 1995; 5–8.

————. "The Nameless City," *The Dream Cycle of H. P. Lovecraft: Dreams of Terror and Death.* New York: Ballantine Books, 1943, 1995; 55–65.

Milton, John. "Areopagitica," *Selected Essays of Education, Areopagitica, the Commonwealth.* New York: Kessinger Publishing, 2005; 31–141.

Muller, Max (trans.). Chandogya Upanishad. *www.hinduwebsite.com/ sacredscripts/hinduism/upanishads/chandogya.asp*

Nietzsche, Friedrich. *Thus Spake Zarathustra.* In *The Portable Nietzsche,* Walter Kaufmann (ed. and trans.). New York: Penguin Books, 1954, 1976; 112–439.

Nin, Anaïs. *Henry and June: From a Journal of Love.* San Diego: Harcourt, 1966, 1989.

Plato. (Benjamin Jowett, trans.) *The Republic,* vols. 1–3. Buffalo, NY: Prometheus Books, 1986.

Poe, Edgar Allan. "Ligeia," *The Complete Tales and Poems of Edgar Allan Poe.* New York: Vintage Books, 1975; 654–666.

Pope, Alexander. *An Essay on Man in Four Epistles to Henry St. John, Lord Bolingbroke.* West Brookfield: C. A. Mirick & Co., 1843.

Pound, Ezra. (J. P Sullivan, ed.) "Mediaevalism and Mediaevalism (Guido Cavalcanti)," *Ezra Pound: A Critical Anthology.* Harmondsworth: Penguin Books, 1970; 98–99.

Rand, Ayn. *Anthem.* New York: New American Library, 1946.

Rice, Anne. *Interview with the Vampire.* New York: Knopf, 1976, 1989.

Shakespeare, William. *Hamlet.* In *The Complete Works of William Shakespeare,* William George Clark and William Aldis Wright (eds.). New York: Grosset & Dunlap Publishers, 1911; 1007–1052.

————. "Sonnet 116." In *The Complete Works of William Shakespeare,* William George Clark and William Aldis Wright (eds.). New York: Grosset & Dunlap Publishers, 1911; 1302.

Stoker, Bram. *Dracula.* New York: Bantam Books, 1981.

Tennyson, Alfred, Lord. "In Memoriam," *Tennyson's Poetical Works (Illustrated).* Boston: Houghton Mifflin/Riverside Press, 1899; 217–259.

Whitman, Walt. "Song of Myself." In *The Oxford Book of American Verse.* F. O. Matthiessen (ed.). New York: Oxford University Press, 1950,

1957; 279–253.

Wordsworth, William. "Lines Composed a Few Miles above Tintern Abbey." In *The Longman Anthology of British Literature,* vol. 2, David Damrosch (ed.). New York: Longman, 1999; 328–331.

FURTHER READING

The following texts are some of the most basic and common books of interest to the Strigoi Vii. Be aware this is far from a comprehensive list. Some of these books may not fully embrace the vision of the Mysteries; however, they are excellent sources from which the individual should form their own opinion of Our philosophies and Mysteries. If the Strigoi Vii is True, they shall instinctively seek out that which aids their Zhep'r.

33 Strategies of War, The, by Robert Greene
48 Laws of Power, The, by Robert Greene, with Joost Elffros
Akhkharu: Vampyre Magick, by Michael Ford
Anthem, by Ayn Rand
Art of Seduction, The, by Robert Greene
Art of War, The, by Sun Tzu
Beyond Good and Evil, by Friedrich Nietzsche
Book of the Law, The, by Aleister Crowley
For the New Intellectual, by Ayn Rand
French Women Don't Sleep Alone, by Jamie Cat Callan
How to Win Friends and Influence People, by Dale Carnegie
Liber Null & Psychonaut, by Peter J. Caroll
Magick in Theory and Practice, by Aleister Crowley
Metaphysics, by Aristotle
Millionaire Mind, The, by Thomas J. Stanley, PhD
Monsters, by John Michael Greer
New Encyclopedia of the Occult, The, by John Michael Greer
Power of Positive Thinking, The, by Norman Vincent Peale
Prince, The, by Niccolo Machiavelli
Psychic Vampire Codex, The, by Michelle Belanger

Reading People, by Jo-Ellan Dimitrius, PhD, and Wendy Patrick Mazzarella

Republic, The, by Plato

Rich Dad, Poor Dad, by Robert T. Kiyosaki, with Sharon L. Lechter, CPA

Satanic Bible, The, by Anton Szander LaVey

Satanic Witch, The, by Anton Szander LaVey

Secret, The, by Rhonda Bryne

Thus Spake Zarathustra, by Friedrich Nietzsche

Vampire Bible, The, by the Temple of the Vampire (TOV)

WEB RESOURCES

Official Strigoi Vii Sites

strigoivii.org—the official portal page of the Strigoi Vii and Sanguinarium movement.

sanguinarium.net—the online community of the Strigoi Vii.

kaladra.org—a private virtual temple for the members of the Ordo Strigoi Vii.

strigoivii.com—free web-based email.

Affiliated Sites

alchemygothic.com—makers of the Legacy Ankh pendant.

fathersebastiaan.com—the blog of Father Sebastiaan.

sabretooth.com—custom-made fangs.

endlessnight.com—the website of the New Orleans Vampire Ball.

konstantinos.com—homepage of the author of our foreword.

Unaffiliated Sites of Interest

ted.com—a great site with hundreds of videos from geniuses of our times.

secularhumanism.org—the homepage for the Council of Secular Humanism.

mfoundation.org—homepage of the Methuselah Foundation, dedicated to curing aging.

alcor.org—homepage of the Alcor cryonics provider.

lof.org—Life Extension Foundation, a great blog and provider of information.

ABOUT THE AUTHOR

Father Sebastiaan, most commonly referred to simply as "Father," is one of the central personalities of the Vampyre/vampire subculture. He joined the community in 1992 and is now known as an authority on Vampyrism, fangsmithing, and Strigoi Vii. He is also an avid student of Chaos Magick and esoteric studies.

Sebastiaan is the founding father of numerous organizations and businesses, including the fangsmithing company SABRETOOTH, event coordination company Endless Night Productions, and the Fangsmith Guild. In addition, he has coordinated various legendary events such as the Vampyre Ball of Gotham (now Masque), Long Black Veil at MOTHER, Black Lutetia "Le Klub Vampyre" in Paris, Black Xion in Amsterdam, and the Endless Night Festival in New Orleans. He also is the editor-in-chief of the *Vampyre Almanac* and the originator of the Black Veil, code of ethics for the Strigoi Vii and Sanguinarium.

Over the years, Sebastiaan has appeared on television multiple times, including programs on A&E, CNNfn, Discovery Channel, History Channel, and National Geographic and episodes of USA's *Up All Night* and MTV's *Oddville*. He was also featured as a central character in the French documentary and book *Vampyres: Reality Is Stranger than Fiction,* by Laurent Courau, as well as Katherine Ramsland's (Anne

Rice's biographer) book *Piercing the Darkness: Undercover with Vampires in America Today.* He has been featured in *Cosmopolitan, The New York Times,* the *Financial Times, InStyle* magazine, *Glamour, Skin Two,* and *Time Out New York.*

Sebastiaan has lived in New York City, Amsterdam, Philadelphia, Dubai, and Berlin; however, he considers himself not an American but instead a New Yorker. He now resides in Paris, where he is pursuing his writing career. For more information on Father Sebastiaan, please visit his website at *www.sabretooth.com.*

Finis Coronat Opus

TO OUR READERS

Weiser Books, an imprint of Red Wheel/Weiser, publishes books across the entire spectrum of occult and esoteric subjects. Our mission is to publish quality books that will make a difference in people's lives without advocating any one particular path or field of study. We value the integrity, originality, and depth of knowledge of our authors.

Our readers are our most important resource, and we appreciate your input, suggestions, and ideas about what you would like to see published. Please feel free to contact us to request our latest book catalog, or to be added to our mailing list.

Red Wheel/Weiser, LLC
500 Third Street, Suite 230
San Francisco, CA 94107
www.redwheelweiser.com